'Terrific reading . . . Amid all the sexual braggadocio and the recital of druggy excesses, Wally reports some terrific battles' *Independent*

'This is a book about his wicked, wicked ways, not a story that hinges on penance' *New York Times*

'His stories of the whispering venality of the image-obsessed young Michael Jackson wanting to renege on deals while appearing squeaky clean are very revealing . . . An entertaining book, his sex life alone being of Olympian proportions' *Daily Mail*

'This entertaining autobiography details his Brooklyn childhood, corporate manoeuvres and eventual religious awakening, all salted with outrageous personal behaviour' *Rolling Stone*

'It's a riveting insider dish for those who are interested in seeing and smelling the music industry's dirty laundry' *Fortune*

'Unquestionably a work written upon sober reflection, and it becomes more extraordinary as he crawls from the wreckage of his career. The story of his rebirth as a devotee of the 12-Step programme, as an AA counsellor who can't stop talking about himself, and his honesty about how tedious a born-again sober guy is to everyone else, is unusually moving. Humility, though learnt late, suits him' *Mojo*

'It's safe to say that they no longer make record company bosses like Yetnikoff, and more's the pity – a maverick, colourful figure . . . The devil may have all the best tunes but Yetnikoff certainly has all the best tales' *Irish Times*

'It provides a stream of fabulous anecdotes – a fight with Mick, a shared mistress with Marvin, and several disturbing encounters with MJ, who called him "Good Daddy"' *Arena*

'Walter Yetnikoff is partially responsible for shaping popular culture as we know it . . . This is the ultimate story of narcissism and excess, candidly told and pulling plenty of punches. Yetnikoff catalogues the freedom of the '60s, the glamour of the '70s and the excesses of the '80s with such humour, jaw-dropping honesty and insider insight that *Howling at the Moon* is unmissable reading' *Scottish Daily Record*

'The former president and CEO of CBS Records traces his life's arc, from his troubled childhood to his wild runs as a skirt-chasing fat cat' *Maxim*

'An unputdownable repository of A-list gossip and narco-fuelled weirdness' *Blender*

'Walter Yetnikoff was a pop music mogul back when people in the music industry still had fun . . . He also hoovered a fair bit of coke and went through his fair share of women and booze. *Howling at the Moon* is his hilarious tell-all memoir of his time in the business' *Sunday Independent*

'*Howling at the Moon* is the story of how this pompous, blustering and boorishly aggressive man rose to the top of the corporate tree, promptly plunged himself into a snowdrift of cocaine and then had to pick up the tab at the end of the decade . . . as deliciously gossipy and trashily entertaining as memoirs get. Highly recommended' *Irish Sunday Business Post*

'In the first chapter, Yetnikoff leaves his wife, comforts Jacko, ignores Mick Jagger, lunches with Jackie O, tells David Geffen where to go, snorts a sugar bowl's-worth of cocaine and is informed that he has three months to live' *Sunday Herald*

'Another fine addition to the canon of tales of debauchery in the entertainment industry . . . Fantastic stuff' *Irish Evening Herald*

Ritz and Velvel

Walter Yetnikoff is a 1953 Phi Beta Kappa graduate of Brooklyn College and received his law degree in 1956 from Columbia University. He joined CBS Records in 1962 and quickly rose through the ranks. In 1975, Yetnikoff was made President of CBS Records Group, spearheading the operation for fifteen years and creating the most profitable and prestigious stable of artists in music history. Yetnikoff is generally credited with developing and nurturing the careers of superstars such as Michael Jackson, George Michael, Barbra Streisand, Billy Joel, Living Colour and Public Enemy. He is currently involved in many projects, including contemporary performance poetry, the production of soundtrack CDs and counseling new artists. He recently joined the New York board of the Caron Foundation, an addiction treatment facility. He lives in New York.

David Ritz is the only four time winner of the Ralph J. Gleason Music Book Award. He has collaborated with many famous performing artists on their autobiographies, including Ray Charles, B. B. King, Aretha Franklin, Smokey Robinson and the Neville Brothers. He won a Grammy in 1992 for Best Album Notes and wrote the lyrics to 'Sexual Healing'. He lives in Los Angeles.

Howling at the Moon

The True Story of the Mad Genius of the Music World

WALTER YETNIKOFF

with

DAVID RITZ

An *Abacus* Original

First published in the United States of America in 2004 by
Broadway Books, New York
First published in Great Britain by Abacus in 2004
This edition published in 2005

All photos courtesy of the author with the exception of:
Yetnikoff, Michael Jackson and Emmanuel Lewis (Webster)
© Roz Levin 201–944–6014
Yetnikoff and Paul McCartney © Roz Levin
Yetnikoff and Marvin Gaye © P. Cunningham 1983 212.533-8006
Both photos of Yetnikoff (excluding motorcycle photo) in Part IV
© Jeremy Liebman
Walter Yetnikoff and David Ritz © Roberta Ritz

A CIP catalogue record for this book
is available from the British Library.

ISBN 0 349 11890 6

Typeset in Caslon by M Rules
Printed and bound in Great Britain by
Clays Ltd, St Ives plc

Abacus
An imprint of
Time Warner Book Group UK
Brettenham House
Lancaster Place
London WC2E 7EN

www.twbg.co.uk

For my sons Michael and Daniel
and their mother June

ACKNOWLEDGMENTS

Thanks to Brother Leo Sacks, who brought us together; Dan Strone; Shelly Schultz; Charlie Conrad; Constance McCord; Sara Roby; Cy Leslie; Arthur Irk; Monsignor Vincent Puma; Milton Ritz; Roberta Ritz; Alison Ritz; Jessica Ritz; Elizabeth Ritz; Cynthia Yetnikoff; Harry Weinger; Alan Eisenstock; Henry Tietel; Bill Wilson and Dr Bob; the guys at GSO; Tim Collins; the Road Recovery mavens – Gene Bowen and Jack Bookbinder; the Eva's Village crew; the Bowery Transitional Center; Ann Price; Nancy Miller; Bo Rucker.

All praises to Heshie.

WY & DR

CONTENTS

The First Lady and
the Last Man

AFTER HER THIRD ORGASM, JACKIE O LOOKED AT ME
with a mixture of gratitude and awe.

'Jack was a powerful lover,' she said. 'Ari was a passionate man.
But you, Walter Yetnikoff, you're nothing short of astounding.'

I smiled a knowing smile. I knew I was good, but I'd never
before satisfied a woman of such standing. After all, for those who
came of age during Camelot, Jackie was our queen.

'Be my king,' she said. 'Love me like this for the rest of my life.
Take me, Walter. Take me again . . .'

I was on the verge of doing just that when a blast of
jackhammers shattered the reverie. Jackie wasn't there. Jackie was
a dream. The jackhammers were real. Outside my apartment
window jackhammers were messing with my head. A skyscraper
was going up. My dick was going down. Jackie was disappearing
into the fog of my early morning mind when I realized something
almost, but not quite, as good as the dream: In real life, I was having
lunch with the real-life Jackie O. In three or four hours, we'd be
exchanging pleasantries at '21'. In her role as book editor, Jackie

was soliciting my autobiography. I was flattered, but my boozy brain was also convinced that it was me she wanted, not simply my tell-all memoirs in which I exposed the antics of everyone from Barbra Streisand to Mick Jagger. And if Jackie wasn't quite ready to embrace me romantically, I would woo and win her. I would charm her, coax her, show her that if she'd be my first lady, I'd be her last man. To do this, though, I needed a drink. Now. Now I really needed the goddamn jackhammers to stop hammering.

I crawled out of bed, stumbled onto my balcony and did what any reasonable man would do – screamed my head off.

'Turn off those machines! Stop the noise!'

No one heard me; no one cared. I lit a Nat Sherman cigarette and poured a stiff drink. I screamed some more. From his terrace, a neighbor in a pinstriped suit looked at me like I was a crazy drunk. I raised my glass and toasted his concern. Vodka in the morning is good. Vodka in the afternoon is even better. Not to mention healthy snacks of coke and grass. Maybe my neighbor didn't approve of a middle-aged businessman like me getting blasted at 8 A.M. Maybe he was on his way to Wall Street where his world was neatly ordered. Well, my world was wildly disordered. And I liked it, liked it because I thrived in it, ruled it, worked it where it made me rich and so infamous that the queen was coming to call. Because Jackie had changed her name to Onassis, only one question remained – would she change it to Yetnikoff?

'Jackie Weds Walter,' the newspaper would read. 'Peace At Last Between Gentiles and Jews.'

The wedding would take place at the Plaza, the same hotel where I wed Cynthia, my current wife, who was twenty years younger and for years my secret lover. Now that the secret was out, the love was losing steam. Maybe I was afraid *I* was losing steam. Maybe that's why I cultivated other secret lovers, why Jackie would find me so fascinating and ultimately set me free from my obsession with women. Jackie would settle me down, and I would sex her up, and we would live happily ever after. If only Cynthia would answer the phone. The phone was ringing off the wall.

'I'm on the treadmill!' Cynthia shouted from the exercise room in our two-story penthouse.

'I don't care. Answer the phone.'

'Answer it yourself.'

It was Nurse Nancy from my doctor's office.

'Dr Covit needs to see you today.'

'Impossible.'

'He says it's urgent.'

'Put him on the phone.'

'He's not here.'

'Then what's so urgent?'

'He'll tell you.'

'I'll call you back.'

I started worrying. It'd been a week since my checkup. What did he find? I didn't want to know. I didn't want to hear his speech about how I had to stop drinking and drugging. I lit up another Nat Sherman, hit the vodka a little harder and headed back out to the balcony. I still hadn't shaven or dressed. Mr Wall Street was gone. But his well-built wife was there, watering the plants. I watched her bend over and considered the convenience of having a secret lover in the same building. That would result in chaos. I liked chaos. But I didn't like answering my own phone, which was ringing again.

'Cynthia!'

She ignored me. The ringing wouldn't stop, so I schlepped back inside and picked up the phone. There was a whirling noise on the other end of the line. Through the cacophony, I couldn't mistake the high-pitched voice of Michael Jackson.

In 1989, Michael Jackson was still the biggest star on the planet. The eighties belonged to him. *Thriller* had set the world on fire –

over 40 million copies sold – and *Bad* was a blockbuster. I'd known Michael since 1975, when he and his brothers joined our Epic label, and watched his career zoom into orbit. I might have even helped. Anyway, we were close. He called me his Good Daddy because his biological Bad Daddy, whom he feared, was threatening and remote.

'My father never hugged me,' Michael told me one afternoon while taking me on a tour of his Neverland ranch.

'You want a hug, Michael? Here's a hug.'

I gave him a good hug, praised him inordinately and reassured him continually – yes, you are the greatest. I meant it. Who doubted his fabulous talents?

My role as Michael's corporate caretaker, though, was not without complexities. At the end of 1987, I'd arranged the sale of CBS Records to Sony, a deal that bloated my already overbloated ego and consolidated – or so I thought – my power. Part of that consolidation rested in my relationship with our big moneymakers, Michael chief among them. I assured Sony – and Michael – that the transition would yield fatter profits for everyone. That meant the key players – the big brass in Tokyo and the artists in America – were more dependent on me. My maneuvers put me in the middle of the action: an indispensable monarch, the King of Records comforting the King of Pop.

I both relished and resented the role. I liked being the guy who gave the orders, but on days like this, with Jackie O and jackhammers on my mind, the last thing I wanted was Michael kvetching. Michael loves to kvetch.

'Walter,' he said. 'I'm in a helicopter flying over Long Island.'

'You with the monkey?'

'Bubbles is back in California. This is important, Walter. David Geffen just called. He's producing the soundtrack for Tom Cruise's new movie, *Days of Thunder*. He wants to use one of my songs. And I don't want him to. But I told him yes.'

'Why did you say yes when you wanted to say no?'

'Well, you know Geffen . . .'

'Too well. I once proposed marriage to him.'

'You *what*?'

'I'm kidding, Michael, I'm kidding.'

'Anyway, I couldn't tell him no, but I want you to. I don't want my music in that movie. My music's getting spread too thin.'

'Fine, Michael, I'll tell him no.'

'But I don't want him to know that I'm saying no. I don't want him mad at me. I'm saying yes. You're saying no.'

'So he should get furious with *me*?'

'You like it when people get furious at you.'

Michael wasn't entirely wrong Besides, the King of Pop was right even when he was wrong. In this case, Geffen had been working behind my back to get Michael's ear. Once a friend, soon to be a nemesis, Geffen spent all his waking hours manipulating the fortunes of famous artists. Fuck Geffen. I welcomed the chance to burn his bitchy ass.

'Anything else, Michael?' I asked, my head throbbing.

'When are you coming back to Neverland?'

'When you get rid of the zoo. Your peacocks hate me. They're jealous.'

Suddenly the chopper got louder and Michael's voice got thinner. He started talking about copyrights – he wanted to buy Jobete Music from Berry Gordy – but his words were breaking up. Good. I didn't want a prolonged discussion about Michael's publishing empire. I wanted another drink. But before I could get to the vodka, Michael was back on the line. He was off and running – ranting about being not only the biggest artist in the world, but the biggest mogul. It wasn't that he didn't say it in a nice way – Michael's a nice guy – but with Michael there's nothing but business. And bigness. Every new venture has to be bigger than Disneyland.

Well, what's wrong with that? Isn't that the dream of every record exec – an artist obsessed with sales? Yes, as long as his obsessions don't overshadow my own.

'Michael,' I said, 'why don't you buy one of those nice little Eastern European countries? Why don't you find Bubbles a wife? Why don't we talk a little later?'

'You'll talk to Geffen?'

'I'll talk to Geffen.'

'And you'll make the soundtrack problem go away . . .'

'Like magic.'

Goodbye, Michael; hello, milk. Milk was my code word for coke. When I called home, I'd ask Cynthia, 'Do we need milk?'

I needed a little milk, not a lot, just a friendly snort to blow away the morning blues. Clear out the cobwebs. Ease the jackhammers. Focus my attention on Jackie. But the phone, the goddamn phone wouldn't stop ringing.

'Answer it, Cynthia!'

But Cynthia, still pounding the treadmill, wasn't budging, even when my screams grew more insistent. Frustrated, I went to the exercise room and banged on the glass door. She ignored me. I banged and banged until she finally looked up. She saw the fury in my eyes and, rather than express sympathy, she mouthed the words 'You're drunk.'

That's when I flew into a fury and tore two posts off our antique four-poster bed. I smashed them against the wall, scaring the shit out of Cynthia. Then I picked out a nice suit, got dressed and went to the office. After all, this was the day that Jackie O, whether she knew it or not, was falling in love.

My office on the eleventh floor of Black Rock, CBS corporate headquarters in midtown Manhattan, had a small adjoining room with a black leather couch. The couch was my playpen, scene of a long and happy series of sexual exploits over the years. It wasn't enough to confine my fun to hotel rooms or girlfriends' apartments. The office was my domain, where instant gratification was mine for the asking. I asked for a screwdriver. My secretary Eileen asked whether I wanted to talk to Cynthia.

'No.'

'Well, she says she's changing the locks and sending over your clothes in a trunk.'

'Good.'

'She says, "Don't come back."'

'Even better.'

My response was to call my girlfriend, the same girlfriend I'd picked up the night of my bachelor party two years ago – the party preceding my fancy wedding to Cynthia with *People* magazine covering and a slew of stars attending. My girlfriend would understand. My girlfriend wasn't home, but David Geffen was. He was calling from Malibu. Just what I needed.

'Walter,' he said, 'I spoke with Michael this morning . . .'

'You've spoken with everyone this morning,' I told him. 'You get up five in the morning and start calling the world. I must be your fiftieth call. I thought I was important, but I didn't even make your top ten . . .'

'Don't start in with me, Walter.'

The screwdriver arrived. Thank God.

'Michael said I could use a song on the *Days of Thunder* soundtrack,' Geffen continued.

'Forget about it.'

'What do you mean, forget about it?'

'It's not going to happen.'

'What are you talking about? Michael himself agreed. Your artist gave me his word.'

'He doesn't know what he's doing. Besides, you bully him. You bully everyone.'

'Who's the bully here?'

'This conversation is useless, David. You're not getting the song.'

'That's Michael's call – and he's already made it.'

'You're wrong. I'm making it. And I'll make it stick. Find some other song. And if you want to be useful, teach my girlfriend to give better blow jobs.'

I hung up and looked over my littered desk – memos, calls-to-return slips, copies of the soon-to-be-released Rolling Stones CD, *Steel Wheels*, reminders that Jagger was looking for me. Jagger could wait.

Mick required far less hand-holding than Michael. Signing the Stones, though, had required a full frontal assault worthy of General Patton, one of my heroes. The final battle exploded at the Ritz Hotel in Paris back in '83. After months of relentless pursuit, I had them. All they had to do was sign when suddenly at 3 A.M. Mick goes mental and calls me a 'stupid motherfuckin' record executive.' I lose it. I reach for his throat. I have a vision of punching out all ninety-eight pounds of him. I stop myself, envisioning tomorrow's headline – 'Yetnikoff Kills Jagger.' Jagger relents, signs and from then on it's wine and roses. It was Mick – wily and witty Mick – who later that year plotted with my girlfriend, the one called Boom Boom, to throw me a surprise fiftieth birthday bash where Henny Youngman emceed and Jon Peters, Barbra Streisand's boyfriend and my pussy-chasing buddy, made his famous claim as the man who brought the fine art of cunnilingus to California.

The knock on my door broke my Stones reverie. Tommy Mottola, former Hall and Oates manager whom I had anointed my second-in-command, was standing there, practically in tears. Tommy's a street guy – I'm partial to street guys – good with music but bad with business. When it came to delicate corporate matters, he turned to mush. These days his involvement with his new signing, nineteen-year-old Mariah Carey, wasn't exactly helping his marriage. Tommy was obsessed with Mariah.

'This isn't about Mariah,' he was quick to say. 'It's about the Jews.'

'What about the Jews?'

'The Jews are unhappy.'

'Which Jews? And what are they unhappy about?'

'The Simon Wiesenthal Center is calling about Public Enemy.'

Public Enemy, the controversial rap group, was one of our big sellers.

'This guy in Public Enemy named Professor Griff is making anti-Semitic remarks,' explained Tommy.

'What'd he say?'

'Something about Jews being responsible for a lot of the wickedness in the world.'

My first instinct was to can Public Enemy and throw Griff in the East River. But that wouldn't work. Their *It Takes a Nation of Millions to Hold Us Back*, a brilliant work, sold millions, and their new one, *Welcome to the Terrordome*, was poised to sell even more. I had a responsibility to CBS shareholders. I was a responsible guy. But this was Tommy's problem.

'You handle it,' I told him.

'I can't handle the Wiesenthal Center,' said Tommy, his voice filled with uncertainty. 'They've been calling every half hour, wanting to know our position. I don't know those people. I don't know what to tell them. They're Jewish. You're Jewish. You talk to them.'

'I gotta handle the rappers,' I said. 'I gotta handle the Jews.'

'You're the boss.'

Eileen broke in over the intercom. 'It's Dr Covit's office. He has to see you today. They want to know when?'

'You have medical problems?' Tommy wanted to know.

'Don't sound so hopeful. He just wants me to give up vodka for carrot juice.'

'What time should I tell Covit?' asked Eileen.

'Four. After Jackie O.'

'You're seeing Jackie O?'

'It's strictly personal,' I assured Mottola. 'She wants me.'

'Billy Joel wants to talk to you,' Eileen broke in. 'He's in his car.'

'Talk to Billy,' said Mottola. 'I'll tell the Wiesenthal people you'll call them later.'

'Walter, I'm with Christie,' said Billy, referring to Christie Brinkley. 'We're calling to thank you.'

'For what?'

'For being a friend. For telling it like it is.'

'You're thanking me for telling you that I want Christie?'

Billy laughed. He understood my twisted humor. 'I'm thanking you for the dinner last month.'

I remembered the evening: me and Billy at Fontana di Trevi on Fifty-seventh Street; over fettuccine Alfredo and a river of red wine, him telling me how he had to sell his apartment in the city to Sting to buy a bigger house for Christie in East Hampton; me wondering why Billy Joel, whose copyrights are worth millions, has to ditch his Manhattan digs; him telling me he's strapped for cash; me telling him that I smell a rat, that he needs to audit his people; him telling me to mind my own goddamn business; me ordering more wine.

'You were right,' he was now saying. 'The audit was an eye-opener. I was being robbed blind. Now I'm suing. So thanks for the wake-up call. Ever since we were in Moscow together and you went to see the refuseniks, I knew you had balls.'

'My balls are none of your business, Billy. But if Christie is interested . . .'

Billy got off the phone and Eileen got on. 'Just want to remind you,' she said, 'that you need to call Ohga and Morita. They want to know about management for Columbia Pictures.'

Ohga and Morita were my bosses, the heads of Sony, who bought out CBS Records for $2 billion and kept me on as ringmaster. I loved them for many reasons, one of the biggest being I no longer worked for Larry Tisch, former CBS chairman, whom I called the Evil Dwarf. I called Ohga and Morita the Happy Japs. The Happy Japs were delighted to have me run the waterworks from New York while they ate sushi in Tokyo. Especially when a dollar could buy more yens, and the music biz was booming. The Happy Japs – whom I had known since I helped put together the initial CBS/Sony joint venture in the late sixties – understood me. When I was in Tokyo, they locked me up in my hotel room at night; during the day, they had me followed as I went carousing to make sure I didn't wind up lost, arrested or dead. Now, on my suggestion, Ohga and Morita were on the verge of paying three or four billion for Columbia Pictures. They were looking to me to pick management. I was looking to oversee this colossal operation of music and movies. That's why all the Hollywood moguls – Michael Eisner, Barry Diller, Michael Ovitz, Rupert Murdoch – were calling. They wanted in on the action and needed my vote.

So another small drink before lunch was in order. Schmoozing with Jackie O was no small challenge. Especially two hours after my wife had thrown me out. Especially when I had to make nice between the rappers and the Jews. Especially with my doctor lecturing me about my excessive lifestyle. What *did* that goddamn doctor want?

First thing you notice about '21' are the silly statues of white jockeys guarding the entryway. I nearly stumbled over one of those little schmucks. I wasn't drunk, just eager. A steady stream of vodkas was a normal part of my daily routine. I drank booze like normal people drink coffee. Just to keep me loose and limber. I was never incoherent. Never out of sync. Always ready, willing and able to conduct serious business.

'Mrs Onassis is waiting for you upstairs,' said the maître d'.

Good; she's here early; that means she's even more eager than I am.

I made my way up the stairs, careful not to stumble in the darkly lit room, where I was escorted to a quiet corner table in the back. Jackie smiled sweetly. She was wearing a conservative blue suit and a few pieces of modest jewelry. Her makeup was minimal. She was as beautiful as her pictures. She took my hand and shook it warmly. I was thrilled. I felt all eyes on me – *Who's the man lunching with Jackie O? Is he a business associate or her new lover?*

I sat down and asked if she'd like a glass of wine. She preferred water. I preferred a vodka martini. She spoke so quietly in a little girl voice that I had to lean in to listen. She spoke confidently. Her easy charm had me wondering whether there really was more than business at hand.

'Mr Yetnikoff . . .'

'Walter,' I urged.

'Walter it is. I've been eager to meet you ever since I worked with Michael Jackson on his autobiography, *Moonwalk*.'

I'd forgotten Jackie was Michael's editor.

'Michael has a high regard for you.'

'The feeling's mutual.'

'A number of your artists – James Taylor is another – speak of you with great fondness. They see you as their champion.'

The bullshit had begun. And I was eating it up. How could I resist? Sweet-talking Jackie was sweet-talking me.

'To be truthful, Mrs Onassis . . .'

'If you're Walter, I'm Jackie . . .'

'To be truthful, Jackie, because I have no talent, I'm in awe of my artists.'

'The list of those you've cultivated comprises a Who's Who of American music. Cultivation of talent is certainly its own talent.'

Shouldn't we be talking about her? Wasn't she the most admired woman in the world? Wasn't she our only true aristocrat, our once and future queen? Who cared about me?

'Care to order?' she asked.

She ordered greens; I ordered meat. She continued to maneuver the discussion in my direction. I sat there wondering – why doesn't she pull on her hair or adjust her dress? Why doesn't she squirm? Why doesn't she do something to let me know she finds me attractive? She was so centered, so self-composed. All talk was on business. She wanted a book out of me. And flattery was getting her everywhere. I couldn't get over how she couldn't get over me. An aide undoubtedly had given her my résumé on an index card, but she rattled off Yetnikoff facts as if she herself had followed my career.

'To take a company to a point where yearly sales have quadrupled to $2 billion,' she said, 'must give you a deep sense of satisfaction.'

'It's the artists,' I said, struggling to sound modest. 'It's not me. And that's the truth.' The real truth, I wanted to tell her, thinking about my vicious run-in with Paul Simon, was that I had successfully created a mutual balance of terror between me and my artists.

'To have won the loyalty of artists as diverse as Barbra Streisand and Bob Dylan,' Jackie was saying, 'requires singular skill. I'm also interested in your time line. You began working at CBS in 1961. That means you've witnessed – and been an integral part of – many of the major developments in our music. I'm intrigued by how you view the relationship of those movements to our overall history. For example, Dylan's impact on the sixties is probably as great as any politician's.'

I was about to ask, 'As great as JFK's?' but decided against it.

'Along those lines,' she added, 'I've been toying with the title *I Wuz There: The Music That Changed the World*. What do you think?'

I thought I wanted another vodka martini. I thought I'd never been sold so easily. But did she really want a highbrow book from me or just gossip about the Stones? I suspected gossip, but she was too classy to come out and say it. The best book I could write would be *Philandering and Abandoning F*, the story of me and women.

'So you're talking about a serious book?' I asked.

'As serious as it needs to be. I think you have a point of view. I think you have humor. I read the profile *Esquire* ran on you and got the impression you have a unique voice.'

'The article was interested in showing my crude side,' I complained, even though the article, in many respects, cleaned me up.

'The more sides the better,' said Jackie.

I wondered what she meant by that, but didn't ask. Food had arrived. The chitchat turned to my earlier life. She knew I'd graduated from Columbia Law School and been on *Columbia Law Review*. She knew I'd been hired by Clive Davis. She mentioned Bill Paley, the CBS founding father, and other luminaries – Ahmet Ertegun, Clive Davis – wondering what I thought of them. I followed her genteel lead. I didn't say a bad word about anyone. I thought of asking her questions, but what? How's your love life? How are the kids? In her own subtle way, Jackie took charge of this lunch by keeping the focus on me. Now she was describing me as the guy who got MTV to break the color barrier and play videos by black artists; now she was calling me an architect of the modern global record business; now she was saying I shepherded the careers of more stars than anyone since Samuel Goldwyn. Of course I knew she was kissing my ass. She was an acquisition editor looking to acquire. It was all business. She paid the check, assuring me that the book would be wonderful. The book would be important. I was important. She was delighted and honored; I was honored and delighted; we shook hands and I left.

I was giddy. Her attention got me higher than the line of blow I zupped up back in the office.

'How'd it go?' Eileen wanted to know.

'She wants me,' I said.

'You got a half hour to get to your doctor's,' Eileen replied, ignoring my shtick, 'but you better talk to Jagger first. He's furious.'

'Why?'

'You never returned his call.'

'He's under contract. He can wait.'

'Alright. When you get back, it's Jagger, then California, then Japan. You promised Mike Ovitz you'd get to him today.'

Today was Jackie's day, and nothing else mattered. So what if I had lost it this morning. So what if Cynthia threw me out. So what if Geffen thinks I'm Satan. Jackie likes me. Jackie's offering me a deal.

'Know who I had lunch with today?' I asked Dr Covit, one of those geniuses with twenty degrees on his wall. His face was the same starchy white as his smock.

'I don't want to socialize, Walter. I want to get to the point. I need to stress the gravity of the situation.'

The word 'gravity' stopped me cold. My heart started hammering. 'Shoot,' I said.

'You'll be dead in three months if you don't stop drinking.'

'Dead as in "dead tired" or dead as in "six feet under"?'

'It's no joke, Walter. It's a certainty. It's your liver. Your liver count is off the charts. It's about to go.'

I sat there as Covit explained liver function and dysfunction and why mine was pickled. Of course I knew why. My brain had known for a long time. But my brain had buried that information because the rest of me wanted booze and blow I'd thought of giving up blow, but not booze. Booze was the soul and substance of who I was. It gave me courage. It was the only way I could cope. I never considered living without it. Until now. Now the doctor had gotten my attention with one small word: death.

I was scared to death. I was scared *of* death. I was scared enough to sit there like a little schoolboy, my usual bravura deflated, my heart racing, my throat dry with fear. I was not only afraid of dying, but afraid I couldn't stop drinking.

'There must be a medicine that kills the desire for drink,' I said. 'A pill.'

'I'm afraid it's more complicated than that. It's emotional as well as physiological.'

'Emotions aren't my strong point. What do I do?'

'I'm recommending rehabilitation.'

'Where?'

'Hazelden in Minnesota.'

'That means leaving the city and my work.'

'For an extended stay.'

'And after three or four weeks, I'm cured?'

'As I said, it's more complicated than that.'

'I don't want complicated, I want simple.'

'Everything alright?' asked Eileen back in the office.

'Everything's fine. My wife's thrown me out, I have three weeks to live, but Jackie O wants my story.'

Eileen laughed. She wasn't sure – no one could be sure, myself included – when I was kidding.

'Should we start returning the calls?' she asked.

'Fine,' I said, still numb with the news of my impending death. 'Call 'em all.'

'Jagger is first.'

'Listen here, mate,' said Mick, 'when I signed with you it's because I wanted your personal attention. You bloody well promised I'd have it. Well, calling you for two days without hearing back is hardly personal attention. I haven't seen a promo budget on *Steel Wheels* and . . .'

'Mick, I've got a few problems.'

'You're paid a fortune to solve problems. I'm hardly sympathetic. You still haven't given Keith enough attention.'

'Keith Richards gives a shit about me?'

'There's not an artist anywhere who doesn't want attention from the label boss. Besides, Keith still sees you as my man. Now he needs to see you as *his* man.'

'Fine. Tell Keith I'll come to his house and listen to blues records all night. We'll have a pajama party.'

'You're joking, but that's the right idea. That's what Ahmet did.'

'Ahmet would strip naked and jump into the Seine if you said so. Ahmet had his nose so far up your tushy he couldn't breathe.'

'Ahmet has genius. You don't understand him.'

'You don't understand *me*. We need to talk another time.'

'Now's the *only* time. The street date is less than a month off. I haven't seen a promo budget.'

'You've seen the ads. They're beautiful.'

'But how much bloody money are you putting into the ads?'

'A fortune. Such a fortune that the Japs are calling me crazy.'

'Crazy like a fox. You're the guy who got me to write that lousy song for that lousy movie you produced. I can't even remember the name.'

'*Ruthless People.*'

'It was a clunker.'

'It made money.'

'Everything you promote makes money. You're the greatest promoter since Colonel Parker.'

'Does that make you Elvis?'

'I hope to Christ not. Elvis was a financial moron.'

'I wish I had a few morons like him on my label.'

'So you could fuck them out of royalties?'

'So they wouldn't fuck me, like you do, with your London School of Economics education.'

'This is a brilliant conversation, Walter, but I still don't know the size of the budget.'

'Same as the size of my dick, Mick. The more excited I get, the bigger it gets.'

'I want you excited, I want that giant CBS cock up the arse of every radio station and record chain in every major market around the world.'

'I'm asking you, Mick, to defer this conversation. I'm not feeling so good.'

'Am I to feel sorry for you?'

'If I told you my liver's about to blow, would that elicit sympathy?'

'I presume you're kidding.'

'Wish I were.'

'Dear God, Walter,' said Mick, his tone suddenly changing, 'you best take care. I know doctors in Switzerland who perform miracles. They brought Keith back from the dead.'

'I'm not quite dead yet, but close.'

'Let me know if you need names. I'll do anything I can.'

The Jagger conversation did me good. Banter always did me good. I got turned on by the sound of my own bullshit. I felt my bravura coming back. I wanted a drink, but hesitated. What about pot? The doctor said nothing about pot. Pot takes off the pressure. I found a joint stashed in the top drawer of my desk and lit up. Felt better immediately. Fear started to subside.

'Get me Tokyo.'

Tokyo was happy to hear from me. Tokyo was always happy to hear from me. Ohga and Morita were hot to trot with Columbia Pictures. The Sony board had approved the purchase last month at their meeting in Cologne. Now it was a matter of finding the right people to run the studio. The Happy Japs didn't know Hollywood. I did. Or I thought I did. I was their entrée, they my sugar daddies. The movie moguls needed me to get to Sony.

'I'll set up the meetings,' I told my Asian bosses. 'I'll introduce you to the executives with the most experience and best track records. There's only one small problem.'

'What's that?' they wanted to know.

'My health. I may have to go to rehab. I'll be taking the Sony jet. Shouldn't be gone for more than a couple of weeks.'

Ohga, who had suffered a series of heart attacks, was especially concerned. 'Let me know if we can help.'

I was touched. These guys cared about me; they also cared about superprofitable CBS Records, which, in their minds and mine, couldn't run without me. I didn't go into specifics about my health problem, but I figured they knew. Everyone knew. I'd been a legendary lush for longer than I cared to remember.

Ovitz was next. 'Ovitz, you toothless prick,' I said, 'what are you bothering me about today?'

'The Sony meeting. When can we set it up?'

'Soon.'

'How soon?'

'Next month.'

'And it'll be discreet?'

'You mean secret?'

'Yes.'

'Everything with you is secret.'

'I'm still running CAA and wouldn't want the agency to know I'm meeting with studios.'

Ovitz was something. He had his army of agents on one hand, and his army of clients – Dustin Hoffman, Tom Cruise, Steven Spielberg, Robert Redford – on the other. He was the most powerful man in Hollywood, but now wanted more. Like Napoleon, he wanted a worldwide empire. Because he'd studied aikido and read up on Japanese management, he figured he was perfect for Sony. Problem is, he saw himself running movies *and* music. He saw me reporting to him. Funny, but I saw him reporting to me. I was running a far larger operation than Columbia Pictures. So how could he take over Columbia and leverage it into my reporting to him? But that was Mike, a master at flipping the script. No matter, this wasn't the time to power-play him into a corner. He had a huge reputation. I had set up a meeting with him and the Happy Japs and he wanted to meet again.

'September,' I told Mike. 'We'll get together when Ohga and Morita come here in September.'

If I'm still alive. My brain starting reeling. *Dr Covit's death notice. My wife's eviction notice.*

'Did you want to call the Simon Wiesenthal Center?' asked Eileen.

And now the Jews. And the rappers.

'And what about Michael Eisner and Rupert Murdoch?'

'I gotta stop,' I said.

'I thought we just started.'

'Today's different, Eileen. Go home early. But before you do, book me into the Carlyle Hotel.'

'For a meeting?'

'For a bed. I'm sleeping there tonight.'

Eileen knew enough to stop with the questions.

It was six o'clock and I was through. Mottola came by to say something about Springsteen disbanding the E Street Band. Shouldn't I call him? Not now. A couple of my underlings checked in to see if I wanted to do lines in my office. My office was a get-high spot for execs and artists alike. It took me years to realize that people in the ABC building, right across the street, had a bird's-eye view. So I closed the blinds and got higher. Coke spread out on the coffee table, a hot shtup on the black leather couch – nothing off limits, nothing too crazy because nothing got in the way of sales. Nothing was wrong.

Now suddenly, staring into space, nothing was right.

I felt nothing inside.

I wanted a drink.

I wanted to escape.

I wanted to call Jackie O and have her tell me how great I am, again and again.

I wanted to call Dr Covit and have him say he was kidding.

I wanted to call my girlfriend and tell her to meet me at the Carlyle.

I wanted to be alone.

I wanted company. I wanted new women with huge breasts and wet pussys.

I wanted the title of President of CBS Records *and* Columbia Pictures.

I wanted to best Mike Ovitz.

I wanted to best Steve Ross, my sometimes-friend/sometimes-foe, who ran Warner Brothers and had earned more love and respect than anyone in the industry.

I wanted love and respect.

I wanted to sleep.

Sleep wouldn't come when I checked into the Carlyle. I tried to tire myself out at the hotel bar, but the sight of the vodka bottles had me salivating. They were like naked women, these exotic pieces of glass sculpture. I saw their long Russian names – Stolichnaya, Kremlyovskaya, Volganaya, Gorbatschow – as confirmation of my ancestral heritage. I needed to taste my heritage. But I resisted. I ordered a diet Coke that tasted like a chemistry experiment gone bad. I tried listening to the combo, but their brand of Republican jazz was limp as my shmeckel. I went upstairs, closed the blinds and got under the covers. I didn't have pajamas, I didn't have clean underwear, I didn't have a decent relationship with my wife. I didn't even have the motivation to repair the relationship. I didn't know from relationships. I just wanted to sleep.

I started to shake. I felt surrounded by fear. I wanted to order up one of those beautiful vodka bottles, but I didn't want to die. I couldn't die. I had to take care of Michael Jackson, Billy Joel, Mick, Keith, Barbra and Bruce. I had to take care of Public Enemy. I had to take care of the Unhappy Jews and the Happy Japs. But now I saw that, for the first time, I didn't know how to take care of myself. I didn't know what that meant. I had to go away to a place which I knew nothing about to undergo treatment I didn't understand. I'd been in therapy before, but the ambiguities of therapy confused me to where I needed a drink.

The shaking got worse. I turned on the TV and tried watching *Honeymooners* reruns. Jackie Gleason could get the rage out of his system. I couldn't. Jackie Gleason could act. I couldn't do anything but shake and fight this fear that was making me feel like a schoolboy scared of the dark, a schoolboy scared of the world around him.

When sleep came, I became that schoolboy, curled up in bed, silently screaming at my mother:

'Ma,' I yelled, *'my liver's going to blow!'*

'What are you talking about?' she said. *'You're a big shot.'*

'Ma, I'm dying.'

'You're making a fortune. They're writing about you.'

'Ma, I'm scared.'

'You have millions. How can you be scared with millions?'

'Ma, will you stay with me?'

'Are you crazy? You gotta get up. Today's a celebration. Don't you know what today is?'

PART 1

Brooklyn and Beyond

Velvel and Grandpa

Velvel at ten

Velvel's bar mitzvah

V-J Day

ON AUGUST 15, 1945, I'D JUST TURNED TWELVE AND recently learned from my friend Harvey that the act of rubbing my dick until white fluid erupted was called masturbation. I also learned that the Japanese had surrendered and the war was over. They were dancing in the street.

I jumped out of bed, ready, eager, happy to get to my summer job at the hardware store. I wanted in on the celebration. My father Max was already gone. He worked for the city painting hospitals and was out of the house by dawn. My mother Bella, who worked as a bookkeeper, and her mother Miriam were in the kitchen. Ma was reading the paper to Grandma, my bubbee, who was proficient in Yiddish and Polish, but not English. The headlines in the *New York Daily News* looked ten feet tall:

END OF WAR! EMPEROR ACCEPTS ALLIED RULE!

Grandpa Lazar, a tailor who worked at home, was crowing about what a great country we lived in. A first-generation immigrant and superpatriot, he was going into the city to celebrate in Times Square. Always overanimated from nipping at his mysterious

Green Valley booze, Grandpa walked around the house with his fly open. When he disagreed with his children, he spit on them or on the floor. That's why no one walked around without shoes. His story of arriving in America was legendary – how he avoided persecution by walking across Europe, how he saved his pennies for five years to bring over his wife and ten kids, five of whom survived. He said he came from Austria, but Mom said it was Poland. No one knew for sure. No one asked him too many questions. He dressed in old shmatas and needed me to thread his needle. For all his crudeness, his children adored him. I didn't know what to make of him.

'Let's hope the end of the war doesn't mean wages will go down,' said my mother, whose two gods were money and fear. 'Wages are low enough as is.'

'They'll get better,' said Bubbee, the eternal optimist.

'If things really do get better,' Ma projected, 'Walter will get a better job when he graduates from school and get us a beautiful home. Isn't that right, Walter?'

'The best job my Velvel can get,' Bubbee insisted, using my Yiddish name, 'is to help others.' She pinched my cheek while I wolfed down a bialystoker and ran out the door.

I couldn't wait to skip out. Our Brooklyn home bristled with tension. The two-family house on 464 Miller Avenue was owned by my mother's parents, a fact that shamed my father, who couldn't afford one of his own. The further fact that Grandpa and Grandma kept kosher, and that Bubbee did all the cooking downstairs, never sat well with Ma. She resented how her parents ran her life. And, even deeper, she resented that we lived in a poor working-class neighborhood in a narrow and rickety row house on a block where everyone struggled to makes ends meet.

But I liked the block, I liked the streets, I liked the bustling neighborhood of pushcarts on Blake Avenue where old-world Jews peddled everything from pickles to piece goods, where the smells

Grandpa Lazar and Grandma Miriam

of fresh-baked breads and the shouts of hungry merchants and excited shoppers collided with the radios on windowsills playing swingtime Benny Goodman and Artie Shaw. This was the tenement-heavy Brownsville section of East New York where everyone lived and died by what the Dodgers did at Ebbets Field over in Flatbush, where Leo Durocher was the manager and our Bums always broke our hearts, this year trailing the Chicago Cubbies by ten games. Compared to the gloom at home, the streets felt happy. And today, with the mightiest country in the world having won the mightiest war in history, the streets were delirious – strangers hugging strangers, kids jumping for joy, people waving flags, women kissing sailors, couples frolicking down the street like Gene Kelly and Judy Garland in *For Me and My Gal*. It was beautiful.

I didn't mind old man Levine, the owner of the hardware store, even though he was cranky and tightfisted with a buck. He was a tall good-looking guy who, in his sixties, had a full head of black hair slicked back Sinatra-style, a foul mouth and an eye for shapely broads. I encouraged him to talk about his exploits with women, the more graphic his descriptions the better. Levine also loved talking about the neighborhood, how Danny Kaye had

grown up around the corner and Bugsy Siegel and Murder Inc.
were born on these very blocks. He liked to hang out with tough
guys. Levine liked me because I listened to his stories with rapt
attention, I'd lie to his wife when he'd steal away on one of his
afternoon adventures and I had energy to burn. I'd sweep up,
carry heavy boxes, wash windows. He'd scream at me when he
found a smudge but wink when I'd point out some buxom doll
sashaying down the avenue. Today he was screaming less and,
like everyone else, smiling more. He had the radio blaring with
the sound of President Truman's salute to our soldiers and the
Andrews Sisters singing 'Ac-Cent-Tchu-Ate the Positive.' He was
so elated that he decided to close down early. All that random
kissing out on the streets had him fired up. Levine wanted in on
the action.

'Go get yourself some,' he urged me.

'Some what?'

'Tuchus!' He made a squeezing gesture with fingers,
mimicking the act of squeezing ripe female buttocks.

With a couple of empty hours in front of me, I decided to go
over to Harvey's. We'd shoot BB guns, find a stickball game and
play until dark. I couldn't remember being happier. The blocks of
my neighborhood – Livonia, Dumont, Pitkin – had turned into an
outdoor party. The Polish lady at the candy store was handing out
free lollipops. The Italian guy was giving away ices. The world was
at peace. I was walking down Atlantic Avenue, with the elevated
subway roaring above me, thinking how I never wanted the day to
end. In the past, the dark shadows cast by the massive steel poles
and girders holding up the track were scary. There were gangs in
Brownsville, and I'd sometimes imagine them lurking in those
shadows with their switchblades and zip guns. Today the shadows
were smiling. And just as I came upon the playground, where
Harvey usually hung out, I paid no attention to two guys coming
toward me.

When they stopped in front of me, not letting me pass, I saw that they weren't smiling. They were sixteen, maybe seventeen, and big.

'Where you going?' they wanted to know.

'To play.'

'No you're not.'

'Yes I am.'

'Fuck you.' And with that they threw me down, landed a couple of swift kicks and took the new wallet my parents had given me the week before for my birthday. Inside was five bucks, a fortune. I struggled, managing to kick one guy in his nuts, but that made it worse for me. He retaliated by bloodying my nose.

I was ashamed to cry, but the tears flowed. I was dazed and confused. Nothing like this was supposed to happen on the happiest day in history. Victory Day turned into defeat. Filled with humiliation, I didn't want to see my friend Harvey. I had to go home. But that wouldn't be easy. Ma would be hysterical. She'd told me to use the wallet only on special occasions. And she'd also see that, in running out of the house, I hadn't worn my tsitsis, the miniature prayer shawl that Orthodox Jewish practice required me to wear under my shirt.

And so it happened: The second I walked through the door Ma screamed at the sight of my bloody nose, my torn shirt, the absence of my tsitsis. She immediately guessed I'd been mugged, a fear of her own that she harbored all her life.

'How much they get?'

'Five dollars.'

'My God, what are you doing carrying around that kind of money? Trying to play big shot? And don't tell me you were carrying your new wallet.'

I had to admit it. She'd find out anyway. Now her screams got louder. I held my ears. She woke up Grandma, who'd been napping. When Grandma rushed in and saw me, she started crying.

She was worried about my well-being; Ma was worried about the money.

'Wait till your father gets home,' said Ma. 'Wait till he hears about this.'

'Leave Velvel alone,' Grandma admonished. 'Come, boychick, let me wash off the blood.'

I went off with Grandma to clean up. She did all she could to calm me down, but the calmness didn't last long. Grandpa Lazar and his son Morris walked through the door, screaming at each other. Hysteria was in full force.

As a lawyer and the first professional in the family, Morris was usually able to keep things calm. Not today.

'You, what do you know?' Grandpa chastised Morris. 'You were going to pay off the cops.'

'I was going to pay your fine – either that, or leave you to rot in jail.'

'What's this with jail?' Grandma wanted to know.

'Ask your son the lawyer,' said Grandpa. 'The fancy pants lawyer has all the answers.'

'Papa was coming back from the city,' Morris explained. 'He was smoking on the subway. A cop asked him to extinguish the cigarette. Papa refused.'

'I told the cop it's a free country,' said Grandpa. 'I'll smoke if I want to smoke.'

'So they took him down to the station and booked him,' Morris continued. 'That's when I got the call. All they wanted was a three-dollar fine. "Pay the fine," they said, "and we'll let you go." But he refused. When they locked him up, he wouldn't eat dinner because it wasn't kosher.'

'I wasn't eating,' said Grandpa, 'and I wasn't paying.'

'Did *you* pay?' I asked Uncle Morris.

'No, he didn't pay,' answered Grandpa. 'Fancy pants lawyer or not, I wouldn't let him throw his money down the toilet.'

'So what happened?' I asked.

'He screamed so loud and long,' said Morris, 'they threw up their hands and let him go.'

'Because they knew I was in the right,' said Grandpa.

'Thank God Morris was there,' said Grandma.

'Morris shmorris,' said Grandpa. 'Morris did nothing. Morris saw what I've been telling him is the God's truth – that he's better off being a tailor. Now he sees how the *goyim* twist their laws against us whenever they want. Now he realizes they can chase us out of the country whenever they see fit. And when it's time to run, his law degree is worth nothing. But a tailor, a tailor always finds work. Pants always need mending. Cuffs always need cuffing.'

'*What's all the commotion?*' It was my father, smelling like paint, his overalls smeared, his five o'clock shadow dark and ominous. A short handsome man, he had a barrel chest, thick powerful arms and a trigger temper. He was never happy when he got home. The subway ride was long and his stomach growled with hunger. My hope was that Grandpa's story would supersede mine. But Ma made sure it didn't. She quickly related what had happened to me, stressing how it was my *new* wallet that was stolen and how I'd neglected my tsitsis.

'To this one,' my father said, pointing to me, 'you can't say a thing. You know why? Because he's the smartest kid in the class. He's already smarter than me. He only understands one thing.'

Bubbee saw the rage rising in Pop; she knew what was coming. She'd seen what happened the day I came home with an 85 on my test when Pop wanted a 100. That was bad enough. She knew this would be worse. She tried to stop him, pleading, 'Max, the poor child only . . .'

'Don't interfere, Miriam,' Pop warned. 'This may be your house, but he's *my* son.'

And with that, he whacked me so viciously with the back of his hand that I flew across the kitchen. My head hit the wall with a thud. I slid down and started to cry. Pop came over. *Good*, I thought, *he'll see how he's hurt me*. But my thought was wrong. Without hesitation, he took my head and banged it on the linoleum floor, banging and banging until the terrible screams of my grandmother shamed him into stopping. Even then, my uncle and grandfather had to restrain him from continuing the assault.

'Have you learned your lesson?' he kept yelling in my face, his forehead bathed in sweat, his eyes blood red.

'No!' I screamed back in defiance. 'I'll never listen to you! Never! Not as long as I live!'

That night, alone in bed, my head still throbbing, I waited – I wanted – for my mother to come comfort me. It was Bubbee, though, who came instead.

'Velvel,' she said. 'If you want to cry, cry. There's no shame in crying.'

'I hate him,' I said, holding back the tears as she stroked my cheek and kissed my forehead.

'He has troubles,' Bubbee explained. 'Everyone has troubles.'

'I don't care. I hate him.'

'When you grow up you'll see the world's not easy.'

'When he grows up,' said my mother, who'd been listening at the door, 'he'll make enough money to take us out of this misery.'

Six months later I was sitting next to my father as the train slowly pulled out of Penn Station. I was excited to be making our annual winter overnight pilgrimage to Montreal, home of Pop's relatives. We were alone in the compartment when a striking young woman, no older than thirty, glanced in.

'Join us,' my father said. 'Have a seat next to my little boy.'

At twelve I was small but hardly a 'little boy.' I understood, though, that I was bait. The woman went for it. She smiled, took off her long fur coat and sat next to me, directly across from Pop. Under a fuzzy red sweater her jutting breasts looked like torpedoes. Her sweet perfume made me dizzy. My father, who rarely engaged

My father Max and my mother Bella

me in dialogue of any kind, engaged her immediately. I tried not to stare at her tits, so I looked down and studied the seams on her nylon stockings. When she crossed her legs, the sound of nylon brushing nylon electrified me.

The chitchat between the lady in red and my father gained momentum as the train gained speed. The night was pitch dark, our compartment overheated. My proximity to the woman – her abundant flesh, her intoxicating smell – made me weak. Remembering Ma's warning before we left – 'I'm sending Walter with you, Max, so you'll have to behave' – made me laugh inside. Max was trying to impress the woman. 'I'm a Boy Scout master,' he told her. 'I help out all the kids in the neighborhood, not just my own.'

How about me? I wanted to say. *You were a scoutmaster before I was born, never when I was of age to join. You're every boy's best friend but mine. Everyone in the neighborhood thinks you're a great guy, but no one knows how you whack the shit out of me for no good reason. You're a hypocrite.*

'That's wonderful,' the lady said, spreading on a coat of fresh fire-engine-red lipstick. 'Little boys need older men to show them the way.'

The discussion was turning my stomach. I turned away from the adults and closed my eyes, the rhythm of the ride making me sleepy. It was well past midnight as I drifted off into a dreamless haze. Hours later the light of dawn broke my reverie. I looked around and saw that I was alone in the compartment. Where had they gone? I didn't care. The world outside the window was magical, soft rays and rainbows of sunshine illuminating a landscape of pure white snow. A new day in Canada. Every tree, every branch, every twig covered with gleaming icicles. After an hour or so, Max returned. The lady was with him. They were expressionless. I never asked, I never knew, I was never told anything.

My grandfather Beryl, born in Russia, ran a general store in a rural section of Montreal. Like Pop, he was mysterious and distant. Behind his house was a barn with goats and sheep. My cousins and I would leap from the top of the barn into the great snowdrifts and stuff ourselves on thick sandwiches of spicy smoked meat. Surrounded by his family, my father seemed a little more relaxed. I was a little more relaxed.

I met a French-Canadian girl with long black hair and dark mysterious eyes. She said she was fascinated by my New York accent. 'You're the one with the accent,' I said. Her laugh was infectious, and when we went for walks through the old quarter of Montreal she took my hand. No girl had done that before. She led me into dark alleys where she stopped and kissed my mouth. I felt her tongue, her breasts, the wet softness between her legs. I felt like a man. This went on for days. And then one afternoon, strolling back to my grandfather's, she offered me a cigarette. I accepted. I put it in my mouth and, oblivious to all the world, was about to light up when a fist struck my chin with such force I fell to the ground. I hadn't seen my father approaching. He stood over me and, as if the first blow wasn't enough, kicked me in the side. Then kicked me again.

'Big shot,' he said. 'You're nothing but a little putz.'

The girl ran, disappearing from my life.

Back in Brooklyn, I spent the rest of the winter preparing for my bar mitzvah. I wasn't happy. My mother wasn't happy because my father's work wasn't bringing in enough. My father wasn't happy because my mother never left him alone for not making enough. He and I hardly spoke. Once, after Friday night services, we were walking home together when he turned to me and said, 'If I had to live this rotten life over, I'd rather not be born.'

Things got worse when my Aunt Frieda and her daughter Marilyn came to live with us. We were all at each other's throat: my bedroom was given to Marilyn and I was given a cot next to my parents' bedroom. Why was I supplanted when my little sister wasn't? I was enraged. I was also put off by my aunt, who spoke with a fake English accent and, because she worked for master builder Robert Moses, thought she was superior. This was the same aunt whose cleaning compulsion had her up past midnight washing walls and dusting lightbulbs.

'Enough with this goddamn cleaning!' my father would scream. 'Get this woman out of my house!'

'It's not your house,' Ma would remind him. 'If you ever figured out a way to make a real living, maybe we'd have a real house.'

'What kind of house is this,' Aunt Frieda would ask, 'when a man with an open fly goes around spitting on the floor?'

'That man is your father,' Bubbee would answer. 'Isn't it enough that he provides?'

'The woman is your daughter,' Pop would tell Bubbee. 'So why do you stick her and her kid upstairs with us? Let them live downstairs with you.'

'Look who's complaining,' Grandpa would say. 'A man who pays no rent.'

I'd cover my ears, run out the door, jump on my bike and ride as far and long as my legs held out. Brooklyn was my playground, my paradise. I'd ride over to Ebbets Field and, if the Dodgers were playing, find a way to sneak in or peak through the knotholes, where the warmth of the crowd and the sweet intimacy of the ballpark made the world seem right. I'd ride down Flatbush Avenue through Prospect Park, with its flowers and lakes and gorgeous girls sunbathing on lawns. If the weather was good, I'd cycle all the way down Ocean Parkway – past Borough Park, past Bensonhurst – until I reached Coney Island, where, hungry as a wolf, I'd inhale a Nathan's Famous frankfurter.

By the time I got back home, I was practically too exhausted to walk up the stairs. But if Bubbee's arthritis wasn't acting up, and if she wanted to take me to the Miller movie theater just down the street, I never refused. I'd sit there and watch a long melodrama in Yiddish, only half-understanding the dialogue, but loving the pleasure it was giving my grandmother. Then she'd sit there while I watched some gorgeous femme fatale – Rita Hayworth or Barbara Stanwyck – ensnare her clueless man.

'Now you'll go home and read Torah,' she'd say. 'You should know that nothing will make me prouder than when my Velvel reads from Torah.'

My bar mitzvah was a bust, a strictly low-rent affair. The women came in flower-print dresses, the men in fedoras and double-breasted suits, a few friends, a few relatives, a tiny synagogue across the street, a small reception in the downstairs part of our house, a modest spread of deli food, my mother complaining that we couldn't afford anything better, my father telling her to shut up, one uncle boasting about his butcher shop in Harlem, another about his booming *shmata* business on Seventh Avenue, Aunt Frieda whispering in my ear, 'When you're eighteen, I'll buy you

a car,' which I knew was a lie, Uncle Morris whispering, 'If I can
help you become a professional, I will,' which I knew was true,
Bubbee whispering, 'You're a good boy, you're going to help
people not so fortunate as you.' Meanwhile, I didn't feel fortunate.
There was no band, no music, nothing that brought me joy or
made me feel like a man, just an Esterbrook fountain pen.

'Tushy and pussy,' Levine said it plainly. 'There are men who go
in the back door and men who work from the front. Personally, I
like both.'

While I swept his hardware store or opened boxes in the back,
Levine loved describing his latest sex adventure in glorious detail.
I was a willing listener. It never occurred to me that he was
exaggerating or inventing. He was offering anatomical insights
about women I'd never before considered. That he was the hero
of every story – 'I couldn't count the number of times I made this
wild one come' – seemed only logical. But while he was obviously
sex-obsessed, Levine was also a sharp merchant. No one could
steal from him. When he caught kids trying to pocket a key chain
or penknife, he slapped them so viciously they ran screaming.
Unlike my father, though, his violence made sense – try and hurt
me and I'll hurt you worse.

It was through Levine that I saw a reaction to the Holocaust
markedly different from my family's. After the war, when the
horrific facts became known, my parents and grandparents were
speechless. They shook their heads, Bubbee wept, but nothing
was discussed. We endured the tragedy in a conspiracy of terrible
silence. Levine's attitude became clear one afternoon when he and
his buddy Nushky, a bear of a man with the face of a bulldog and
the voice of a frog, were drinking schnapps in the back room after
hours. I got the feeling Nushky was connected.

'Now take Nushky here,' said Levine. 'He'd slice the nuts off
those Nazi bastards. He'd stuff their schlongs down their throats.'

'They'd get the point,' Nushky explained.

'They can call us thugs,' Levine went on, 'but I'd rather be an alive Jewish thug than a dead Jewish pushover.'

It was this same impressive Levine who introduced me to the girl he called 'our own Anne Frank.' I'll call her Erika. She worked next door at the five-and-ten-cent store. She was my age, fifteen, and hauntingly beautiful – raven-black hair, dark faraway eyes, high forehead, high cheekbones, sensuous mouth, alluring figure. She was a Dutch Jew. Levine knew her parents and their story – how they and their only child Erika hid in an attic for twenty-one months until the war was over.

'She's shy,' Levine said. 'And so are you. You both need to get over it. She needs a boyfriend and you need a girlfriend. So here's a buck. Go. Ask her out. She knows who you are. I told her you're a good boy.'

She worked in the sewing department selling ribbons and bows. I went there twice before I found the nerve to say hello. Then one afternoon I waited till she was off work and offered to walk her home. That's when I noticed her severe limp. With each step, she made a sound, a small grunt, that came from deep within. She said very little. 'Would you like to go to Coney Island on Sunday?' I asked. Her lips turned up into a half-smile that I took to mean yes.

We started out early on a cold April morning. The subway wasn't crowded. Erika wore a brown raincoat big enough to be her father's. We ate hot potato knishes and drank cream sodas on the boardwalk. Watching the sun break through the clouds, we felt the day begin to warm. Erika began to warm. She said she liked rides so we went on the Cyclone. Later we stopped at a trinket stand, rode the bumper cars, pitched pennies. I threw a baseball at bottles and won a small teddy bear which I proudly presented to her. She seemed pleased but said little. Then we went to the freak show along Neptune Avenue.

The strong man had rippling biceps big as footballs. The hairy woman looked like an ape. There were snakes with four heads and midgets with scales for skin. The worst was a small child with a wrinkly face and a protruding neck that made him look like a goose.

'That's too horrible,' I said.

Erika studied the freaks and didn't say a word until we walked to a remote part of the beach and sat beneath the boardwalk. Covered by shadows, we sat alone. She spoke softly but deliberately.

'I've seen things much more horrible,' she said plainly.

For the next several minutes, she described the small attic that hid not only her and her parents but six other adults. She spoke of the fear each time she heard footsteps, each time a siren screamed, each time she grew sick and had to suppress her coughs. She slept inside a trunk so small that her legs were permanently twisted. It made me sick to hear how they dealt with their waste. When one of the men died of heart seizure, they had to live with the decaying corpse for two weeks before removing it. It confused and enraged me to hear how her loved ones – friends, aunts, uncles, all her cousins – had perished. All because they were Jews.

I had no words of comfort. The fact that my old man beat me whenever the mood possessed him hardly seemed comparable.

'You must be happy to be here,' I finally offered, looking at the open sky and the crashing waves.

Rather than answer, she slipped off her raincoat and kissed me. I was surprised and aroused, even more so when she urged me to remove her bra. I fumbled until I finally managed. She let me kiss her nipples, the most erotic act of my young life. She made sounds I'd never heard before.

'That's all,' she said. 'That's all we can do.'

I was relieved because I didn't know how to do the rest. I also felt guilty. Was this something I should be doing with a girl who

limped and had been locked up in an attic? Wasn't she a heroine?
And wasn't it wrong to kiss the naked breasts of heroines?

When I called the next week, her father said she couldn't talk
to me. I never learned why. In fact, I never saw her again. That
summer she and her parents moved to Long Island. In our
neighborhood, whenever anyone moved to Long Island it meant
they were making money. 'Her father made a mint in styptic
pencils,' Levine told me. That same summer Levine's wife caught
him humping a woman in the stockroom and filed for divorce. She
won a big settlement, he went broke, and I lost my job.

I wasn't a superstrong kid, but I wasn't weak either, and by the
time I was sixteen, when I'd grown to normal height, I made up
my mind that next time my father whacked me I'd whack back. I
was fed up with being his whipping boy. Besides, why the hell *was*
he still taking out his frustrations on me? At Brooklyn Tech, I
made good grades in advanced engineering courses. For all Ma's
endless complaints, I obeyed her. I adored my grandmother and
treated Grandpa with respect. What was my father's beef – that I
got home five minutes late? Or my shoes weren't shined? Enough
was enough.

The showdown came in 1949. My father was infuriated because
Ma told him I hadn't taken out the garbage. I was at the kitchen
table doing math homework when he walked over to take a swipe
at me. I caught his arm and wrestled him to the floor. Ma
screamed, Bubbee came running, Grandpa started spitting at us.
We awkwardly rolled around until Pop got on top of me, trying to
punch my face. I could stop him but had trouble landing any
punches of my own. Exhausted, we finally gave up. 'You're a little
shit,' he said, realizing, given my size, verbal punishment was an
easier way to go.

Meanwhile, family tension grew worse. For high Yiddish drama,
you couldn't beat the Yetnikoffs. Ma was furious with Bubbee that

Frieda was still living with us. Bubbee was furious that Ma wasn't nicer to her sister. The resentment between the two sisters got so bad that Frieda called their older brother Abe, the big shot in the *shmata* business, to complain about Ma.

'Tell that sister of ours,' said Abe, 'that I'm coming to slap the shit out of her – right now.'

Ma got hysterical.

'My brother's going to attack me! He's a man with a terrible temper! He'll wind up killing me!'

My first reaction was to round up my friends to protect Ma. So I ran out of the house to recruit the troops. Like my father, Abe was a violent man, and no telling what he might do. My friends were up for the defense of motherhood. We rushed back to our house, only to find that Uncle Abe had already arrived, but so had my father. The two men stood in my grandparents' downstairs living room, face-to-face. Pop ordered Abe out of his house. Abe reminded Pop that it wasn't his house, that Pop and Ma had no right to treat Frieda like dirt. 'You'll mind your own business,' Pop demanded. 'You'll make that sister of mine act like a human being,' Abe replied, 'or I'll teach her a lesson she'll never forget.' 'You and what army?' asked Pop. Then the shoving began, a prelude to what looked like an all-out brawl. My heart beat like crazy. I'd never seen my father in such a position. With my friends watching, my emotions ran wild. Part of me wanted Abe to deck him, for all the harm Pop had done to me. But a bigger part wanted Pop to prevail and use his fury for a noble cause. Then Pop collapsed.

It wasn't anything Abe did. The two men never came to serious blows. It's just that Pop's face turned red, his eyes grew vacant, he moaned in pain, clutched his arm and fell to his knees. You can imagine the shrieking – the sisters, the grandmother, the brother. Animosity turned to alarm, everyone hysterical – call for an ambulance, call for a doctor – me frightened and confused but knowing enough to race down the street and burst into the office of the neighborhood physician, yelling that my father was dying, running back home with Dr Weinstein by my side.

'Max has had a heart attack,' the doctor said after a quick examination.

Pop survived, but he was never the same.

I'd always seen my father as a defeated man, but a defeat that came at the hands of the world. Now his own body was defeating him. Now the defeat was complete. It was nothing I wanted to see, and it went on for years.

'Your father,' my mother would tell me, 'can no longer satisfy me.'

At first I thought she meant financially. But she was careful to make sure I got the big picture. 'He can't satisfy me in bed.'

This was more information than any son wants to know about a father.

'He can't make a living, he can't please his wife,' Ma went on. 'What good is he?'

'Stop, Ma,' I demanded. 'I don't want to hear it.'

'Now I'm in charge of changing his diet. He can't eat this, he can't eat that. Who needs the aggravation?'

'Who needs this goddamn rabbit food?' asked Pop.

'Your old diet will kill you,' said Ma.

'Better dead,' Pop shot back, 'than living like this.'

'You don't think I'd like to live like my cousin Louie?'

'Are we going to hear about Louie and his Manischewitz dealership again?'

'You should be so lucky to have such a business.'

'Louie's never helped a living soul,' Bubbee broke in. 'You could be starving on the streets and he wouldn't lift a hand.'

'Louie's a go-getter,' said Ma.

'Because he's rich you think he's a genius,' said Pop.

'I think he's a provider,' Ma insisted.

'You think every rich man is a genius,' said Pop.

'Our Walter is a genius,' Ma boasted. 'He has the IQ of a genius.'

'But if he doesn't get rich, by you he'll be a bum,' said Pop.

'He'll get rich.' Mom gave the final word. 'He has to.'

Domestic Dreams

THE FIFTIES WAS A CONFORMIST DECADE AND, IN many ways, I conformed. I wasn't looking to buck the system; I was looking to get in it. Like thousands of other working-class kids who went to Brooklyn Tech High and Brooklyn College, I was looking to rise to the middle class and realize my parents' aspirations for me. No matter how I felt about Ma and Pop, no matter how deep my confusion and ambivalence, no matter how bitter my resentments or angry my attitudes, I saw myself as their champion. The first son, the first grandson, the anointed over-achiever couldn't afford to fail. The hopes and dreams of many generations were weighing me down and spurring me on. Nothing could get in my way.

High school and college were basically tuition-free. I worked nights and weekends – a garbage man at the beach, a delivery boy in the city – to pay for my books. I dropped engineering, which bored me, and took up pre-law. My Uncle Morris made good on his promise to help. When I completed undergraduate school in three years, he saw I was serious, paid for my Phi Beta Kappa key and covered my first-year tuition to Columbia Law. It wasn't that I felt a calling for jurisprudence. It was a matter of choice. For good Jewish boys looking to get ahead it was medicine, dentistry, accounting, engineering or law. Law seemed least taxing.

All this time I lived at home. Pop grew more morose, Ma more frustrated, Bubbee more understanding, Grandpa more eccentric. One afternoon after the long subway ride from the Columbia campus in Manhattan's Morningside Heights to Brooklyn, I saw Grandpa running down Miller Avenue, chasing a group of teenaged boys. His shirttail was flying out of his pants, Yiddish obscenities flying out of his mouth. He caught the kids and smacked each one across the face. Later I learned how they'd taunted a young retarded girl, threatening her with sexual assault. It was Grandpa whom the girl came to for protection. And it was Grandpa, still spitting on the floor for no apparent reason, who provided it.

While it's true that I conformed to the aspirations of the age, my appearance at law school didn't fit the norm. While everyone in the mid-fifties wore nice Ivy League pants to school, I wore dungarees. When I was told that crewneck sweaters and blue blazers were considered cool, I replied that I didn't own any. I owned a couple of sweatshirts, which I wore not out of rebellion but because they were all I could afford. In the social hierarchy of law school, I quickly saw that I was on the bottom rung. Still shy, still a green tourist from Brooklyn roaming the sophisticated streets of Manhattan, I stayed to myself. Part of me felt lucky to be at such an elitist institution. And as an outsider, I realized my only way in was through my brain, not my sense of fashion. So I studied. First year I was third in my class, won a scholarship for the next two years and was invited to join the *Law Review*.

To a large degree, I was a loner. That superextroverted character − that out-of-control lunatic − wouldn't emerge for another couple of decades. I didn't know it at the time, but the maniac was hiding inside. Outside the good boy prevailed, even if, after a sterling first year, I dropped dramatically in class ranking. A quick study, I saw I could work less and still succeed.

Pop also got me a job as a night watchman at Bellevue Hospital's Psychiatric ward. That's where he still worked painting the hallways. As I walked those corridors listening to patients cry and scream, I thanked my lucky stars for my sanity. That sanity meant going straight through law school and finding a job. It also meant finding a woman.

I fell in love walking down Utica Avenue in Brooklyn. I fell in love with a girl minutes after meeting her. It was springtime, the trees were budding and the air was soft. I heard a distant radio playing 'My Foolish Heart.' That's when I knew that I had a heart, that I could love a woman, that life, rather than being barely endurable, could actually be sweet.

My cousin had set me up on a blind date. It happened when I was twenty-two and she had just turned twenty-one. Her name was June May Horowitz, and she said she was born in April.

'June May born in April,' I said to her. 'Sounds like a poem. Are you a poet?'

'A painter.'

'I knew you were an artist.'

'How'd you know?'

'Something about you. The way you look. The way you smile.'

Her smile was radiant and her look Bohemian. She had lustrous blond hair worn straight and long with bangs that covered her forehead. Her eyes were blue as the April sky, her jewelry turquoise and silver. She told me how she studied at Pratt Institute, how sketching and sculpting consumed her time and excited her imagination. She suggested that we go to Greenwich Village.

I'd never been to the Village. I didn't know about art or poetry. I knew nothing of the world of beatniks. As we strolled in and out

In love with June

of art galleries, June explained the emotions behind the paintings. As we sat in an espresso bar and listened to a folksinger strum his guitar while describing the dead heart of the Era of Ike, I couldn't keep my eyes off June. Afterward, at a tiny Italian restaurant on Jane Street, surrounded by other young people discussing existentialism and abstract expressionism, I felt part of a brave new world. Spaghetti never tasted so good. At a reading held in an old church from another century, a bearded man got up and read from Allen Ginsberg's just-published poem called 'Howl.' The opening line hit me between the eyes: 'I saw the best minds of my generation destroyed by madness.'

On the subway home, she described her life. She was about to move out of her parents' place to share an apartment with a girlfriend and a black man. I wondered about the sleeping arrangements. She assured me they were all just friends, that the three of them would often go to Harlem to hear jazz. From where I came from, this was radical stuff. Her unconventional attitude added to her allure. As the subway rolled under the East River into Brooklyn, I put my arm around her. 'June May born in April,' I kept saying to myself. When she moved closer to me, my heart skipped a beat. When we got to her house she invited me in to meet the folks. I took that as a good sign. They obviously had a little money, but didn't act like it. Her father owned the toy company that had invented G.I. Joe. I liked telling him – and he liked hearing – that I was at Columbia Law School. When I left, she kissed me on the cheek and said, 'Call me tomorrow.' That night, tossing and turning in my childhood bedroom on Miller Avenue, I planned my marriage proposal. It took a year to say it, but when I did, she accepted.

Basically I wanted the one thing I never had – a happy family. I had no model for a healthy male/female relationship, but I was certain that June's sweet disposition and beautiful way of looking at the world would see us through. For reasons I still can't fathom, she also believed in me. Emotionally we were perfectly compatible. It took a while for the sex to get good – I was still an inexperienced fumbler – but soon that, too, became a source of joy. Her supple body, her artistic sensitivity, her loyalty to this schlep from Brooklyn she was certain would go far . . . everything about June made me feel like a winner.

'She looks like a shiksa,' Ma said when she met her the first time. 'You sure she's not Gentile?'

'Positive.'

I hesitated before introducing her to Pop. Our relationship was still distant. This was the first time I'd brought home a girl for him to scrutinize. In his weakened state, he'd become even grumpier.

'You won't like this guy,' I warned June.

Turned out she loved him. And he loved her. Somehow the spark of her personality ignited a spark within Pop. In her company he became more animated, even charming. He asked her questions about her work and even asked her to show him her paintings, delicate watercolors of summertime scenes in the Botanical Gardens, sketches of the old boathouse in Prospect Park, renderings of the New York skyline seen from the promenade in Brooklyn Heights.

'Lovely,' my father said. I'd never heard him use the word 'lovely' before.

My mother liked June – everyone liked June – but worried that marriage might interfere with my monetary goals.

'When you marry,' she said, 'it means you need to make more, not less.'

'When you marry,' Bubbee added, 'you need to ask your heart only one question – do you love this woman?'

'I do.'

'Then God will bless you.'

With Bubbee's blessing, we married in 1957. By then I'd graduated from law school and been drafted into the peacetime Army. I was stationed in Germany but got a leave to fly home for the ceremony, held in a small reception hall on Eastern Parkway. That morning Pop had bought me a shiny fifty-dollar suit (with two pairs of pants) at Robert Hall, the discount clothier. My best man forgot to arrange for a honeymoon hotel. Brooklyn best men didn't know from such things. So June and I wound up spending the night back at my parents' place on Miller Avenue. I saw it as a fitting way to say goodbye to the only home I'd known for twenty-four years.

We lived in a little town outside Frankfurt for the final months of my military stint. I was a good soldier. If I was inclined to rebel against authority figures reminiscent of Pop, my pragmatic Jewish mind realized the Army was the wrong place to do so. I worked in the legal office and, in the most dramatic chapter of my service, helped a master sergeant falsely accused of rape beat the charge. Then there were a couple of episodes that should have warned me – but didn't – about my aberrant behavior to come:

Twice I became crazy drunk. The first time, riding the bus back to the barracks, I shit my pants. And the second time I ran through the parade grounds screaming, 'The Russians are coming! The Russians are coming!' until someone emptied a bucket of cold water on my head. Both incidents, though, happened before I married. Once June arrived and I settled into a domestic routine, I couldn't imagine booze being a problem. Besides, when I was discharged and we moved back to New York, providence was shining on me – June was pregnant and I had a job with a classy law firm.

At the end of the fifties, my slow climb up the ladder of middle-class success had begun. My first job was with the firm of Rosenman and Colin. Sam Rosenman, a former judge, had written speeches for FDR and counseled Truman as well as Roosevelt. Ralph Colin was William Paley's lawyer, the same Paley who owned CBS. This was a blue-chip firm, and I was hired as junior litigator. In law school I'd gained a reputation as an adept analyzer of tricky legal problems. As a student, I'd also been hired to work part-time for Jack Weinstein, aka Blackjack Weinstein, a law school prof (and later a famous federal judge) who had been revising every procedural New York statute, a job that drove me a little nuts. Nuts or not, the experience with Blackjack showed me I could hang with heavyweights.

The Rosenman firm weighed heavily on the side of the establishment. Among the young lawyers were a group of guys, not unlike myself, highly motivated to make it. I related to one guy in particular. His name was Clive Davis, and he'd graduated from Harvard Law. A little rotund and already balding, he appeared to be your prototypical nerd. We were roughly the same age, though he'd arrived at Rosenman slightly ahead of me. We had much in common – a Jewish Brooklyn background, deep statistical knowledge of the Dodgers, the challenge of being a new husband and father. Clive had lost his New York accent at Harvard, but his sense of street competition was acute. He was a go-getter who burned with ambition. I saw him as someone I could learn from.

We were both living in Queens, a step up from Brooklyn. Sometimes we'd ride the subway together.

'The trouble with the Rosenman firm,' Clive would say, 'is that it's all about Rosenman. Rosenman and Colin bring in the business and reap the rewards. We're there to serve them.'

'It's a job.'

'With severe limitations. I feel fenced in. I could recruit clients, I could earn a lot more.'

'I could earn a lot less. I could be out on my ass without work.'

'You'll always be working, Walter. You're too smart not to be. The challenge is to find work that works for you, not for others.'

'It's a decent beginning.'

'It's a dead end.'

'So what's the alternative?'

'Remember Harvey Schein?'

'He used to work at Rosenman. Now he's at CBS.'

'Right. He's general counsel for Columbia Records.'

'I didn't know he knew anything about music.'

'You don't have to know music, you have to know contracts. Harvey's practically alone in the legal department. He wants to bring me aboard.'

'To fiddle with contracts all day? Isn't that a bore?'

'It's what I've been doing here, only Harvey's offering me more money. He's also convinced there's a future in the record business. To tell you the truth, Walter, I'm tempted.'

Temptation won. Clive went to CBS, I stayed behind at Rosenman, but we kept an eye on each other.

Meanwhile, our first son Michael was born in 1958. My dream of a family had come true. A year later, though, my original sense of family, always ambivalent, was shattered. At age fifty-six, my father died of a heart attack.

That morning I'd been reading constitutional law in the firm library. Sam Rosenman was to appear on a TV show, and I'd been instructed to help with research. When the receptionist called to say that Uncle Morris was in the waiting room, I knew something was wrong.

Because he was a lawyer who never felt successful, my uncle was especially proud to see me in such a prestigious firm. In Morris's eyes, Rosenman was God.

'Some office you have here,' my uncle said, running his hand up and down the rich wood paneling.

'What's wrong?' I wanted to know.

'I would have called, Velvel, but this is something I had to tell you in person. Your father passed this morning.'

'When did it happen?'

'An hour ago.'

I couldn't cry, couldn't do anything but think how I'd denied this moment would ever come. For all his weakness, I assumed he'd hold on forever. My first feeling was fear. Though he'd been a tyrant and then an invalid, he'd also been a protector. I no longer had protection.

I went back to the house at 464 Miller, where the odor of death filled every room. Maybe it had always smelled that way. Maybe the dusty musty old-world feeling of my childhood home had always been oppressive, constraining, dark. Now the darkness enveloped us all.

I've blocked out memories of the funeral – of Ma and Bubbee and Grandpa Lazar, of Pop's family and cousins and the week-long shiva period during which we mourned. All I remember is coming home to June and having her hand me a legal-sized envelope with the words 'For Walter' written across the top. I presumed it concerned work. When I opened it, though, I saw it contained a single sheet of white sketch paper. In a black-and-white etching, June had drawn a likeness of my father's face that shook me to the bone. She saw beyond his uncertainty and confusion; she caught a gentleness in his gaze, a sweetness in his demeanor that I never detected, not once. Through June's eyes, he looked at me with such compassion, such undeniable vulnerability, that I found myself, for the first time, able to weep for a man I never knew. June showed me my father's soul after my father was gone. She held me in her arms that night, kissing my forehead while, like a little frightened boy, I cried myself to sleep.

When John Kennedy took office in 1961, things started shifting. Youth, energy, glamour – the country came alive. In my own way, I came alive, convinced that an offer from Clive Davis to join him in the legal department of CBS Records was the right move. My move, however, was not without equivocation. My first reaction was to say no. I was afraid of becoming a corporate legal hack. But two things convinced me otherwise:

First, Clive was persuasive. He pointed out that at Rosenman I was going nowhere fast. He also offered an incentive – $10,000 a year as opposed to my current $8,000. As a kid in Brooklyn, a salary of $10,000 had a magic ring. It meant success. I doubt if my father ever made $5,000. The real clincher, though, was my visit to Columbia Records at 799 Seventh Avenue, in the heart of Tin Pan Alley.

Walking down the hallways, I heard music. A chorus of pretty girls was rehearsing in the stairwell, singing enchanting harmonies. More pretty girls worked in the reception area. The atmosphere bristled with hustle-bustle energy. Mitch Miller rushed in one door while Jerry Vale rushed out another. I couldn't help but be impressed.

'This would be your office,' Clive said, pointing to a nice-sized room with a desk and phone with three buttons. My phone at Rosenman had no buttons.

'Emily will answer your phone,' Clive added.

Emily was another pretty girl, young and vivacious.

'I'm still a little afraid of being a cog in the corporate wheel,' I admitted. 'I don't want to spend my life doing legal grunge work.'

'That's not going to happen. The music business is open-ended. And Columbia Records is its own entity, in many ways independent from CBS. That's why we're on Seventh Avenue and Paley and his boys are on Madison. The man who runs records has his own fiefdom over here.'

'What's his name?'

'Goddard Lieberson.'

Coolest Character
of the Century

I CALLED GODDARD LIEBERSON POTTED LIEBERFARB.
Poking fun took the edge off his perfection. Because if any record
exec seemed perfectly suited for the job, this was the guy.

Accepting Clive's offer in 1961 marked the start of my twenty-
nine-year corporate career, all at CBS. I began as a junior lawyer,
learning the complex contractual lessons of the music business. I
didn't meet Goddard until the winter of 1962 when I was called
into his office. Of course I'd seen him in the hallways – a tall
handsome man who dressed with subtle panache. His shirts were
custom-made in London; his tweed jackets sported leather elbow
patches; when he occasionally wore an ascot it seemed
appropriate, never pretentious. He was said to have a dry wit and
sharp intellect. His wife, once married to George Balanchine, was
the former ballerina Vera Zorina. Along with Mitch Miller, who
also served as Columbia's chief A&R (artist-and-repertoire) man,
Lieberson had attended the Eastman School of Music, where he
wrote chamber music and choral pieces to texts by Elizabethan
poets. He was credited with making Leonard Bernstein a star. At

his urging, CBS had invested in the Broadway musical *My Fair Lady* and made a mint. Alone among his executives, the class-conscious Bill Paley considered Goddard his social equal. Paley's aristocratic wife Babe loved lunching with Lieberson, as did Groucho Marx, Ira Gershwin, Aldous Huxley, Noel Coward and Mahalia Jackson. He had written a novel, mastered Japanese and turned Columbia Records into the most prestigious music merchandiser in the world.

You can understand why I was anxious when his secretary said he wanted to see me. Ushered into his office, I sat across from him as he spoke on the phone. He acknowledged me politely, indicating he'd be off in a minute. In his early fifties, he had a full head of dark hair that grayed dashingly at the temples.

'Yes, it was wonderful,' he told his caller. 'Going to the White House is always wonderful. President Kennedy was honoring Pablo Casals and, believe me, Pablo played like an angel. The First Lady couldn't have been more gracious. Jackie spoke of Pablo's work with firsthand knowledge. Yes, Arthur Schlesinger was there, chatting it up with Stravinsky. Then when Lenny Bernstein arrived he embraced Igor so theatrically the President remarked, "Why all this hugging and kissing and none for me?"'

When the call was over, Goddard turned to me and said, 'I wasn't trying to impress you, but I actually was at the White House last night and had to report the gossip to my mother.'

'My mother wouldn't let me go to the White House without her.'

'Aside from our mothers,' he retorted, 'there's the matter of Johnny Mathis. Clive's out of town this week but he tells me you're a quick study. I'd like you to review Mathis's contract versus his sales figures. He's up for renewal.'

'What are you looking for?'

'What a serious record man is always looking for – ways to make the artist happy while making our blessed corporate accountants even happier.'

He nodded politely, indicating the audience was over, but not before saying, 'Thank you, Walter,' thrilling me with the fact that he knew my name.

Until the advent of the Beatles, the record business in the early sixties was still low-key and, in certain instances, ancillary to bigger ticket items like nightclubs and concerts. In addition to Mathis, the big names at Columbia were Andy Williams, Andre Kostelanetz and Tony Bennett. Bob Dylan was making some noise – John Hammond, the man who brought Goddard to Columbia in 1939, signed Dylan and produced his first album – but his revolutionary impact had yet to hit. Barbra Streisand, whose style reflected an earlier era, would soon emerge as a budding star. Miles Davis was Columbia's cutting-edge jazz icon, but Miles's sales, while decent, were never spectacular. The same was true for Goddard's beloved classical catalogue – big prestige, small profits. Gargantuan profits – profits beyond our wildest imaginations – were a not-so-far-off reality that no one quite saw. In the radical transformation of popular culture that became the hallmark of the sixties, the music business would expand and explode.

Starting in the fifties, RCA got a taste of the phenomenon with Elvis. Now Capitol was seeing the same amazing surge with the Beatles. Columbia was slow to catch the wave. Goddard's talents were tremendous and his popular tastes broad, but rooted in previous epochs. Broadway was his bailiwick. He was, in fact, the man who packaged and popularized original recordings of Broadway shows. As Broadway fell, though, and rock and roll rose, Columbia was caught between generations. Even the man some saw as the most powerful producer of the pre-rock era – our own Mitch Miller – wasn't what he used to be.

Miller used to be the Great Guru of pop hits. Like Goddard, he was a highbrow who understood commerce. A world-class oboist, Miller ran a hit machine that had produced everyone from Rosie

Clooney to Percy Faith to Marty Robbins. With his manicured goatee and his undulating baton, he'd also turned himself into a TV star with his *Sing Along* show. By the middle of the decade, though, Miller, who issued anti-rock and roll edicts with imperial authority, would start to fade.

I say these things now as if, back in the day, I had some socio-musical overview. I didn't. I wasn't thinking about cultural changes; I was struggling to save enough money to buy a house. When I hit thirty, I was just another company man living in a modest place in Queens with a wife and two kids (Daniel was born in 1962). June kept painting and sculpting, but without designs on a career. She seemed content to raise the boys and leave the moneymaking to me. I was content to go from making $10,000 to $15,000. I had a knack for mastering the intricacies of contracts. I kept my nose clean. I wasn't loud or raucous or even pushy. I was observant. I saw how Goddard never worked up a sweat and was out most days by five. I saw how Clive always worked up a sweat and stayed most nights till eight. Goddard had arrived. Clive was trying to get there. Goddard was riding the crest of a glorious past. Clive was looking for the wave of the future.

'It's a business of relationships,' Clive would say to me on our subway rides home, 'and the most important relationships are with the artists – those signed and even, more critically, those unsigned.'

'Isn't that what the A&R guys do?' I asked. 'Aren't lawyers supposed to be lawyering?'

'There's no reason to restrict ourselves. Record judgments are as much about business as music, maybe more so.'

'In my judgment, Harvey Schein is doing a great job setting up these CBS-owned foreign subsidiaries for Columbia product,' I said, referring to the man who'd hired Clive. 'He's revolutionizing the international arena.'

'Harvey's a brilliant guy, and if you're interested in international, I can push you in that direction.'

'Any push is appreciated,' I acknowledged as the train pulled into the Flushing station.

'But keep your eye on the artists, Walter. The artists and the money are one and the same.'

The first time I saw Bill Paley, Our Father Who Art CBS, was just after we'd moved to the new headquarters in the superclassy supercold skyscraper called Black Rock on Sixth Avenue and Fifty-second Street. Designed by Finnish architect Eero Saarinen, Black Rock was an elegant monument to corporate conformity. CBS had been dubbed the Tiffany Network and Paley, starting out in the twenties, had built an empire based on news, music and entertainment. His father had made money in the cigar business, but it was young Bill who had the vision to see the future of radio, phonograph records and television. Black Rock was a concrete manifestation of that vision.

When he welcomed an assembly of employees to our new home, Paley had a princely air about him. He smiled easily and spoke glibly, yet always with reserve. Everyone knew he was Jewish, but everyone also knew he didn't like talking about it. He liked mingling with the High WASP Society. He appeared unapproachable. His number-two man, Frank Stanton, ran the vast operation like a Secretary of Defense. It was Stanton who set down the regulations for Black Rock.

Moving to Black Rock meant leaving the hustle bustle of Tin Pan Alley. I'd miss the old-school ambience of tunesmiths, song pluggers and Broadway delis. Black Rock was ominous. Black Rock was thirty-six stories of rising ambition, an impossible-to-miss metaphor for many of us looking to move up. A homage to the Man in the Gray Flannel Suit, it had an exterior of charcoal-gray granite – tasteful, unyielding, permanent. Its interior was dictated by an Ayatollah Committee headed by Stanton. Every detail down to the last pushpin conformed to code. One employee was busted for hanging a small rug on his wall. Another was accused of plant abuse for feeding his ficus an extra cup of water. Corporate hierarchy was explicit everywhere, from the dimensions of your office to the size of your wastebasket. My wastebasket was small.

In this button-down world of extreme standardization, Columbia Records lost a measure of its individuality. Working in Tin Pan Alley, Goddard had cultivated the élan of idiosyncrasy. But now that we were lumped in the tower with every other CBS division, something was missing. At the same time, we started feeling new pressure from above. From the executive suites where Paley and Stanton ruled the roost came not so subtle reminders that profits and profits alone were, in fact, the mortar that built Black Rock.

Goddard took it all in stride. He had long complained that, compared to news, music was undervalued. Clive had long complained that, compared to rival labels, we were underpaid. Clive continued to outwork, outthink and outmaneuver his colleagues. His designs on artists and repertoire were more apparent, and in 1965, just a year after moving to Black Rock, Goddard anointed him administrative vice president, granting him authority over the A&R men. I was moved up to general counsel.

I was good at summarizing, analyzing and remedying intricate contractual issues. I discovered I was also good at dealing with difficult characters. For example, I found myself face-to-face with one such character who could have come out of the smoky backroom of Levine's hardware store in Brooklyn.

The task was simple – go to Roulette Records and collect the $400,000 that its owner, Morris Levy, owed Columbia for manufacturing. If Levy was infamous at the time, I didn't know it. Still in greenhorn Jimmy Olsen mode, a mild-mannered lawyer for a great metropolitan corporation, I wasn't privy to inside music biz gossip about tycoons with mob connections. I knew Roulette had enjoyed success with R&B artist Frankie Lymon and jazzman Count Basie. Levy had also owned nightclubs, including Birdland, as well as a big music publishing firm. He was also in the cutout business – buying and reselling discontinued records from other labels at discounted prices. Beyond that, I strolled into his office clueless.

He sat behind his desk where he clipped coupons from stock certificates. In those days, you got dividend payments only when you submitted coupons. I waited a long while before he looked up. When he did, I was a little startled, maybe even a little scared. He had a helluva mug – big head, piercing eyes – and huge hands. When he stood, he towered over me like a mountain. His rough-hewn face was covered in a scowl. Rather than talk, he barked. His accent was guttural New York street.

'Whadya want?'

'Mr Levy, I'm here to discuss the matter of your debt to Columbia Records in the amount . . .'

'You don't think I know how much I owe?'

'I'm here because . . .'

'You'se here because you're a fucking lackey. What's your name again?'

'Yetnikoff.'

'A nice Jewish boy.'

'I don't know about the "nice" part.'

'You're one of those goddamn legal beagles.'

'I am a lawyer.'

'Don't say it with such pride. The biggest schmucks I know are lawyers. You work for Clive?'

'I do.'

'And Clive didn't warn you about me?'

'He called you a gentleman and a scholar who always honors his debts.'

That got Levy to laugh. 'So Yetnikoff is a wise guy.'

'Yetnikoff is looking for wisdom, Mr Levy.'

'Call me Moishe. I like your chutzpah, Yetnikoff, but I still don't see how the fuck you're going to collect this debt.'

'The contract is explicit.'

'I use contracts to wipe my ass.'

'Then I imagine you have quite a sore ass.'

'You still don't know who I am.'

'I know I'd like to go back to the office and report a successful transaction.'

'You got a lot to learn, Yetnikoff. Successful transactions don't have shit to do with contracts.'

'Then what *do* they have to do with?'

'Moxie. Raw fucking moxie.'

A week later, a check to CBS for $400,000 arrived along with a scribbled note that read, 'To bright boy Yetnikoff – I'm not paying because I gotta. I'm paying because I wanna. I'd hate to see you in trouble so early in your career. That'll come later. Moishe.'

It was 1967, and Tokyo was ablaze in neon. I walked around the Ginza a little dazed. This was my first big trip for the company as chief counsel. This was also my first big deal. I was helping put together an arrangement between Sony and Columbia for a joint record company in Japan. I didn't know it at the time, but the association would change every aspect of my life for decades to come.

I flew the first leg of the trip with Goddard. We told each other our life's story a couple of times over while consuming more than a couple of martinis. Goddard was an intellectual. God knows I wasn't. Maybe that's why he found it easy to talk to me. He didn't have to impress me with insights into Jean-Paul Sartre. If he had, I'd be bored. Instead he told war stories of amorous adventures. He had many. In fact, when he traveled to Japan, he did so with his customary cool. He stopped in L.A. and then in Hawaii for R&R.

Meanwhile, I schlepped in on the all-night flight and arrived exhausted.

Harvey Schein, head of international, was already there. Harvey was the guy who got the idea of the hookup one day while walking the streets of Tokyo. He looked up, saw a huge sign that said SONY and decided to call. They were interested and soon the makings of a deal were in place. My job was to actually write the contract. I'd worked on a draft for weeks.

The three of us – Goddard, Harvey and myself – went to Sony headquarters, then housed in a creaky old building. When two short men, unassuming and unfailingly polite, greeted us in blue cotton work jackets, I presumed they were receptionists. They were, in fact, the bosses, Akio Morita and his younger number-two man Norio Ohga. Morita was one of the great pioneers of consumer electronics. Ohga, who headed his music division, was a Renaissance man who, like Lieberson, was an accomplished classical musician as well as a business wizard. With a flair I later came to understand as gracious efficiency, they whisked us into a conference room to discuss the deal. Proudly, I pulled out my carefully worded contract which ran over fifty pages. Just as I was about to go over the salient points, Goddard stopped me and began speaking Japanese. Morita and Ohga were stunned and delighted. Next thing I knew, the four of them were off in another room while I was left to cool my heels.

'Don't worry, Walter,' said Goddard. 'We'll have it worked out in no time.'

Three hours later the group emerged with a dramatically different deal. Rather than have Sony distribute product, our new joint venture would create a distribution entity of its own. This meant an extensive contract rewrite.

'You don't mind, do you, Walter?' Goddard asked with gentlemanly aplomb.

'Not in the least,' I lied.

A day later I emerged with a pile of new papers. I added some points of my own. By the time I left Tokyo, the deal was done. It was 50/50. CBS kicked in a million and so did Sony. Twenty years later that investment would earn the corporation some $100 million in profits per year. The association would give me power I never dreamed of, not to mention untold misery.

Meanwhile, back at Black Rock, Goddard made another monumental move. In 1967, just after returning from the Monterey Pop Festival, an event of seismic proportions, Clive was named President of Columbia Records. Suddenly everything shifted. The corporate climate would never be the same. Every aspect of recorded music was about to change; the dynamics of power – the interplay between the artist and the label – would be radically redefined. Mass culture was being revolutionized. The old order was dying while a new Age of Aquarius was being born. Few understood the implications. I know that I didn't. But Clive did. As a result, Clive was crowned Emperor, a role he relished to the point of no return.

Piece of My Heart

TO CONSUMMATE THE DEAL WITH BIG BROTHER AND the Holding Company, Janis and her band marched into the conference room where Clive, myself and a few other execs were assembled.

'The way we celebrate,' Janis said, 'is that we all take off our clothes. And Clive, I get to fuck you.'

Clive turned green.

Clive, who signed the hippest of the hip young contemporary artists, was a square. I don't say that disparagingly. I was a square myself. With the exception of Goddard, whose cool could never be questioned, most of us were squares. But where Goddard's acumen rested in the realm of classical and Broadway pop, Clive saw how the youth culture was rewriting the rules. Clive was a button-down lawyer, a universe away from the hippies. In some ways he – and the rest of us – were the ultimate company men, the sort of establishment figures the counterculture liked to mock. But at the Monterey Pop Festival, Clive had an epiphany. He came back transformed. He described it in lofty terms. 'I have,' he said, 'caught a glimpse of the new world.' He spoke of the sweetness of the flower children and the transcending nature of their music. He put on a necklace of love beads. He became a convert, deeply identifying with the purity of hippie sentiment. He started wearing Nehru jackets and tinted glasses. I think Clive was sincere. And just as sincerely, inside his head I believe he saw dancing dollar signs.

Monterey was where he first heard Janis and her Big Brother and the Holding Company. As a result of his California experience he also signed the Electric Flag, the Chamber Brothers, Santana and Blood, Sweat & Tears. Clive cut a label deal with Lou Adler, a producer of Monterey Pop, and immediately hit with Scott McKenzie's 'San Francisco (Be Sure to Wear Flowers in Your Hair),' which became the anthem of the Summer of Love. Suddenly everything started to pop – Simon & Garfunkel, who had been huge sellers since the 1965 'The Sound of Silence,' had a number-one smash with the 1968 'Mrs Robinson.' The Chamber Brothers had 'Time Has Come Today.' Blood, Sweat & Tears had 'You've Made Me So Happy.' Clive got even happier when Donovan, another one of his signings who earlier had 'Sunshine Superman' and 'Mellow Yellow,' went top five with 'Hurdy Gurdy Man.' Through manager David Geffen, Clive recruited Laura Nyro, the great singer/songwriter. At a time when FM radio was emerging as a power and albums (in the aftermath of *Sgt. Pepper's*) were seen as whole artistic entities, Nyro's *Eli and the Thirteenth Confession* was a smash with music critics.

I watched all this from afar. Clive's upward climb was impressive and, at times, funny. One afternoon I dropped by his office and saw he was taking dancing lessons so he could shake his ass to the contemporary music he was championing. Clive doing the boogaloo was not an inspiring sight. He looked like a robot.

'Loosen up,' his teacher would urge. Clive tried, but rather than resemble the free-flowing free-loving hippies he'd seen at Monterey, he looked like Dr Frankenstein's unwieldy monster.

Clive was obsessed with success. I'd accompany him to midtown Manhattan record stores to inspect the placement of our product. When Columbia Records weren't in the front of the bins, Clive would move them there. Clive wouldn't hesitate to call me at home on weekends, regardless of the hour.

'Laura Nyro wants to see her contract,' he'd say. 'Geffen's hysterical.'

'Geffen's always hysterical.'

'Have it on my desk Monday morning.'

'Clive, it's Sunday night.'

'I want to keep these people happy.'

'These people can wait,' I said, convinced I was dealing with Clive's compulsion to please the artist rather than any real deadline.

'What's wrong with you, Walter, I need it right now. Do it!'

I didn't do it till the next day.

Clive's relationships with artists and managers marked another major difference between himself and Goddard. Artists sought out Goddard while Clive sought out artists. As the sixties came to an end, the paradigm of power was turned on its head. The artist no longer had to go to the label, hat in hand.

Goddard was the gentleman executive, Clive the hungry go-getter. Goddard did what he liked. Clive did what he had to. He sold like crazy. He fought off fierce competitors like Ahmet Ertegun and Jerry Wexler at Atlantic, seasoned vets with vast music backgrounds. By haunting concerts and hanging out backstage, Clive stayed on the scene. By carefully cultivating his persona as a hitmaker, he drew ambitious artists into his circle. He and his PR staff worked the press. Clive couldn't get enough press and soon began believing the hype surrounding his

ascension. Rather than opine, he pronounced. He was the new
Pope of Pop.

I was named executive vice president of international in 1969.
Setting up subsidiaries and selling our records in foreign markets
intrigued me. I was good at it. I liked the travel and the open-
ended sense of opportunity. I also liked the company conventions.
As my managerial responsibilities grew, so did my schmoozing
skills. Tokyo, Paris, London, Los Angeles, fancy hotels, loose
women, open bars. It was at such a meeting in L.A. that I first
faced the test of sexual temptation. In spectacular fashion, I
failed.

Sex had always been the subtext of these corporate get-
togethers, especially in the late sixties and especially in the music
business. The guys tended to go nuts. If we were square
businessmen watching the sexual revolution play out in the music
we sold, we sure as hell wanted free and easy sex for ourselves.
Some execs were growing long hair, smoking pot and sporting love
beads, but most were just Old School Horny. That tried-and-true
standby – pay-for-pussy – was the music biz norm. Hookers in all
forms did a bustling business during these meetings. And, believe
me, things got kinky. One well-known gent gained fame for his
endurance as a practitioner of nonstop cunnilingus, performed
before a cheering crowd of wide-eyed colleagues. I watched with
interest, but wasn't ever inclined to buy sex – maybe because it
seemed a little tawdry, but probably because my marriage was, at
least to my mind, in good shape. I loved June, she was a great
lover, so why cheat? Besides, she'd been a tremendously
supportive wife and beautiful mother to our sons.

Then on one particular afternoon in the pool of the Beverly
Hills Hotel I felt warm flesh rubbing against my leg. I looked up
to see a smiling lady whom I knew as the wife of a famous literary
figure. I had met her a few times but only to chat briefly. I smiled

back, she moved closer, and then closer, before whispering in my ear, 'Let's go to your room and fuck.'

So we did. She was wild. I was wild. She was insatiable. I was insatiable. She said her husband didn't like to shtup. I didn't mention my wife. I tried not to think of my wife. I was surprised at how quickly I fell into the three-day affair. Surely I was guilty, but the guilt didn't stop me. I could say it was the naughty ambience of the music biz meeting, the fact that we were all oversexed, the phenomenon of aggressive out-of-town businessmen looking to party. All that was true, but the deeper truth is that when she said, 'Let's fuck,' I said, 'Okay.'

Before the week was over, I was feeling secretly proud of the number of orgasms I had set off in this woman. I felt bold. I felt like a big shot. It didn't matter that we'd never screw again. She wandered back into her life and I carried on with mine. Sex was just sex, instant gratification, a way to release tension, nothing more, nothing less.

At a company dinner during the convention, Clive came over to my table.

'Looks like you'll soon be taking over international,' he said. 'But before that happens, I wish you'd get a little hipper.'

'What are you talking about, Clive?'

'Your shirt collar. It needs to be spread out over your sports coat. You've got it tucked in.'

'I like it tucked in.'

'Spread it out.'

'I'm keeping it tucked.'

'The spread is where it's at.'

'Look, Clive, you spread, I'll tuck.'

The next afternoon Clive invited me to a bash hosted by his friend Abe Somer, a big-time L.A. music lawyer. In the late sixties, Abe was in the middle of the mix. His parties were legendary. This was the era of Hollywood hippie dippies mingling with showbiz moguls, trading cultural tips over pipes stuffed with hash. Tiny Tim was there, and everyone was singing something about 'Captain Jack will get you high, Captain Jack will get you high.' Who the hell was Captain Jack? Unable to posture effectively, I felt like a fool. I thought – *what in hell does any of this have to do with me?* Clive worked it well, but I was an awkward tourist. Maybe my tucked-in collar should be spread out.

When I got home to Great Neck, I was exhausted. I was also guilty for having banged Mrs Hot Box back in L.A. But walking into the impressive suburban house we'd just bought in Great Neck, I started feeling better. This was our first big house. When my mother saw it, she started crying. This was the American dream, and if I'd been a bad boy for a couple of nights, I was entitled. Look how I provided.

'Looks like I'm being appointed president of international,' I told June, who was sitting at the kitchen table chalking in the outlines of a face on a sketch pad.

'So that means you'll be gone even more?'

'It means I'll make more money than ever before.'

'That's good, Walty.'

'You don't sound too thrilled.'

'I have nothing to complain about.'

'And nothing to be happy about? You don't like the house?'

'Of course I like the house. I picked out the house. But I feel . . . well, a little trapped out here. I never thought I'd wind up in Great Neck.'

'We talked about living in the city, but you said it was better for the boys out here.'

'And it is. It's just that . . . it's like living in a beautiful cocoon. Maybe it's too beautiful, maybe it's all too good.'

'But you draw, you paint, you make your sculptures.'

'I'm making them less and less.'

'So you'll find something else to do.'

'I'm sure I will.'

'And I'll try to keep the trips to a minimum.'

'That's not going to happen.'

'Probably not.' I had to agree.

'Anyway, welcome home, Walty. I'm going to bed.'

She came over and kissed me on the forehead. I felt her sadness, and when I looked at the sketch she'd drawn I saw the face of a deeply depressed woman, a poignant self-portrait in blue. She left and I sat alone.

I turned on the radio to catch the news. 'Janis Joplin died today in Hollywood,' said the broadcaster. 'Early reports indicate a drug overdose.' Then he played 'Piece of My Heart,' the song that jump-started her career. 'Just take another little piece of my heart, baby,' she kept singing over and over again. 'Just take another little piece of my heart, baby.' Upstairs I thought I heard my wife crying.

PART 2

Corporate Climbing

Clive Davis at the head of the table. Walter on the extreme left, sitting across from June

A nerdy junior lawyer presents Johnny Cash with a gold record

James Taylor, just after he signed

Pillow Talk

STORMING INTO THE SEVENTIES, COLUMBIA RECORDS really caught fire. In death, Janis sold more than in life. Clive couldn't miss – Santana, Johnny Winter, Blood, Sweat & Tears, Chicago. Simon & Garfunkel's 'Bridge Over Troubled Water' broke the bank. The hits kept coming, the numbers kept climbing, the stakes got higher.

The business was changing fast. Within a year, even Barbra Streisand would release a rock album, *Stoney End*. I wanted in on the action. As head of international, I became interested in artist acquisition. Everyone congratulated me when we signed Johnny Nash, then living in England, to our sister Epic label. Nash's rock-reggae *I Can See Clearly Now* was a smash. Bit by the bug of talent recruitment, I sought other such signings, but few came through.

As I hit the international highway, as I ran from one swanky hotel to another, as my salary and status rose, so did my sexual hunger. Such would be the case for years to come. My first full-blown affair, which lasted four years, was with a woman in the music business, an exec who understood the exciting nuances of both boardroom and bedroom. I'll call her Diana. The fact that she was married to a sexually indifferent schlemiel only fueled *her* rationale. Our rationales, though, were bullshit. We simply liked fucking each other. I liked her scent; I liked the intrigue; I liked viewing myself as a man who could satisfy more than one woman; I liked all the slipping and sliding and ducking and hiding.

In opulent suites at the Inter-Continental Hotel in London or Paris, we'd screw like rabbits and then talk business. Because she knew the cast of characters who dominated the melodrama at CBS, our postcoital conferences were as hot as our shtups. My increasingly twisted mind viewed her demanding nature in a good light. She demanded superenergized performance from me – as a sex partner and as a corporate manager. My ability to rise to the occasion in both arenas, hitting her G spot while mastering the complexities of Columbia Records' worldwide operation, made me feel great. Like all adulterers, I started leading two lives.

In 1972, CBS boss Bill Paley retired his longtime second-in-command Frank Stanton. A couple of years earlier he had canned his lawyer, buddy and close adviser of forty years, Ralph Colin of the Rosenman and Colin firm, with the chilling statement 'You were never my friend, Ralph. You were my lawyer.' I had yet to experience a one-on-one with Paley, but the tone he set surely exacerbated my – and everyone else's – nervous condition.

'Paley can be whimsical when it comes to dismissing staff,' Goddard told me during a moment of candor. 'The closer he gets to you, the more he sees your warts. So you learn to keep your distance.'

The distance between Goddard and Clive had noticeably widened. The greater Clive's success, the less use he had for his predecessor. Goddard was a tough act to follow, but Clive had done it. Now his own legend rivaled Goddard's. Clive's picture appeared in *Billboard* more often than pictures of most of our artists. He was credited for everything short of the Vietnam peace treaty. And he liked it, encouraged it, never tired of cultivating his image of infallible starmaker. In the process, he made Lieberson seem a relic of the past. I don't think Goddard objected – his eye was on a comfortable retirement – until the insult became too blatant to be ignored. That happened at a monumental Columbia Records convention in London.

Ever since anyone could remember, Goddard always ended the four-day affair with an illuminating overview, a speech that never failed to entertain and reaffirm his role as *éminence grise*. This year, though, it was Clive, in an especially self-serving mode, who gave the speech. He excised Goddard from the program. We were stunned. And in his own quiet way, Goddard was pissed. Relations between the two men never healed.

The corporate climate got even chillier when Paley appointed Arthur Taylor President of CBS.

'Taylor,' said Goddard, 'is Paley's view of himself as a young man.'

In his thirties, Taylor came from International Paper, where he'd been exec vp. He had no background in broadcasting, news or entertainment. But he was tall, charming and handsome; he was the kind of WASP Paley saw as a symbol of CBS class. The office joke was that Taylor got the job because he was a good tennis player.

The first time I met Taylor, he falsely mentioned that he had a Jewish grandmother.

'Actually, Arthur,' I explained, 'I'm not Jewish at all. My real name is Rensaleer Yeats. My father was an English nobleman and my mother a Moscow-born scholar who served the Queen of England as a translator and political adviser. On a state trip to Russia on behalf of the Crown, my mother, pregnant with me, was kidnapped and raped by Cossacks. She was rescued by the

Queen's secret agents. But the tragedy killed my father – when he heard the news, he dropped dead of a heart attack – and so traumatized my mother that she reverted to her maiden name, Yetnikoff, and remained secluded in a nunnery outside London for the rest of her life, devoting herself to a study of the saints. I was born in that nunnery and sent to America, where I was raised by Franciscan monks. That's where I learned Latin and Greek.'

'Is that true?'

'Of course. Call me Rensaleer.'

Rather than humor Taylor, Clive resented him. He resented the fact that Taylor was younger than him. He'd point out that Taylor's former employer, International Paper, didn't do the volume of Columbia Records. Some thought Clive was miffed that he hadn't been chosen, but I didn't see it that way. Clive viewed himself – and still does – as a record man. He had no interest in running the daddy corporation. But neither did he want any interference with his day-to-day operation. He made it clear that he and he alone understood the vagaries of pop music. He had set up a fiefdom that defied scrutiny by outsiders. How could they possibly understand how to deal with Bob Dylan, Sly Stone or Bruce Springsteen?

'Please, Arthur,' Clive would chastise his boss at big managerial meetings, 'do *not* question my judgment. You simply do not understand the market. You do not understand the music business.'

Clive was right, but Clive was arrogant, and arrogance – he would learn, I would learn, everyone eventually learns – has a way of taking down the mighty.

The fall took us by surprise. It came in 1973 during the time of Watergate when conspiracies and plots had us all half nuts. The fall came after 'A Week to Remember,' the unintentionally ironic title of Clive's concert presentations of the dazzling talent assembled under his leadership – Bruce Springsteen, Earth, Wind & Fire, Miles Davis. It happened in L.A., and everyone was there. Dressed in white from head to toe, Clive was the host-with-the-most, the impresario-on-the-scene, Johnny-on-the-spot at every show.

Not long after Clive was back at Black Rock, he was called to Arthur Taylor's office and canned. Just like that. He was also served with a civil complaint by CBS for expense account violations and escorted out of the building. You can imagine the fallout.

I wasn't privy to the particulars, but I never believed that Clive was guilty of anything more than minor monetary indiscretions, if that. I believed that the corporation – and Taylor in particular – overreacted. The plain truth was simple: Clive had made CBS untold millions; compared to his counterparts at rival labels, Clive, as he often complained, was underpaid. If Frank Stanton had still been in charge, he would have laughed the charges away. But straight-arrow Taylor was naive and, I believe, miffed at Clive's condescending attitude. He panicked. He mistakenly thought the scandal might lead to CBS losing its broadcasting licenses. Taylor lost his common sense.

How did Goddard react? With his access to Paley, couldn't Goddard save Clive? Maybe, but Goddard, like Taylor, had endured Clive's condescension. If Clive had shown Goddard a bit more respect, Goddard might have intervened. But Clive never gave him his due. Consequently, Goddard was content to let Clive twist in the wind. Besides, Paley and Taylor were calling on Goddard to head the records group and replace the man who had replaced him. Karmic elements were in play.

Meanwhile, Irwin Segelstein was brought over from CBS-TV and given the job of running the domestic record company, reporting to Goddard. The rest of us were beset by a bevy of legal committees, all scrutinizing our files to see if we'd been stealing. Everyone was scared shitless. The code of the music business, especially in promotion, was loose. If you hired a hooker for a company party, you buried the charge among the flowers and wine. This had been going on since Eve ate the apple. Now suddenly the corporate buzz brains, under Arthur 'Mr Clean' Taylor, were putting the screws to us.

'We have a serious problem, Yetnikoff,' Taylor said to me after closing the door to his private office.

'What?'

'Your car. You're driving a company Mercedes that's not authorized for your use.'

'You're worried about my car, Arthur?'

'Most definitely.'

'Well, here's the story of my car. I had a ten-year-old Buick. Clive saw it and said, "When you pick up clients coming in from Europe and Asia, is this the car you use?" "Yes." "Well," Clive said, "show a little class. Get a Benz." That's the story of my car.'

'Mr Davis doesn't remember it that way.'

'Of course he doesn't. Who remembers that kind of detail except a putz like you. I happen to have a written memo authorizing the purchase. But I have no intention of showing it to you.'

The Spanish Inquisitor sat there with his mouth open.

I blew up. 'Look, Arthur, I run a huge international division. Subsidiaries in dozens of countries. Deals with thousands of suppliers. If I wanted to steal, I could steal millions. I could steal you blind. If you want to investigate me, do it thoroughly, but please, don't insult me with this car business. It's bullshit.'

The bullshit, though, went on for months. The troops were demoralized by the questioning, which turned up nothing. More infuriating was a report aired by CBS News, our sister division, pointing fingers without proof. Even Segelstein was outraged at his former colleagues for making a mountain out of a molehill. We both complained to Taylor but Taylor pleaded ignorance.

Later that year, the United Jewish Appeal honored Morris Levy with a banquet. I was there, along with everyone else in the business. Everyone was discussing Clive.

'So, Moishe,' I asked him, 'what about this Clive business?'

'CBS has their head up their ass. Clive is a Cub Scout. If he took, he took peanuts. Do they think they're running a record company or a fucking nunnery?'

'It's a clean-cut corporation.'

'Ain't no such animal. How do you think Paley signed Bing Crosby? You don't think someone got greased? In this business, someone's always getting greased. It's the American way.'

'What do I know?'

'You know the same fucking thing we all know. It's about getting hits. Now what's going to happen to my bright boy Velvel?' he asked, using my Yiddish name.

'Not sure, Moishe. Segelstein is in.'

'Segelstein doesn't know the business. Lieberson knows. And Lieberson knows that Yetnikoff knows. Lieberson is class. Stick with Lieberson.'

I did.

'You have an artist in England named David Essex,' Goddard told me. 'Are you familiar with him?'

'He just cut an album.'

'With at least one strong song. I heard it the other day. "Rock On" is a hit. Get behind it.'

Turned out that Goddard's instincts went beyond Bartók, Stravinsky and Percy Faith. By January of 1974, 'Rock On' was top five.

That same winter I was in Paris. My suite had a view of the Eiffel Tower, an erect inspiration for the nonstop sex I was enjoying with Diana. Our relationship had gotten steamier. We'd manipulate our schedules to maximize our secret meetings. The more exotic the locale, the longer we lingered. Diana was one of those modern women who swore that sex and sex alone was enough to sustain her. She didn't need to hear about love or commitment. Naturally I loved her attitude and wondered why there weren't more women like this when I was growing up. Our connection, though, was more than sexual. She was as passionate about my career as I was. After a serious screw or two, our pillow talk would turn to office politics.

'Segelstein will never stay. They want someone else to run records,' she said.

'I'm not sure.'

'I am. And I think Taylor likes you. He knows you're honest. And he knows you see the big picture. He sees you can run the whole operation. Can't you see that?'

'I'm beginning to.' After successful shtuping, I was beginning to believe I could be President of the United States. In fact, my fantasies of taking over – of being the new Clive or the new Goddard – increased in direct proportion to my adulterous activities with Diana. The more I got, the more I wanted.

'You're a self-made man,' she said. 'Everything you've accomplished you've accomplished on your own. There's no end to those accomplishments.'

There seemed no end to the sex. Friday turned to Saturday, Saturday turned to Sunday. 'Sorry,' I said to June when I got home. 'Got delayed by business meetings all weekend long.' More and more, June withdrew to her drawings, which seemed sadder and sadder. My world excluded her. If she knew about my secrets, as I suspect she did, she said nothing. My secrets emboldened me, my job consumed me. I was flying to Brussels, to Rome, to Berlin.

I was whipping the international division into tip-top shape. Profits were strong. By the time I got off the plane in Tokyo in 1975, my Sony friends, Akio Morita and Norio Ohga, were delighted to see me. Our joint venture had proven lucrative for all. The soundtrack for Barbra Streisand's *The Way We Were* seemed as big in Japan as it had been in America.

'I'd like to talk with you,' said Ohga, 'but big boss wants to talk to you first.'

'What big boss?'

'Mr Arthur Taylor. He say, "Soon as Walter arrives, have him call."'

Taylor got right to the point. 'Walter, Goddard is retiring. I'm appointing you President of the CBS Records Group and a vice president of CBS Inc. Congratulations.'

How did it happen? I later learned that pillow talk helped my case. Turned out that an extremely close female friend of Taylor's was a passionate advocate of me. It also helped that Arthur and I shared the same lawyer, Stanley Schlessinger, who argued my case. The victory made me giddy. Within a few minutes, though, I found my equilibrium and swung into action. I made weekend reservations at the Kahala Hilton in Honolulu. On the way home, I'd stop over for a tryst with Diana. If I was going to celebrate, I was going all the fucking way.

All the Way

TO TRACE A LOST SOUL IS TRICKY BUSINESS. I SUPPOSE if I knew where I had lost it, I could go back and claim it. But in my case the loss was incremental. It happened over an extended period of time, the result of not one but a series of events. The loss was confusing and, most important, something of which I was unaware. I see it now. I sure as hell didn't see it then. What I do see, though, is that the series of events began on the day Taylor appointed me Great Führer. The appointment went to my head, went to my dick, and over a period of years turned me into a madman. The more powerful I became, the greater my rewards, the deeper my lunacy.

I knew I needed help, which is why I turned to Goddard. I figured I'd do the opposite of Clive. Rather than marginalize Goddard, I'd maximize him. I'd keep him right there by my side. I saw him as a seasoned warrior who'd won a half-century's worth of bloody battles. I was happy to grant him any title he wanted – over me, beside me – just as long as he advised me. But it wasn't meant to be. Goddard didn't explain the friction

The gang's all here.
From left, Arthur Taylor, Goddard Lieberson,
Katherine Pelgrift, yours truly, Norio Ohga

between him and Paley, but I knew it was there. Some said
Paley was forcing Goddard into retirement. Goddard told me he
had been ready to leave years before. His dream was to move to
Santa Fe to write novels and compose music. I tried to convince
him to stay part-time. My notion was to make him a roving
ambassador for Columbia Records, allowing him to travel the
world, evaluating the state of our business in foreign markets.
'Fine,' he said, 'as long as I'm not required to go to a single
corporate meeting.'

I took the idea to Taylor; Taylor took it to Paley; Paley said no.

'It's no use, Walter,' Goddard conceded. 'One must learn to exit
with grace.'

No one had greater grace than Goddard. I held a memory of
when he met David Clayton-Thomas, lead singer for Blood, Sweat
& Tears. David had perfect pitch. He asked Goddard to take a fork
and strike a glass half filled with water. David accurately called out

the note. Goddard returned the favor by asking David to strike four glasses of water, each filled to varying degrees. Goddard accurately called out all four notes. Then the two men – the pop rocker and the erudite gentleman – embraced affectionately.

Great affection for Goddard was reflected in the retirement party given by Bill Paley. Maybe it was Paley's wife Babe, the regal swan, who insisted on honoring Goddard, or maybe Goddard had melted the old man's heart of stone. Either way, it was my first time at the Paleys' swank Fifth Avenue apartment, filled with early Picassos, English antiques and the kind of tchotchkes that turned me into a bull in a china shop. I was sure I'd break some ashtray worth $7 million.

Goddard was in his element, surrounded by his sophisticated circle of friends and admirers, Adolph Green, Betty Comden, Leonard Bernstein. Even Paley, stingy in praise, was saying nice things.

'Here's the man who understood and supported my passion for *My Fair Lady*,' said the chairman.

'Come on, Bill,' said Mrs Lieberson, 'you hadn't heard of *My Fair Lady* till my husband dragged you to the show – and made you invest.'

'Ah, spousal loyalty. Isn't it wonderful?'

Always the great ballerina, Vera spun around and kicked her leg high over her head, a breathtaking physical response that ended the verbal joust. Goddard embraced his wife and downed another vodka martini. Toward the end of the evening, I approached him to say goodbye.

'I'll miss you, Goddard. I'm not sure I can do this job without you.'

'You'll do splendidly, Walter. You're a little rough around the edges, but that's what the job requires. You've got the guts.'

'May I call you?'

'Every day if you like.'

Smart son of a bitch, I thought, *getting out while the going's good. He's got money, he's got health, he's got an incorruptible reputation, a sexy wife, creative talents, everything a man needs to be happy. If anyone deserves to ride off peacefully into the sunset it's my hero Potted Lieberfarb. God bless him.*

But God didn't bless him. In my view of things, God blew it. Goddard got liver cancer and, within two years, was dead. His hard-earned retirement turned into a nightmare. Maybe I didn't understand God; maybe I misdefined God; maybe I was confusing God for the devil, but any way I looked at it, I saw injustice. If one man deserved years of unfettered bliss, it was Goddard. He'd paid his dues. So where was his reward? Goddard's cruel demise convinced me, at least then, of a single truth – the only rewards that mattered were those I could taste in the here and now. And right now I was in a position that was entirely new to me. I was President of the CBS Records Group. In that position, I suddenly realized I had to figure out who the hell I was.

On the primary level, I was just another guy who worked for Bill Paley. That reality hit me hard when he called me into his office for our first one-on-one.

The office was eclectic – a cigar store Indian over here, an original Picasso over there. Paley himself was enormously charming, or least could be. He could be warm and friendly or distant and cold. His insatiable appetite for press had swollen his ego. He was brilliant, and never tired of hearing outsiders tell him so.

'Arthur Taylor is high on you,' he said to me, 'and, as you know, Taylor's a shrewd judge of character.'

I thought otherwise, but now was hardly the time to argue.

'Taylor feels you're smart as a whip and honest as the day is long,' Paley continued. 'But what Taylor doesn't know is that I've been following you ever since you got here fourteen years ago.'

A blatant lie I gladly accepted.

'Nothing pleases me more. Walter, than to promote a man like you, one of our own.'

'Thank you, Mr Paley.'

'To celebrate, I'm hoping you'll join me for a little lunch.'

The little lunch turned into a feast. I've never seen anyone eat like Paley. When it came to food, his long-suppressed Jewish soul came roaring out. We ate in the private dining room, we were served by a private waiter, but we might as well have been at Katz's Deli on the Lower East Side. There were pickles, potatoes, rye bread, herring, chopped liver, boiled meat, smoked fish, enough food to feed the Israeli Army. I bonded with the boss over cheesecake.

Before I left, though, the boss was careful to tell me a story about his celebrated employee, the fabled Edward R. Murrow, probably the greatest war correspondent in American history. Murrow deserved all the accolades, Paley told me. Murrow was the premier journalist of our time. 'Murrow,' he added, 'was also my friend. But one time Murrow made the mistake of going against me. I was going to fire him, but at the last minute, changed my mind.'

Great, I thought. *If you'd fire Murrow, you'd fire your own mother.*

The emotional fallout from our first encounter never left: I was working for a man I feared. Before lunch was over, however, I took that fear and turned it on its ear.

'Before I leave, Mr Paley, I have a proposal.'

'What is it?'

'That you adopt me.'

'What are you talking about?'

'I'm the right age, the right religion and I'm your neighbor.'

'You are?'

'I have a small house next to your estate on Long Island.'

'You do?'

'Yes, and my mother thinks it's a good idea.'

'Yetnikoff, you're crazy.'

'And that's another good reason for you to adopt me. Now, can I call you Dad?'

He shooed me out of the dining room, but not without a big laugh. I didn't question the fact that I had made an impression. But what kind of impression? I had this great new job, yet I couldn't help questioning my qualifications. I knew the music business, but did I, like Goddard, really know music? I was a lawyer. On the other hand, Clive was a lawyer whose business acumen took him to the top. But Clive had an ear and instinct for popular taste. Did I? I was tone-deaf. Was Clive? Clive acted as though he could scrutinize melodies and critique lyrics. Writers and musicians might mock him behind his back, but writers and musicians also kissed his ass because he could make them rich. However you viewed them, my predecessors had projected themselves as larger-than-life figures. Goddard and Clive were in the Music Mogul Hall of Fame, no questions asked. They had cultivated identities and demanded respect. In this grand scheme, in the storied history of CBS Records, how the hell was I going to fit in?

My sense of myself as a corporate leader took a few years to develop. When I hit my stride in the eighties, people viewed me as a wild man. And I was. But operating concurrently (and improbably) with my wildness was a strong element of caution. I knew that, first and foremost, I had to make money for CBS. The minute that stopped, I was out on my ass. The more I made, the crazier I could afford to be. The job came down to two words: sell records.

My first signing came in my first year, 1975. I approached it cautiously. Ron Alexenburg and Steve Popovich, brilliant promo men who had proven their mettle, were excited about the Jackson

5, who, after years of hits, were ready to leave Motown, where they felt underappreciated and underpaid. The boys' manager and dad, Joe Jackson, wanted big money. I wanted more information. I knew their sales had once been impressive, but I also knew their recent albums had faltered. Because Motown never signed on to RIAA, the Recording Industry Association of America, which certifies sales, no one knew the exact number of records sold.

'Exact doesn't matter,' argued Ron, who then headed Epic, a subsidiary of the Big Red Columbia label. 'Their sales are huge, their potential enormous. Just come out and see their show.'

Their show at the Westbury Music Fair was less than spectacular. Their baby sister Janet, who did a Mae West impression, looked silly. Their dance steps looked tired. The bright spot, of course, was sixteen-year-old Michael, who was lit from within. His dancing was spectacular. But when he stood alone onstage and sang 'Ben' – the theme song for a film about a boy and a rat – I had my doubts. In my new role as president, wouldn't I be a schmuck to authorize a multi-million-dollar deal to a guy pouring his heart out to a dead rat?

'"Ben" was a smash,' Popovich insisted. 'We'll make money on this group, believe me.'

I'm not sure I believed but okayed the deal anyway. We entrusted them to Kenny Gamble and Leon Huff, the producers who had forged an enormously profitable sublabel, Philly International. With their scorching tracks for the O'Jays and Harold Melvin and the Blue Notes, Gamble and Huff were creators of an edgy urban sensibility that blossomed into disco. As Motown had led the sixties, Philly International was defining the seventies. And by mid-decade, that definition had everything to do with dancing and screwing.

I assumed power at a time when hedonism was hitting new highs in our culture. Rather than argue or challenge the trend, I went with it. I chased it, caught it, maybe even expanded it. I brought it into my life and into my office. I started drinking more, smoking more, toking more. I did it not only because I liked it, but because it went with my job. I reasoned – and reasoned rightly – that artists would be more comfortable with an executive who did what they did. It was an era when many artists got high, played high, stayed high. A critical part of my job description was to relate to such artists. Not only was it cool to party with them, hell, it was practically obligatory.

It was precisely such an obligation that brought me to a LaBelle concert at Madison Square Garden. Patti LaBelle, Sarah Dash and Nona Hendryx were a funk-rock girl group signed to Epic who made the Supremes look like Mary Poppins. They flew onstage, Martians in metal, silver-winged, G-stringed, titanium bras, glitter-gold tushy tights, feather headdresses like wild Indians, voices like horny angels. Their epic erotic hit 'Lady Marmalade' was breaking the bank. Their show was making me hard. Backstage, they were only too happy to meet the boss. They were charming, sweet, irresistible.

'Tell me,' I asked Sarah Dash. 'What's the literal definition of the hook of "Lady Marmalade" – this *voulez-vous coucher avec moi ce soir*?'

'"Do you want to sleep with me tonight?"'

'Of course I do. I'd be nuts not to.'

Thus began my affair with the enchanting Sarah Dash. I was in business.

Sarah and I liked to love on the black couch in my back office. We liked loving in bungalows at the Beverly Hills Hotel. We liked joking about the Jewish-black connection. I liked teaching her proper Yiddish pronunciation. I had no notion of the impropriety of becoming sexually involved with a CBS artist. I had no sense of boundaries or appropriate behavior. I was willing, Sarah was willing, so what's the problem? Besides, things were looking up. Before he left, Goddard, God bless him, had advised me to put out the cast album and invest in a musical he was certain had legs. Turned out *A Chorus Line* ran as long as I did, all the way from '75 to '90.

Then Morris Levy called.

'Velvel, I want to put out a compilation pulled from the Columbia Record Club. What do you say?'

I said yes. Moishe was good at compilations. For a reasonable advance, he gave us a healthy profit.

Then Jon Landau called.

'"Born to Run,"' he said, 'is going to be Bruce Springsteen's first hit single. It's going to be big.'

A year earlier Landau, then a journalist, wrote, 'I saw rock and roll's future and its name is Bruce Springsteen.' Now Landau was coproducing Bruce's music and obsessed with Bruce's career. Soon he'd become Bruce's manager. Whatever he was, he was right. 'Born to Run' was a monster hit, Springsteen went on his first national tour and, in the same week, he was on the covers of *Newsweek* and *Time*, rock's newest hero. Sitting in the front row at Springsteen concerts turned me into a believer. He'd turn anyone into a believer. He was a passionate performer with phenomenal charisma. His heart was in every song he sang. As an individual, the guy reeked with sincerity. Springsteen was almost too good to be true.

Then Paul Simon called.

'I'm unhappy,' he said.

'Why?'

'I'm not getting the label support I need.'

'I'll come to your show and we'll talk afterward.'

Paul Simon and Art Garfunkel broke up in 1970. Since then, Paul had had big hits and Grammys on his own, the latest 'Still Crazy After All These Years' and '50 Ways to Leave Your Lover.' I never liked the way Paul left Art. I thought he lacked loyalty. I also considered him disloyal to his former lawyer. As a person, Paul struck me as pretentious and self-important. In his backstage dressing room, his entourage treated him like little Lord Byron, hanging on his every word. When I walked in, he was stretched out on a couch, smoking a joint, pontificating about the nature of poetics. He didn't offer me a puff. I didn't like the guy. And, believe me, he didn't like me. War clouds were rolling in.

Fuck the Bunny

THE LARGER WAR I WAGED WAS ON WARNER BROTHERS, the Bugs Bunny company which, in the wake of Clive's demise, had come on like gangbusters. Warner's Mo Ostin and Joe Smith had clout, but Steve Ross was the big boss. Ross had parlayed a funeral parlor/parking lot business into a multimedia conglomerate. With Warner movies and Warner music at his command, Ross was a smooth operator, a much beloved leader who, unlike CBS, paid his underlings well. With the Grateful Dead, Van Morrison, Black Sabbath and James Taylor, Warner was winning market shares left and right. Ross also had a selling tool – which he undoubtedly was employing with Paul Simon – that I lacked: Ross told artists he could put them in the movies. I had no movies to put them in. But I did have money, deep CBS money, and I was willing to spend it.

I was intent on making noise. As a label honcho, I needed an identity. Artists had images, and in this new era of corporate power so did execs. Ahmet Ertegun – whose Atlantic label was bought by Ross – was a music maven, a sophisticate and suave bon vivant who could party all night. With his flair for self-promotion, Clive's image was genius hitmaker. The scandal behind him – he pleaded guilty to minor charges and was rightfully let off with a small fine and no jail time – Clive was busy starting his new Arista label. He was looking to regain his championship, but how would I gain mine?

By knockout, that's how. By charging out of my corner like Raging Bull. By finding a way to shock my staff – and the industry – with the fact that Columbia Records was ready, willing, able and eager to win at any cost.

'Win what?' one of my associates asked me as I was thinking out loud.

'The war. We're going to war with Warner.'

War required a battle cry, so I had banners printed at our annual convention with slogans that couldn't be faulted for their subtlety. They read, 'Fuck Warner. Fuck the Bunny.'

A few of my people were appalled, but most were pleased. After all, war is exhilarating. War elicits loyalty, solidarity. War gives us purpose and drive. War was what I wanted. War was who I was. The Music Warrior was about to move. I gathered my forces, I gave my hyped-up speeches, I set my sights on the competition and the first thing I saw was James Taylor. Wouldn't it be wonderful to steal JT from Warner? What a way to start the war!

Nat Weiss, James's lawyer, happened to mention that his client felt neglected by Warner, where all attention was on Fleetwood Mac.

'Tell James I'll give his career my personal attention,' I said.

James was interested. We met and hit it off. You had to like James Taylor. As a singer/songwriter, he had that feeling-healing aura that calmed the most tumultuous soul, even mine. As a man, he had manners, charm and elegance. In those days, he also liked to get high. He called me a Yiddish comic and applauded my humor. I called him a WASP prince and praised his talent. He spoke of his loyalty to Warner; I spoke of my ability to promote him like he'd never been promoted before. He said he'd sign. I said he'd never regret it.

Hopes were high. Contracts were drawn. Plans were made. We were to meet at Nat Weiss's apartment for the official signing. I took June along to witness this history-making moment – the luring of a major artist away from a major label. Rumor had it that Warner chief Mo Ostin was flying across the country to undo my deal. I'd also heard Mrs Mo was working on Mrs Taylor, aka Carly Simon, then very pregnant. Poor Mo couldn't handle it alone.

In addition to a fat contract, I brought along a multi-million-dollar check. I arrived early. James arrived late – so late, in fact, we started wondering whether he'd show. It was past midnight when he finally walked it, and he looked ashen. His manager Peter Asher said he'd been going through hell.

'Why?' I wanted to know.

'The Warner people have been working him over,' Peter said. 'They've been lobbying him to stay.'

'Tell those assholes the deal is done.'

'It isn't done, Walter,' said James. 'I have feelings about this.'

'How about *my* feelings?' I asked. 'We've been working this deal night and day. You're getting everything you want.'

'I want my integrity intact.'

'And that's what I'm buying – your integrity as a great artist.'

'The Warner people helped make my career.'

'And we're taking your career to another level. Look, James, this is no time for kvetching.'

'I told James to take as much time as he needs,' said Asher. 'Let him think it over.'

I grabbed Asher and yelled, 'Shut up, you redheaded English traitor!'

James was on the verge of tears. He said how much he liked me. He said how much he liked Mo Ostin. Asher insisted James be allowed further reflection. I insisted we weren't leaving without a contract. James wanted to walk around the block. Fine, walk around the block, but hurry. Before he left, he stood before me and bowed. The gesture was neither gratuitous nor sarcastic. It was the gesture of a gentleman. Hours went by – 2 A.M., 3 A.M. – before James returned. While he was out deliberating, I assured Weiss and Asher that Taylor had only two choices: sign the contract or die by my hand.

He half-signed.

'I'm writing "James,"' he said, 'but not "Taylor."'

'Fine,' I said, 'Put an X if that makes you happy, but take the check.'

We were all exhausted, relieved, ecstatic. I'd pulled it off. I'd acquired one of the premier talents in pop music. Columbia Records was richer for the acquisition. James's first CBS album was a huge success with a number-one single, 'Handy Man.' Fuck Warner.

'Fuck Yetnikoff,' was the word back from Warner. Their wrath took the form of recruiting Paul Simon. Meanwhile, Paul owed Columbia another record. In the spite of antagonism between me and Paul, all parties thought it best to try to negotiate a new contract. So we did. We screamed at each other for months. During one marathon session, I drank a bottle of scotch while Paul drank a bottle of wine. That same night we finally agreed on a number – or so we thought. It was a huge deal, worth $14 million. But when the papers were presented to Paul, he was certain I'd agreed to $14.5 million. I was certain he was bullshitting. I wouldn't budge – and neither would he.

In one last attempt to see eye-to-eye, he came to my office on Passover Eve. By then I knew how intensely Warner was pressuring him to sign with them.

'I've had a brainstorm,' he said sarcastically. 'I've decided to put a series of Elizabethan sonnets to music. That's going to be my new album.'

'It'll sell five copies.'

'I'm not in charge of sales, I'm in charge of songs. I'm fascinated by the Elizabethan era. So that's that.'

'That isn't that. You'll give me an album of regular Paul Simon songs.'

'And you'll bury it.'

'Don't be a jerk. I have a corporate responsibility to sell records.'

'No one's ever accused you of being responsible.'

'For a teeny tiny little squirt you've got a big mouth.'

'If you want an album of Paul Simon songs, you write them.'

'*You* write them, and you deliver them on time.'

'Don't hold your breath.'

'You know, Simon,' I said, 'back in your beloved Elizabethan times, guys like you were wandering troubadours working for a chicken. Do you know how many artists are signed to CBS, and how many want to be signed? Thousands. I'm tired of your whining. Go somewhere else with your demands. I don't want to see you anymore. All I want is a proper Paul Simon album.'

And then I went to my seder.

Paul's next shot was to call other CBS artists – James Taylor, Billy Joel – asking them to record duets with him. Simon thought that if his last Columbia album was a series of duets with Columbia artists, I couldn't bury it. I'd have to promote it. That was his way of outfoxing me.

It wasn't a foolish move. But it didn't work because James and Billy called for my advice. 'Do what you want,' I told them. 'But if the tables were turned, if you were in trouble and needed Simon to sing with you, do you think he'd come running? Besides, I can't control my marketing and promotion people. They aren't going to be happy about your collaborating with Simon. They don't like him any more than I do.'

I made my point. The duets were never recorded. Meanwhile, Steve Ross and Mo Ostin signed Paul, in spite of his obligation to us. The fighting went on. Lawsuits were launched. We finally received a big cash settlement of a million and a half dollars, and that was that. Paul became a Warner artist.

Simon's first move was to write and star in a Warner movie, *One Trick Pony*, in which a sadly misunderstood artist of unwavering integrity battles a heartless and exploitative music label. The film was boring and self-indulgent. Its only saving grace was an evil character modeled after me. Paul called him Walter Fox. Walter is a corporate cad with a sexy wife. In the film, Paul gets to screw Walter's wife. That was Paul's revenge. My revenge was the box office: both the movie and soundtrack were resounding flops.

The battle with Paul made Arthur Taylor nervous. He thought I was dealing too precipitously, too personally.

'Don't be impulsive, Walter,' he warned. 'You're going to make a major mistake. These things need to be thought through.'

'Look, Arthur,' I explained, 'there's a method to my madness. I'm putting out the word that artists can't run over us. We'll pay and pay big for the right artists, but we won't act like we have no leverage. I'm trying to establish a mutual balance of terror between us and the artist.'

I used that balance of terror to define myself as a boss. It was a conscious part of the image I was looking to cultivate. In the case of James Taylor, I saw that I could hang with the artist, charm the artist, lure the artist into a deal. I could convince the artist of my ability to sell and promote his music. In the case of Paul Simon, I saw the opposite – that I wasn't afraid to alienate an artist whom I felt had turned against us. I wasn't afraid to publicly feud with an artist, letting him – and the world – know that CBS Records was bigger than any one act. I realized that a label's greatest bargaining power is the artist's insecurity.

As a corporate captain, I saw myself as a cheerleader. If I didn't have the ear to recruit new musical talent, I had the smarts to recognize others who did. And hire them. I saw myself as a teamster. My job was to get the horses moving in the same direction. My job was to lead the troops into battle. My role model was General Patton. I was struck by something said to me by a friend who'd fought in the Israeli Army: 'No officer will give the command "Advance." The command is always "Follov me."' Maybe my energy was extreme, even crazy. But it worked. It got people moving, it enlivened and emboldened the workplace. When anyone asked me, I could state my philosophy in a phrase – stay in the game. And the game was about hits, hits and more hits.

The hefty paperweight I threw at Arthur Taylor nearly hit him in the head. He ducked just in time.

As I was rushing to catch a plane for California, he had called me to his office to complain about the fancy Cadillacs and long limousines that lined Fifty-second Street next to Black Rock. 'It's bad for corporate image,' Taylor said. 'It looks vulgar.'

'Why is this my business?'

'They belong to people in your division.'

'They belong to guys who work for Philly International Records, an independent label.'

'Well, tell those guys not to park there.'

'Arthur, are you serious? This is what you have to do all day – worry about parking? As long as they keep making hits, they can park in our goddamn lobby.'

'Tell them to move their cars.'

'*You* tell them. I'm leaving for L.A.'

'Walter, this is your responsibility.'

That's when I threw the paperweight. Although it missed him, he fell out of his chair and ran out of his office.

Two days later he called me at the Beverly Hills Hotel. I figured I was fired.

'In the spirit of noblesse oblige,' he said, 'I offer you an apology and expect one in return.'

'In the spirit of Brooklyn, New York,' I replied, 'I accept your apology and hope you never do something that stupid again.'

Back home in Great Neck, June and the boys were seeing less of me. I was running from conference to conference, country to country. As my salary got bigger, June got sadder. I couldn't understand why. Wasn't this America, where happiness and money are synonymous?

She, the former Bohemian, was bored in the 'burbs.

'If you're bored,' I said, 'start a business.'

She did – a travel agency – which meant we saw even less of each other. If someone had accused me of being callous and uncaring about my family, I would have pointed to our luxuries. I was doing too well in my work, getting too successful too quickly, to bother with introspection. Everywhere I looked I was seeing dollar signs.

I was also seeing more of Sarah Dash, but Sarah wasn't enough. I started screwing my secretary, who didn't seem to mind that I was screwing Sarah. Not to mention Diana.

'Walter,' my secretary said, 'I've never seen anyone take off and put on his clothes so many times in one day.'

Michael Jackson wanted to write and produce. Representing his group, he, rather than his father, came to see me. He reasoned rightly that he'd be a better spokesman than his bullying dad. The first Jackson-Gamble/Huff album had spawned one hit – 'Enjoy Yourself' – but the second album bombed. My staff was less than enthusiastic about the Jacksons' commercial prospects.

Sitting across from my desk, Michael was a composed young man. He was dressed in jeans and a plain red T-shirt. He'd grown a few inches in the last couple of years. I saw a tall, good-looking nineteen-year-old with an easy smile and ingratiating manner. He spoke so quietly that I had to lean in to listen. His words were carefully chosen. He was shy but determined, a young man on a mission.

First he discussed a movie he had just made with Quincy Jones and Diana Ross, *The Wiz*, in which he played a scarecrow. He was excited about its upcoming release and pleased with his singing and dancing. I sensed that the project, done on his own without his family, had renewed his confidence.

'I want to do a solo album,' he said, 'but my family feels we should do another Jackson record first. I want to honor my family's wishes.'

'Good, because that will also honor our contract.'

'But I want to write and produce the record myself. My brothers will help me. My brother Randy and I have written some great songs.'

'What about Gamble and Huff?'

'They're geniuses, Mr Yetnikoff, and they've taught me plenty. But I'm ready to step out. Me and my brothers have our own ideas.'

Michael was convincing. I didn't doubt his hard work or his sincerity. I also knew he was driven to succeed. What I didn't know was whether he could produce hits.

'I'll take a chance,' I said. 'But one chance only. If your new record bombs, I'm selling you back to Berry Gordy.'

'You won't be sorry.'

I wasn't. In 1979, an otherwise dismal sales year, the Jacksons' 'Shake Your Body (Down to the Ground)' was a top-ten hit, selling over two million copies. Some consider it the most sensuous dance song in that supersensuous era known as disco.

My regime began when disco fever was flaming. Self-indulgence was everywhere. I was everywhere, running over to Studio 54, where the security guy guarding the door also worked at Black Rock. That meant I was waved in so I could party with my new friend, Steve Rubell, who owned the glittering joint. I told myself it was work. And crazily enough, it was. There was David Geffen, hocking me about some deal he wanted to do. There was Liza Minnelli, recently signed to Columbia, oohing and aahing how thrilled she was to be recording for a company led by *me*. There was Mick Jagger, wondering why I, as opposed to my friendly rival Ahmet Ertegun, the Great Pasha of Atlantic Records, hadn't pursued his Rolling Stones. 'All in good time, Mick,' I said. 'All in good time.'

The very tone and texture of time changed. Everyone wanted my time, which took on new value. Time spent with family diminished. Time spent with artists increased. Important people wanted my time, affirming the fact that my time was more important than theirs.

'Mr Paley wants a little of your time,' his secretary called to say.

I hurried to his office.

'Just wanted you to know that Arthur Taylor is gone,' he said. 'He wasn't the man I thought he was. So I'm replacing him with John Backe. You'll like Backe, Backe will like you. So carry on.'

'And plans for my adoption, Mr Paley?'

'That's between you and your psychiatrist.'

I laughed at the boss's joke, but still felt a chill. When Paley threw the paperweight at your head, he didn't miss.

I ran over to England for our yearly convention, arriving late at the Grosvenor House. Diana was waiting, Diana was angry – 'why can't you spend more time with me?' – but Diana was horny. So was I. I was always horny. We screwed and slept late. They called from the Inter-continental, where the big meeting was starting. John Backe was there. Where was I? Everyone was waiting. I threw on my clothes and raced over. Hurrying into the Inter-continental, I was stopped by Lisa Robinson, a journalist, who insisted I listen to something by this fabulous singer/songwriter.

'Lisa, I'm late. Not now.'

'He's right here, you have to hear him.'

I turned around, and standing on the street, his guitar hooked up to a little amp, was a gawky guy with glasses.

'I don't have time, Lisa.'

'It'll take two seconds.'

'I don't have one second.'

She motioned to the guy to start playing. I heard something, but I had no time to digest it. I was frantic to get to the meeting.

'Out of my way, Lisa.'

'You're making a mistake. He has hits. You must sign him.'

'Fine, I'll tell my A&R man to sign him.'

As a result of that reasoned adjudication, Elvis Costello came to Columbia Records.

I stirred the troops at the meeting, and later, back at the hotel, Diana stirred me when she spoke of other lovers. Out of deep insanity and insane hypocrisy, I insisted she see no other men. She insisted that when it came to philandering, she was no match for me. The more we drank, the hotter our dissonance; she ran out the door; I caught her, embraced her.

'What do you want from me?' I asked her.

'Pull down my panties. Then spank me. Then kiss it and make it better. And then go down on me.'

'Right here in the hallway?'

'Right here in the hallway.'

I did as I was told. I had no idea if anyone spotted us. I was too busy screwing to notice. When we were through she said, 'This relationship is totally nuts. I'm leaving right now.'

'It is nuts,' I agreed, 'but when can I see you again?'

'Never,' she insisted, and disappeared.

Guilty

I ENJOYED GOOD RAPPORT WITH BARBRA STREISAND and even better rapport with her crazy lover/manager/hairdresser Jon Peters. Barbra and I share deep Brooklyn Jewish roots. Culturally, we come from the same place. I saw her as a scared little girl from Ocean Parkway who, at the same time, was gutsy and strong. Sure she was difficult and bossy, but no one was more difficult or bossy than me. We'd scream at each other like spoiled siblings, then make up. I appreciated Barbra as one of the great talents of our time. Her boyfriend Jon was a legendary rogue, but look who's talking.

Like most every artist, Barbra, queen of the Broadway ballad, was obsessed with sales. During disco, when our labels lagged behind the trend, she caught on just in time. Her duet with Donna Summer, 'No More Tears (Enough Is Enough),' went number 1. How to stay hot? Pair her with Barry Gibb of the Bee Gees. *Saturday Night Fever*, featuring Bee Gees songs, had set the industry on fire. The movie and soundtrack broke the bank. I had long believed that the combination of contemporary music and

A UJA dinner honoring Barbra

contemporary visuals would be box-office magic. I had music, but
no movies. Robert Stigwood, the force behind *Saturday Night
Fever*, had both. The Bee Gees were on his RSO label. Barry
Gibb, I reasoned, would be happy to record with Barbra. What
artist wouldn't? Barry quickly agreed, but Freddie Gershon,
Stigwood's partner, urged me to call Robert for Barry's release. I
didn't bother.

Instead, Barbra, Jon and I ran down to Miami.

'We'll swing, we'll spling, we'll bing,' said Peters, who spoke an
abbreviated jive talk all his own.

We flew down on a private CBS jet to where Barry was waiting.
In a haze of herb, the song was cut in a blaze of enthusiasm. Gibb
called it 'Guilty.' Musically, he and Barbra were milk and honey.
We had a smash. We took off a couple of days for high fun in the
sun. Sitting around the pool, Peters never tired of telling me how
he sexually satisfied Barbra. 'When they say I have a silver
tongue,' he explained, 'they don't know the half of it.'

On the day of departure, we set takeoff at noon. But at twelve-thirty Barbra was still packing. I knocked on her door. 'What's taking so long?'

When she let me in, I saw enough clothes to costume a Hollywood musical. And she was doing all the packing herself.

'Where's your maid?'

'What maid? I don't have a maid. Besides, they don't call them maids anymore.'

'Whatever they call 'em, you need 'em. It's crazy for you to do this yourself.'

'A full-time assistant costs a fortune.'

'A full-time assistant costs less than keeping the jet waiting.'

'You'll pay for the assistant?'

'I'll find you extra royalties, I'll do anything to get you to throw your shmatas in the goddamn suitcase.'

It took another two hours before we made it to the airfield. In those days Barbra was a nervous flier. She stood on the tarmac a long while. I reassured her, Peters reassured her, everyone reassured her that the jet was safe. But it was only when the pilot came down and expressed his endless admiration for her talent that her mood changed. Flattered, she found the courage to climb aboard. The flight was bumpy, though, and her anxiety returned. She sat between me and Jon, squeezing our hands and trembling like a scared kitten. When we landed, the kitten turned into a tigress.

'I want to see promotion plans for "Guilty,"' she insisted, 'first thing in the morning.'

'Have your maid come by and pick them up.'

We had rightly predicted that the record would hit. Freddie Gershon had also rightly predicted that, without being consulted, Stigwood would hit the ceiling. With 'Guilty' zooming up the charts, he hit me with a lawsuit from a firm with a name like Higginbotham, Carlyle, Upshaw and Downshaw. I picked up the phone and called him.

'Robert,' I said, 'if you're going to sue me, at least use Jews. What's this WASP firm?'

'My dear boy,' said Stigwood in his best Australian drawl, 'when you employ my artist without my consent, I consider it an effrontery.'

'Well, consider this my apology. I messed up. I'm sorry.'

'Apology accepted. Now let's forge a more formal reconciliation. Be my guest at my estate in Bermuda. Bring whomever you fancy.'

I fancied a much younger woman named Cynthia Slamar whom I'd met at a music convention. She was gorgeous, smart and stacked, a knockout who worked in the entertainment business. Robert arranged for a private plane. His estate was the size of a small country. He was the perfect host. He had us hike up the side of a small mountain fragrant with flowering plants. When we reached the summit, there was an antique table covered in white linen and a waiter with champagne and fresh strawberries and cream. Next to the table was Freddie Gershon, an accomplished musician, seated at a white piano playing 'Anything Goes.' For once I was speechless.

Because we never struck serious disco gold, the late seventies were challenging. We hung in: Boston was a strong seller, Bruce Springsteen had *Born to Run* and *Darkness on the Edge of Town* and, out of nowhere, Meat Loaf's *Bat Out of Hell* took off. Billy Joel, however, was struggling. Billy paid little attention to the business side of his creativity. His copyrights were scattered and his career had stalled with the release of *Turnstiles*. His then wife and manager Elizabeth called to say he was trying out new material on the road. Would I come to a concert? I did. I spent more time watching the audience than evaluating the music. I let the audience, a better gauge than me, do the evaluation. They loved what they heard.

'I love it too,' Billy told me backstage, 'but we're canceling the rest of the tour.'

'The material is developing beautifully,' I said. 'Why do that?'

'No support money. Elizabeth called Columbia for another eighty thousand dollars and they laughed.'

'Tell her to call again tomorrow morning. Take my word for it, no one will be laughing.'

Billy got the money, the tour went on and the record came out. *The Stranger*, which included 'Just the Way You Are,' shot Billy into orbit.

'I don't want to do another record with my brothers,' Michael Jackson told me. 'Not now. I want to do a solo record.'

To my mind, Michael had proven himself with 'Shake Your Body (Down to the Ground).' Besides, his choice of a producer, Quincy Jones, made it an easy call.

'Fine,' I said. 'Go do your solo record.'

Off the Wall was a perfect piece of pop soul, exceeding all sales predictions. Michael, who wrote three songs and coproduced three tracks, had his first taste of multi-platinum solo action. The album's success excited Michael's ambition. My respect for his talent was growing along with my puzzlement about his personality. He seemed a sweet guy, exceedingly eager to please. *Off the Wall* retooled his child-like image. Now he was pictured as a dark-skinned handsome young man in a bow tie, tux and fashionably coiffed Afro. He was ready to rock, and his love songs, especially 'Don't Stop Til You Get Enough,' suggested adult sexuality. When you spoke to Michael, though, the adult was not present.

'I never had a childhood,' he kept telling me – or anyone else who asked. His education had been truncated. All he knew was singing and performing. His focus was on his career and career alone. 'Understand,' he told me, 'that I was a star when I was six.'

Sometimes I felt that he was still six. I wasn't sure he could name the President of the United States. He had no social skills. He was a child who sought the company of other children. He sought my company only because I was the man who controlled the hype machine. And if Michael understood anything outside the value of music, it was the value of hype.

Michael liked to call me his Good Father. That's when I was okaying big promotional plans for his record. At other times, he dropped the affection and reverted to normal artist behavior – whining. Michael was a world-class whiner.

After *Off the Wall* won only a single Grammy, he called me to complain.

'You're complaining to the wrong guy,' I told him. 'I have nothing to do with who wins.'

Michael's high, almost inaudible voice changes tone when he's unhappy. He becomes an angry little boy who won't be happy until he gets all the candy in the candy jar. 'Mine was the first solo album to have four Top Ten singles. That means I should get at least four Grammys.'

'Be happy with one.'

'I know the labels have influence over the Grammys. Can't you use your influence?'

'Beyond talking you up and taking out ads, there's nothing to do.'

'I want more Grammys.'

'Make more records and you'll get more Grammys.'

'My next record will win every Grammy there is.'

'From your mouth to God's ear.'

Turned out God was listening.

'Mr Paley,' I said to my boss, 'meet Meat Loaf.'

'Do I call you "Meat" or "Mr Loaf"?' asked Mr Paley.

'Up to you, Bill,' said the rocker as he looked around the chairman's office. 'I dig your setup.'

This all came about because Meat Loaf, a big star on our Epic label, was dying to meet the man who started CBS. I wrote Paley a short note that made it easy for him to decline. He shocked me by accepting.

Meat Loaf showed up looking like, well, a meat loaf with long hair. He was wearing overalls and combat boots. Paley was wearing Brooks Brothers and Turnbull & Asser. Meat Loaf came carrying a box of glazed jelly doughnuts. Paley was sipping Earl Grey tea.

'Have a doughnut, Bill.'

'Don't mind if I do, Meat.'

'So how did this little operation get started?'

Paley gave a five-minute rundown while Meat Loaf inhaled a half-dozen doughnuts. Then, while Meat Loaf responded to the chairman's question – 'Tell me about your hit song' – Paley downed the other half-dozen.

'It's called "Paradise by the Dashboard Light."'

'I'm sorry to say I haven't heard it yet. What's the theme?' asked Paley.

'Humping.'

'Oh, I see.'

'Phil Rizzuto is announcing a baseball game while me and this chick are getting it on. That's the paradise part.'

'Paradise indeed,' Paley said, a big smile on his face.

'You ought to come to my show.'

'I understand tickets are hard to come by.'

'I'll stick you in the first row, Bill. Even better, I'll put you on the band bus and you'll go on the road with me. What do you think?'

'The directors might not approve.'

'Bring those fuckers along.'

Paley turned and asked, 'Do you think that's a good idea, Walter?'

'Sure,' I said. 'In another lifetime.'

Something didn't compute. A Columbia artist and an artist on Big Tree Records released the same song at the same time. Big Tree had the hit and we didn't. I couldn't understand why. So I called Big Tree owner Doug Morris and asked, 'How'd the hell you pull that off? We had the bigger artist with bigger ads.'

'Two words,' said Doug. 'Fred DiSipio.'

Fred DiSipio, a little guy and a big Navy hero in World War II, was an independent promoter who'd gained a reputation as a hitmaker. The other prominent name in the field was Joe Isgro. I invited DiSipio to dinner. We met at Patsy's Italian Restaurant on Fifty-sixth Street, Sinatra's favorite.

I was blunt. DiSipio was even blunter.

'If this is payola, I can't touch you,' I said. 'I work for a corporation that makes J. Edgar Hoover look like a hippie. We count paper clips. We scrutinize our consultants. We'll make you sign enough documents to sink the English Navy. At the tiniest irregularity, we'll sue you out of your underwear.'

'What are you worried about, Walter?' asked Fred. 'This is legit. If the labels had promo men who knew what they were doing, you wouldn't need me. But you do need me because I know what radio wants. Radio is hit with so much product they need to weed. Radio knows I can weed. Radio respects me. Radio listens to me. What I bring them, they play. I'm the maître d' who decides who gets in the restaurant. Give me a hit record, I'll make sure it's played. I don't handle anything but hits. There's only three questions I'll ever ask you about a record – Is it a boy or a girl? Is it black or white? Is it fast or slow?'

'I'm telling you, Fred, if this isn't as clean as Snow White, we'll not only get our money back from you, we'll come after your ass.'

'It's supersalesmanship, Walter. Hire me and you'll be adding a supersalesman to your staff. If you don't see results in a month, dump me.'

'I will.'

I didn't. DiSipio came through. He and other indie promoters were the reason we were able to stay in the game. They cost a fortune. But to make a fortune, I reasoned, you had to spend a fortune. I wasn't shy about using corporate resources to gain market share. Some complained that I was killing off competitors who couldn't afford outside promoters. Bullshit. I was looking for hits, pure and simple, and willing to pay the price.

I like street characters. DiSipio was one, Moishe Levy was another. I never asked Moishe about his so-called underworld connections. It wasn't my business. When he asked me to invest in an Irish stud racehorse improbably named Malinowski, I put in 100K. I thought it'd be fun. When the stud started producing, I thought I'd see big returns. I never did. Every year I'd get a check for 30 or 40K. When my investment was paid back, the checks stopped. So I called Moishe to ask why.

'You got your money back,' he said. 'What else do you want?'

'A profit.'

'I'll send you another twenty, but that's it.'

'We have a contract, Moishe, we have a detailed agreement. You've never sent me an accounting.'

'You want an accounting, call my accountant.'

'Give me his number.'

'He just had a stroke. He's out of commission.'

'Moishe, you're giving me the runaround.'

'Velvel, you're breaking my balls. You don't want to break my balls. You'll make a couple of dollars on this deal. That's it.'

The phone went dead.

Another Levy deal went dead, only this one had to do with

CBS. Moishe was in the business of cutouts – discontinued records at discount prices. Somehow he had gotten hold of 800,000 Electric Light Orchestra albums which, according to our contract with the band, shouldn't have existed. So when I was told Moishe was selling them in England without authorization, I called him. He never called back. I thought about it for a day or so. This wasn't a racehorse, this was company business. The numbers were not inconsiderable.

'Sue him,' I told our lawyers. 'Get an injunction.'

We did. We forced him to stop selling the product. I confess to being a little nervous about my decision. I looked over my shoulder and wondered about ominous-looking cars riding past my house in Great Neck. Moishe's reputation was intimidating. Moishe was intimidating. And, besides, I liked the guy. But I liked my job more, and my understanding of my job was basic – I had to operate on the square. For all my wackiness, I was what a writer once called 'cash-register honest.'

The honest truth was that, in contrast to intellectuals or corporate creeps, guys like Levy appealed to me. I was drawn to tough-talking Jews. I liked thinking of myself as a tough guy. And you didn't have to be Jewish to enter my social circle. In my mind, you had to be street, down-to-earth and, most important, impressed by me. I didn't know it at the time, but insecurity and vanity made me an easy mark for ass-kissers. Enter Tommy Mottola and Allen Grubman.

It started at dinner at a midtown Manhattan restaurant in the late seventies. Consider my condition: I had been on the throne long enough for the conflicting feelings of power and emptiness to start to clash. Mitigating those feelings meant more drinking and womanizing. I was drawn to drama, especially with women. Cynthia had wisely broken off with me, but Sarah and my secretary were still around, not to mention an L.A. kook I'll rename Ophelia who lived on pills she called Black Beauties, Red Planets and Green Buzzards, forms of speed that kicked her already overheated libido into Looney Tunes land. Ophelia was the kind of gal who'd show up at my hotel room in a trench coat, high heels and nothing underneath. Ophelia was so toxically irresistible that I once left L.A. in the middle of a convention to fly to San Francisco, where we spent forty-eight hours rocking and rolling in a houseboat on the bay. The next day she accompanied me to the airport and, without a ticket, got on the plane, swearing she'd never leave me. It took the security guys to drag her off.

If I needed women who needed me, I was the same with men. Two such men – Tommy Mottola and Allen Grubman – were especially solicitous. Mottola was a music man, a former singer and promoter, and the manager of Hall and Oates. Grubman was Tommy's attorney. He had a few other clients but was hardly at the top of the profession. What he did have – what they both had – what, in fact, we *all* had – was blind ambition.

Tommy was savvy and street in a way that made me comfortable. He was a man's man who knew guns, boats and women. Unlike corporate types who bored me to tears, Tommy entertained me with tales from the fast lane. Sensing my need for a protégé, he filled that need with brotherly sympathy. He asked about the big decisions I had to make. He listened worshipfully as I described the challenges of running my worldwide operation. He lavished praise on my abilities. He made me feel great.

For his part, Grubman was a grubber. He went along with anything that was said. He sought consensus and relished the good fellowship being forged by the three of us. By evening's end, he suggested that I set up a production deal for Tommy's production company. I didn't hesitate. I wanted to be in business with Tommy. I already felt like the guy's big brother. 'Draw up the papers, Grubber,' I said. 'It's a done deal.'

The deal got undone when RCA, Hall and Oates's label, objected, but my relationship with Mottola and Grubman would grow along with my need for yes-men. 'Tommy manages you like a manager manages a star,' said a close observer. She said it as a warning, but I liked the idea. It might sound obnoxious now, but the truth is that I *was* starting to see myself as a star. And like most stars, my sense of self was dangerously inflated.

As my prowess increased, my temper shortened. I'm not sure whether that was by design or deterioration. Part of me was consciously creating a ferocious character that the industry would respect. Another part of me, increasingly accustomed to getting my way, blew a gasket when circumstances went against me. A case in point was Clive's appearance at an industry-wide convention of the National Association of Recording Merchandisers. He gave a speech in which he blatantly badmouthed CBS. I understood he was still pissed, but I was even more pissed that he was handed a platform to trash us. I went crazy, insisting that he and his new Arista label be thrown out. I ordered the organization board to my hotel suite, where I read them the riot act. They listened attentively, and did nothing. I suppose I was also harboring resentment about a recent lunch I had with Clive when he advised me against signing an artist he considered 'uncommercial.' That same artist was soon doing brisk commerce for Arista.

I displayed another temper tantrum when a committee of CBS Inc. questioned the multi-million-dollar deal I wanted to offer Paul McCartney. I'd spent six months chasing Paul and his brother-in-law attorney John Eastman. The competition was fierce. Everyone and his mother wanted Paul. My ace in the hole was to also offer him Frank Music, the CBS-owned publishing company consisting of Frank Loesser songs. I knew McCartney and his copyright-oriented family would find the deal

Velvel nabs a Beatle

irresistible. That's why when my committee balked I flew into a rage.

'How many times do you think we're going to get a chance to sign the last big Beatle?' I asked. 'Do you think he's going with us because of our illustrious past or our beautiful red label? Pull your heads out of your ass. I've laid out the numbers. The numbers are going to work. The only thing that's not going to work is a committee of buzz brains who don't know their ass from their elbow. But I'm tired of arguing. I'm not dealing with this shit anymore. This is the deal I've worked out. If you want to offer it, Paul is ours. If you want to nix it, Paul is gone.' And with that, I stalked out of the room.

An hour later the committee sent me a note: 'Sign him.'

Between my fury, there were respites of reasonable tranquillity. When Paul arrived at my office to sign the contract, he was with Linda Eastman, whom I found charmingly candid.

'I've come to meet the birds,' said Paul before going around the office and signing autographs for a bevy of female employees.

'You see the ego I have to put up with?' Linda asked.

'You and my woman both.'

Maybe it was because of my wife June and the guilt I bore; maybe it was because of my erratic behavior; maybe it was just middle age and midlife crisis time; or maybe it was because I'm Jewish and Jews go to shrinks. Whatever the reason, I started therapy in 1979. At forty-six, I was beset by anxiety. I knew I had issues. Mommy, Daddy, authority figures, impulse control – you name it. I figured that a session every two weeks might be the only way to grab an hour of calm self-reflection.

I had no problems discussing myself. What narcissist does? I didn't need Freud to see how I feared Father and desperately tried and failed to please Mother. It seemed like dime-store psychoanalysis, but it didn't hurt me to hear it. I was in the middle of discussing my mother's impossible demands when the session suddenly exploded in my face. The door flung open and a screaming Ophelia came running in. She stood in the middle of the room and started screaming, '*How could you have left me?*'

The therapist, who looked a little like Kermit the Frog, jumped out of his chair. He was scared Ophelia was packing.

'Are you crazy?' I asked her. 'How in hell did you know I was here?'

'You were going to call me last week. You were going to take me to the Bahamas.'

'I got busy,' I said. 'You mean, you flew here just to bust into my shrink's office?'

I saw that my shrink was shaking.

'She's not the violent type,' I assured him.

'Says who?' she shot back, reaching into her purse.

The shrink crouched behind his desk. He expected shots.

Instead, Ophelia pulled out a poem about the beauty of our lovemaking. I'm not a connoisseur of verse, but this was definitely not Edna St Vincent Millay.

'You're nuts, Ophelia.'

'I'm not the one going to a headshrinker.'

'But you're the one breaking into a headshrinker's office. They could throw you in jail.'

'Mr Yetnikoff,' said the shrink, still hidden behind his desk, 'get this woman out of here.'

I did. We checked into a motel. For the next two hours, my mother problems disappeared. All problems disappeared. That night I drove Ophelia to the airport. As I parked the car, she gave me one last goodbye blow job. I put her on the red-eye back to California.

'Will you remember me?' she asked.

'Always,' I promised.

And I always have.

Meanwhile the shrink said he no longer felt safe in my presence. So I involuntarily left therapy. I'd go back, but only when I was considerably crazier. As the seventies turned into the eighties, craziness became a way of life.

Bust and Lust

THE BUST-UP OF MY MARRIAGE IS THE SADDEST chapter of my life. It's especially sad because, looking back, I can offer no excuses. June was my soul mate. She was the love of my youth. She believed in me from the start. She stood by me when I was filled with insecurities and fears. She indulged my work mania. She graciously hosted my colleagues. When Sony's Norio Ohga traveled to New York, she made him so comfortable that he stayed in our Great Neck home, an unusual move for a formal Japanese. After a long flight, I remember Ohga falling asleep on our couch with his glasses on. June gently removed them and covered him with a blanket. When he awoke, June had prepared a lovely meal. Over a leisurely dinner the three of us spoke of the value of family and mutual trust. I broke June's trust time and again. When my secretary fell into a drunken stupor and called my wife and son Daniel to confess our affair, even then June wanted to know whether I was willing to work on our marriage. I said I was, but I wasn't. I liked the idea of the family. I felt love for June, Michael and Daniel, but nothing could hold back the floodgates of my raging ego.

When we sold our house in Great Neck and moved to an apartment in Manhattan, I thought things might change. I could get home quicker, spend time with the family, more closely integrate my personal and professional lives. But, in fact, nothing changed except the intensity with which I sought adulterous encounters. I did incalculable injury to June and the boys. I destroyed my family. I did it because the lure of sex, drugs and rock and roll overwhelmed my sense of responsibility. I did it because I was selfish and shortsighted. I made the choice and now live with the remorse. To paint myself as a tortured man, though, would be a lie. I hardly felt the conflict. I hardly felt anything. I just wanted to get high and stay high. And the stimulants – drink, drugs, adulation, corporate power, fast women – made it easy. If you'd asked me if I was troubled, I'd laugh and say, 'How troubled can I be? I'm running the biggest record company in the world.'

The industry suffered a marked decline in the late seventies/early eighties. For our group, the turnaround came relatively quickly. For most, in the eighties, despite a few notable dips, business boomed. The great paradox that sat in the center of my life was that the more I misbehaved, the more the company profited. Profits were my tickets to entitlement, craziness my reward. I could have anything. The more records we sold, the less the corporation understood how we did it, the more absolute my autonomy. The insane profitability of my professional life allowed me to lead a personal life, equally insane, free of reason or restraint.

In a few years, just as cocaine contributed to the decline of what was left of my moral character, Michael Jackson, who never touched a drug, soared into the stratosphere, creating a buying frenzy that consolidated my power base even further. MTV, compact discs – the decade would see a series of innovations that fattened profits and led to excess on everyone's part. Soon the eighties would make the hedonistic seventies appear altruistic.

With Reagan in the White House playing the part of a benevolent laissez-faire father, the marketplace was a free-for-all. On many levels and in many places – CBS Records serving as prime example – a lunatic was running the asylum.

And yet . . .

I think it's fair to say that my business acumen stayed sharp. Ironically, as I slid into alcoholism and drug abuse, I could still steer the ship. Given the eccentric nature of navigating the wild waters of the music biz, my altered state may have even helped. I'm not recommending working high. Lack of clarity ultimately did me in. But there were many moments when my freewheeling whacked-out style of doing business worked.

Some of the artists liked that style. For all my nuttiness, they knew I'd cut through red tape. They saw I had even less patience with corporate procedure than they did. They appreciated my bluntness. When Bruce Springsteen was working on his first album of the eighties, *The River*, I went by the studio. Bruce had been developing the record for over a year. We needed it.

'Where is it?' I asked Bruce. 'Where's my record?'

'It's going to be two records.'

'Oy vey. Why can't you just give me a nice one-record with two or three hit singles?'

'I can't, Walter, because what I have to say won't fit on one record.'

When Bruce spoke that way, who could argue? His artistic sincerity was stronger than my commercial drive.

'Fine,' I said, 'it's two LP's. But finish the goddamn thing.'

A couple of million copies later, Bruce's heroism was reaffirmed. On the other hand, Bruce's manager, Jon Landau, drove me up the wall. Landau saw Bruce as Jesus. He'd call me to report what Bruce had for breakfast – 'he ate the eggs but he skipped the bacon' – not to mention endlessly detailed reports on how they mixed 'Hungry Heart.'

'I don't care if they mixed it with an eggbeater, Jon,' I said. 'It's a hit, and I'm happy.'

But Jon wasn't happy until he told me Bruce's exercise routine, Bruce's political agenda, the books Bruce was reading, the magazines Bruce favored and the movies Bruce saw twice.

'Stop!' I said to Jon. 'I believe in Saint Springsteen, but enough's enough.'

Her nickname was Boom Boom, her real name Lynda Emon. She was a party girl. If I was willing – even eager – to further explore the world of self-indulgence and sleaze, Boom Boom was a willing companion. She wasn't Mary Poppins and she didn't work for the Salvation Army. But she and I did work each other over for a number of years. In any contest for misbehavior, we'd have won the Outrageous Couple Award. We looked stoned, we acted stoned, we *were* stoned. When I abandoned my family, I took up with Boom Boom.

The sexual side of our relationship was especially steamy. That's because it was based on a ménage à trois – Boom Boom, me and cocaine. I had toyed with the drug from time to time, but during my Boom Boom days of the early eighties the toying turned serious. The last thing in the world I needed was the pumped-up power surge of cocaine. Unlike pot, which has interesting creative properties, coke inflames the ego. How does an egomaniac become more maniacal? Give him coke. How does self-absorption, self-obsession, self-aggrandizement take on deeper dimensions? Try coke. I tried it, liked it and made it part of my acting-out operation.

The bungalows at the Beverly Hills Hotel continued to be a prime acting-out spot. I'd check in, get high and get down with Boom Boom. After sex I'd turn to business. During one such trip, my business involved leaving CBS.

Like Clive before me, I liked to complain how, compared to the

Warner execs, I was underpaid. The truth is that although my salary was high, my financial worth remained modest. I needed to be fixed. Sex didn't fix me, although I loved it. Power didn't fix me, although I reveled in it. Drugs didn't fix me, although I gorged on them. Maybe money would. I saw my competitors accumulating great wealth. I wanted great wealth.

I was dreaming of such wealth when Irving Azoff, manager of the Eagles and all-around big shot, came by the bungalow. Azoff's reputation for ill-tempered dealings rivaled my own. Some called him an even bigger prick than me. I doubted that, but didn't doubt his mad drive for success. We started talking. As rivals, we dealt with each other cautiously. At the same time, we saw how working together might serve us both. We both knew music, but we wanted movies. Like Stigwood, we wanted to combine the two. At the same time, we said the same word, 'Warner.'

We agreed to approach David Horowitz, who worked under Steve Ross. The idea was a Yetnikoff/Azoff partnership, a combination music label/movie deal underwritten to the tune of $15 million. In addition to equity participation, I'd also be paid a cool million a year. We pitched the idea to Horowitz, who said he'd think about it. By the next day, his thoughts were positive.

'You two guys can't miss,' he said.

He shook our hands and asked for a week to get approval from Steve Ross. 'Don't worry,' he added, 'Steve's going to love it.'

I'd been with CBS twenty years. Did I feel a tug of loyalty? Was I conflicted about breaking ranks and going over to the other side? Sure, I had reservations, but none that couldn't be erased by a few million bucks. Such thoughts were racing through my head when the phone rang.

'One moment please for Mr Paley.'

'Walter?'

'Yes, Mr Paley.'

'I'm making the announcement tomorrow.'

My heart started racing. I figured he'd heard about my negotiations with Horowitz. The old man was firing me.

'I wanted you to hear it first,' he said. 'I'm getting rid of Backe – he's not the man I thought he was – and bringing in Tom Wyman from Pillsbury. You'll like this guy. He'll like you. He's top drawer. I'll set up a meeting as soon as you get back.'

A few days later when I saw Wyman, I understood what Paley had seen: another tall and handsome golf-playing, tennis-playing WASP. Wyman had gone to Andover and Amherst, lived in Switzerland and England, discussed Irish poetry, charmed the chairman and taken over as his new man. I didn't like him. He sounded like a duck; he quacked rather than talked, speaking in a lockjaw uptight snotty locution that made me crazy. His mind was plodding and predictable. He was enamored of the mechanics of bureaucratic organization, and he was boring to boot. I'd never get along with him – another reason to fly the coop to Warner.

The next week Horowitz asked me to meet him at his New York apartment. It was a hot, muggy summer night. My brain was whirling. I was feeling topsy-turvy. I arrived disheveled. The deal was coming down.

'Have a drink,' Horowitz offered.

'I've already had a drink.'

'Have another.'

'I've already had another. Let's get to the deal.'

'It's not going to work.'

'How can it not work? We had a handshake.'

'We have a problem with Steve Ross.'

'Ross hates me.'

'Ross doesn't hate anyone. He just doesn't see this deal. He's got Alan Ladd, Jr., making movies. He doesn't see the need.'

'Ross hates me.'

'You're taking it personally.'

'Not only that, I'm going to take it out on him. I'm going to eat up so much Warner market share, he'll wish he'd paid twice what I was asking.'

To soothe my aching ego, I could always turn to Mottola and Grubman, two guys who, like the drugs I shared with Boom Boom, did wonders for my self-esteem. Tommy and Allen weren't interested in drugs; they were interested in access and power. Mottola liked going to Joe's Restaurant in Little Italy, where you couldn't tell whether the guys in trench coats and fedoras were the real deal or extras from Central Casting. Sometimes I'd see Moishe Levy down there. 'Velvel,' he'd say, 'your fucking lawsuit is breaking my balls. You're too tough for me.'

'When's my horse coming in?' I'd retort.

'Any day now.'

Meanwhile, Mottola, Grubman and I conspired over linguine and clams.

'Geffen's looking for international distribution for his label,' Grubman told me.

'You're in touch with Geffen?' I asked.

'He's not happy with the deal Warner is offering.'

'Warner bankrolled his label,' I said. 'Warner will do his overseas distribution.'

'At the right price, Geffen would let CBS distribute internationally.'

'That would aggravate the hell out of Ross,' said Mottola.

I thought about it. David had started Geffen Records. He'd signed some big acts – he'd eventually wind up with Guns N' Roses – and the idea of making money on his foreign sales had appeal. I'd be muscling in on Warner territory. I liked the idea, but I wouldn't make it easy for Allen. Like so many music lawyers, Allen was acting as an agent. Torturing agents was one of my chief forms of recreation. Torturing schleppy Grubber was almost too easy.

'What are you getting out of this, Allen?' I asked.

Velvel and yenta Geffen

'The satisfaction of a good deal.'

'You're using me to sell yourself to Geffen.'

'I'm bringing you business, Walter. But I want you to know, my loyalty is to you. Always to you.'

'I'll give Geffen money,' I told him. 'We'll make Geffen happy. But in order to do so, you're going to have to get down on your hands and knees and beg me.'

'You're kidding.'

'Those are my conditions.'

'Right here?'

'Right now.'

Without hesitation, the fat man dropped to his knees and begged.

'Puh-leeze,' he intoned.

I was in business with Geffen and Geffen's lawyer, Allen Grubman.

The rivalry with Ross escalated in the early days of MTV.

Back in the seventies, when I ran CBS International, my colleague Bunny Freidus and I innovated the use of videos as a way as presenting nontouring artists. If a performer wasn't playing in a particular country, we'd use the video to promote the product. It didn't take Einstein to see that rock and roll was a visual medium. The more pictures the better.

When MTV began in the early eighties, I saw it as a natural extension of the same concept. The bright hope of MTV reminded me of the hope we had harbored for FM in the early seventies. MTV could be innovative, shake up the mainstream and inspire creativity. It could also break new artists. More than FM, though, I saw MTV as a new marketing tool. From Sinatra to Elvis to the Beatles and the Stones, pop music had always depended upon iconography. To enhance those icons – to sex up songs with narrative accents and seductive choreography – would inevitably boost sales.

Steve Ross saw the same thing. His Warner conglomerate partnered up with American Express and started MTV, an all-music video cable channel. I was enthusiastic about the new venture. I was certain it would sell records. One problem, though, stopped me in my tracks: MTV wanted free use of all videos. I said no.

'I don't understand your position,' said Steve when he heard about my boycott. 'You don't charge radio for the use of records.'

'Different day,' I said. 'Different medium.'

'The Warner labels aren't interested in charging us.'

'You *are* the Warner labels. You're making money coming and going on this thing. I see it as a source of revenue for CBS. Videos are expensive. They're a form of programming. If we're to provide programming for your channel, we need to establish a fair system of compensation.'

'You're alone on this, Walter. If you want to boycott a sales outlet that your competitors will only too gladly exploit, that's your loss, not mine.'

'Something tells me my competitors will want to get paid for their videos the same as me.'

'We'll see.'

We saw. I held my ground. Some of the other labels did wimp out and give away their videos. But CBS stuck it out, and within a short while others followed our lead. MTV finally saw fit to pay multimillions for exclusive use of our videos. Certain CBS artists – among them Cyndi Lauper – benefited enormously from the arrangement.

At the same time, the industry was crying about the huge payments to indie promoters like Fred DiSipio. They were called unnecessary and excessive. They were said to stink of payola. My answer was always the same – show me proof of payola and I'll cut them off. I never saw proof. But I did feel the pressure, from within my own firm, to cut out the practice of hiring middle men to gain record play. I even went along with a ban. The ban was a joke. When certain songs didn't hit, it became clear that the indie promo guys knew what they were doing.

Given the fiercely competitive nature of the business, an industry-wide boycott never held. If the majors agreed to cut out the indies, you could be sure that Clive would break the ban. Like me, like all responsible company chiefs, Clive wanted hits and would do whatever it took to get one. Besides, the artists themselves were furious when they heard that indies would be eliminated. Artists hunger for hits with as much, if not more, desperation than the labels. To get around the ban, the labels – including our own – would give extra money to the artists or their managers so that they, and not us, would hire the indies. Any way you looked at it, independent promoters were in the game. If you wanted to play the game – and win – you couldn't ignore them. That was the story of the eighties, at least until the shit hit the fan. But that's several years off. Meanwhile, pass the joint.

Sexual Healing

LIFE WITH BOOM BOOM:

New Year's Eve in Acapulco, a costume party at the opulent home of Boom Boom's drug dealer. Fountains of champagne. Fishbowls of blow. Boom Boom's dressed as a tiger. Her tail is dragging, her tits barely covered. I'm the cat trainer, high leather boots, long leather whip. We're whacked out of our minds. Boom Boom's pissed at her drug dealer for not returning her calls. She urges me to confront him. Gladly.

I get in the guy's face. I call him a son of a bitch and an irresponsible motherfucker. 'When my lady calls you, call her back or you'll have to deal with me.'

He responds by nodding to a half-dozen black-suited guys who are suddenly pointing pistols at my head.

'I understand your position,' says the drug dealer in a quietly measured tone. 'But is any woman really worth this?'

I look at the guys with the guns. 'No,' I say.

Back in New York, Boom Boom and I are off for a weekend in the country. High on grass, I'm driving a souped-up Porsche. I flip on the radio. Marvin Gaye's singing 'Sexual Healing.' I beam with pride. After twenty years, Gaye has left Berry Gordy and signed with us. In spite of the fact that his recent Motown records hadn't sold, I approved the deal. 'Sexual Healing,' the first single from his debut Columbia album, is a smash. His comeback is in full swing. Me and Boom Boom are swinging to the stars, radio blasting, engine humming. In the distance are the lights of the Tappan Zee Bridge.

'Trouble ahead,' says Boom Boom.

'What trouble?'

'A roadblock.'

'What are they looking for?'

'Nothing much. Probably just drugs.'

My heart racing, I assess the situation: I'm smoked out on weed; my companion is a half-naked blonde who's shoving several vials of cocaine into her already too tight bra. She's also stuffing a bag of weed into her panties. I myself am carrying a considerable quantity of cocaine in my jacket. As we approach the red-and-blue lights of the cop cars, I frantically try to remember my lawyer's advice in the event of a search.

'If you're asked to leave the car,' he said, 'put the drugs in the glove compartment.'

Or did he say, 'Keep the drugs on you'?

I can't remember. But I better remember because I'm president of Columbia Records, an officer of CBS Inc. and, at this point, a member of the Board of Directors.

This will end my career.

A cop motions me to roll down my window. 'What's you have to drink tonight?' he asks.

'Half a glass of wine.'

'Is that it?'

'That's it.'

'And what about her?' he asks, eyeing Boom Boom, who has

positioned her upper torso so that her nipples are practically winking at him.

'She's had a few more than me, officer.'

'Well, you two behave yourself.'

'We'll try not to.'

He smiles, and I slowly take off. When we get to the other side, Boom Boom is screaming with glee. 'I was so excited I came,' she says.

'While you were coming,' I confessed, 'I was pissing my pants.'

Barbra Streisand was calling from London. When Barbra called, it wasn't to say she loved me. Something was wrong.

'Where's Jon?' she asked, referring to her boyfriend Jon Peters.

'How would I know?'

'I know he's in New York. I know the both of you are running around with women.'

'I'm always running around with women, Barbra.'

'And Jon is with you.'

'Jon is *not* with me.'

'You're lying, Walter, and until you stop lying I don't intend to sing a note.'

'I thought you were directing. Aren't you directing *Yentl*?'

'I'm in a sound studio with a sixty-piece orchestra. This is costing you a fortune. I intend to hold the musicians here for as long as you refuse to tell me where Jon is.'

'Hold them up for the rest of the year. Music costs come out of the film budget, not mine.'

'Why are you protecting him?'

'Why are you hocking me?'

She hung up before I could. Peters, like Mottola, had become a pal with whom I'd exchange pussy stories. But I didn't know where he was, and even if I did, I wouldn't have told. Out in Malibu, I had recently witnessed a scene between Jon and

Barbra that even I, a well-known disturber of the peace, found disturbing:

It was a beautiful afternoon on the California coast, seagulls fluttering, sandpipers scampering. I'd gone out to visit Barbra and Jon in their oceanfront digs. Sue Mengers, Barbra's tough-talking agent, was also there. We sat on the deck, noshing on cheese, sipping wine, gossiping about show business. Then the fireworks exploded:

Barbra accused Sue of not showing her a script. Sue said she had shown her.

'If I had seen it, I would have taken the part,' Barbra insisted.

'You did see it,' said Jon.

'In the future, you'll give me a written record of every submission. Do you have that straight?'

Thoroughly humiliated, Jon turned red with rage.

'Who the fuck are you to talk to me like that?' he screamed.

'Who the fuck are *you* to talk to *me* like that?' Barbra screamed back.

'You're an ungrateful cunt,' he said.

The screaming went downhill from there. Barbra started to cry, stormed off, got in her car and drove away. Mengers and I, hardly innocents ourselves, looked at each other in disbelief. Compared to Streisand/Peters, I felt absolutely sane.

I did, in fact, make several sane decisions.

Springsteen had been working on a new record he wanted me to hear. He and Jon Landau came by my office to play it. As I listened, Bruce nervously walked up and down the hall. At times like these, I always felt funny. I understood how Bruce felt how, in fact, most artists feel when someone is evaluating their music. On the other hand, Bruce is an artist and I'm not. I'm a lawyer, a business guy, a cheerleader for the CBS labels. How much do I really know? But what Bruce knows is this – I decide how much promotion muscle to put behind his music. He's right to be nervous.

He wants to call this new record *Nebraska*. I refer to it facetiously as *Omaha*.

'I like *Omaha*, Bruce,' I tell him when the last song is played. 'I like it a lot. It's folkie, it's sincere, it's strong messages and deep meanings. I like these songs about ordinary people. I can feel the social statement you want to make. But there's no E Street Band, Bruce, there are no rock and roll hits. I'm happy to put it out and promote it, but I'm telling you – sales will be modest.'

'That's fine with me,' he said. 'To grow as an artist, I need this record. I'm not going for sales. This is where I'm at artistically. I have to be true to that.'

'And I'll be true to you.'

And I was. Bruce more than rewarded my patience. His ensuing albums – *Born in the USA* and *Live* – were his biggest records ever.

Billy Joel was another serious artist with serious convictions. In the early eighties he, like Bruce, was developing his social conscience. I applauded the move. When I heard *The Nylon Curtain*, I had to respect his convictions. 'Allentown' was a strong statement about the results of Reagan-era economics. I liked everything about *The Nylon Curtain* except the cover. When I saw the cover, a picture of a body under some cloth, I threw a fit.

'I'm not having it,' I said.

'What's wrong with it?' Billy asked.

'Everything. What's that body doing on the floor? And why is it covered by a shmata?'

'That's the Nylon Curtain.'

'That's the Nylon Shmata. If you want to throw away your album because of a stupid cover, just call it *The Nylon Shmata*.'

'I thought the cover was artistic.'

June, Velvel and a young Billy Joel

'You want arty-farty, Billy, or you want sales?'

Billy wanted sales. We changed the cover and he got them.

I was standing at the counter of the Carnegie Deli, grabbing my order to go, when I recognized the man standing next to me. It was Paley's driver. He was picking up corned beef for the old man.

'Where's the boss?' I asked.

He nodded toward the street, where a limo was double-parked. I went outside and knocked on the window. Paley let me in. He seemed happy to see me.

'We meet over pastrami,' I said, offering him a sandwich which he gladly accepted. In between bites, he turned to business.

'I see you let some people go,' he said, referring to a downturn in record sales that meant firing three hundred employees. 'Do you see a turnaround?'

'Prospects are good, Mr Paley. I'm pursuing the Rolling Stones.'

'I'm sure you'll catch them.'

'Michael Jackson's new album will be ready for release before long.'

'Who's Michael Jackson?'

'The little kid who sang in the Jackson 5. Now he's all grown up. His first solo album sold big. I'm hoping the new one will be bigger.'

'You understand these things, Walter. I don't.'

'I'm not sure I understand any more than you do, Mr Paley.'

'You're good with contracts, you're good with artists, you know the business. To guys like me and Tom Wyman, the record business is voodoo.'

'Are you calling me a witch doctor?'

'I'm counting on you to shore up the division.'

'You'll also be happy to know that we just bought Winterland, the largest retailer of rock T-shirts. I tell you that,' I said sarcastically, 'because I know how you've always dreamed of being in the shmata business.'

'How can I thank you?'

'Bigger salary.'

'It's already too big.'

'Bigger compliments.'

'You'll compliment me by showing up at an affair at the Waldorf next week. I'm being honored at the Family of Man dinner.'

'I already have a table down front.'

'And I want you to behave.'

'Yes, Daddy.'

'Unlike the last function where you wound up screaming at that awful woman, the feminist . . . what's her name?'

'Gloria Steinem.'

'I thought you were going to punch her out.'

'I wanted to. She kept blabbering about the lack of female rock stars.'

'And you kept blabbering about her lack of brains.'

'I'll behave, Mr Paley. As soon as you finalize my adoption papers, I promise I'll behave.'

I broke my promise.

Boom Boom and I walked into the black-tie affair at the Waldorf to discover we were seated at a table with Mike Wallace. I didn't like Wallace. I'd heard he was investigating record companies, including ours. There'd also been a nasty item in a Detroit newspaper that said, in essence, if Paley knew what Wallace knew about Yetnikoff, Yetnikoff would be out on his ass. I saw the guy as a prima donna and a phony. This was our first face-to-face encounter.

'So you're Walter Yetnikoff,' he said after shaking my hand. 'You're the guy who's bankrupting CBS.'

If he meant it as a joke, I wasn't laughing. Making matters worse, he turned to Boom Boom and said, 'Why is a good-looking woman like you hanging out with Yetnikoff?'

I spent the rest of the evening fuming. I didn't say a word to the schmuck.

The next day I went to Tom Wyman, president of CBS.

'I want Wallace fired,' I said.

'What are you talking about?' Wyman quacked.

'He's a pompous asshole who insulted me at a public affair. He also bad-mouthed me to the *Detroit Free Press*. Even worse, he stuck his hand up my girlfriend's dress. He touched her pussy.'

'Is that true?'

'Yes.' The insult was true; the pussy part was a bit of an exaggeration. He did, though, touch her knee.

'What do you want me to do about it?'

'Fire him.'

'Please, Walter, I am not firing Mike Wallace.'

'What would you do if someone touched your wife's cunt?'

'I'd deck him.'

'Then I'm on my way over to *60 Minutes* to deck Wallace.'

'Don't do that. I'll get him to apologize.'

Next day Wallace called.

'Walter,' he said, 'why are you making such a fuss? We're all part of the same family. No harm intended. I had nothing to do with that article in Detroit. But if it makes you feel better, I apologize.'

'In writing, Mike.'

'Don't hold your breath.'

Two hours later, Don Hewitt, executive producer of *60 Minutes*, called.

'Why are you creating these silly problems?' he wanted to know.

'You know, Don, your vaunted *60 Minutes* has investigated the record business for years. Your people have been searching high and low for drugs and payola. Payola is hard to find, but drugs? Just walk out of your own office and you're in Snow Valley. I'm a better investigative journalist than you are.'

'I've never seen cocaine.'

'I didn't use the word. You did.'

By the end of the week, a formal letter of apology from Mike Wallace was sitting on my desk. I felt vindicated and invulnerable; I also felt like a willful little kid who got his way. I liked that feeling. Besides, Boom Boom was impressed.

Jagger liked to fuck with me.

We were in a swanky Parisian restaurant ordering wine that cost more than the gross national product of certain countries. We were both bombed – or at least I was. You could never tell with Mick. He liked to give the impression of inebriation while retaining control. I'd flown over as part as my relentless campaign to sign the Stones. It amused Mick to see hungry record execs chasing his skinny ass around the world. He was a skilled negotiator who never lost sight of his advantage as a pop icon. His image as the prancing prince of rock belied that side of his character that had seriously studied economics. When it came to numbers, Mick was sober as Saint Augustine.

After the caviar, truffles, escargots and wine, we were onto the brandy.

'You have a reputation, Walter,' said Mick, 'as being King of Contracts. They say you can read a fifty-page legal document in five minutes and know exactly what's right and what's wrong. Is that true, mate?'

'I can speed-read.'

'And what about foreign royalty rates? Do you understand them?'

'It's my job.'

'And what about the Value Added Tax in France?'

'It's a bit tricky.'

'Shall we have a go at it? Let's set up a scenario. Let's presume a certain royalty rate and a certain number of albums sold. From there we'll calculate the VAT in France. Are you game?'

What could I say? I was the big macher. This was my territory. I had to take him on. So Mick put up some numbers, and we both began scribbling on our cocktail napkins. Two minutes later he had an accurate reading of the French tax while I was still fumbling. He grinned that sly Jagger smile and announced, 'You need a bloody bookkeeper, Walter.'

'You're hired,' I said.

Signing the Stones kept me running for a year. Meetings in Europe, meetings in New York, meetings in California. Meeting the challenge of Jagger's swagger and sinewy ways took all I had. But I was determined to get them. During our final negotiations at the Ritz Hotel in Paris, I flew off the handle. The highly complex contract was already drafted. It required a dozen lawyers and involved a Dutch Antilles holding company. After months of haggling, all we needed were signatures. That's when Mick balked.

'I'm not letting you pick two singles from every one of our albums,' he said to me.

Velvel eyes Mick and assorted Stones

'I won't pick the singles. You will. The contract just says that from each album two singles must be released.'

'Whatever Mick says is right,' said Keith Richards, glaring through his heavy eye makeup. 'Do you know our music better than we do?'

'Go get another blood transfusion, Richards. Maybe it'll get your brain working again.'

This was the moment when Mick called me a 'motherfuckin' record executive' and I called on the gods of restraint to stop me from shoving my fist in his face. The gods came through, the deal got done. The deal worked out, in part, because we bought rights to a portion of their lucrative back catalogue. The richest part of their catalogue, though, wasn't owned by them but by Allen Klein, the accountant/music mogul who at one time had managed the Stones and the Beatles. I had asked their current manager, Prince Rupert Loewenstein – Prince of what, I never understood – how Klein wound up with the jewels, including *Sticky Fingers* and *Hot Rocks*.

'When they started selling records,' the good prince told me, 'Mick searched for the one man with the skills to beat up on the record companies. Klein was that man. The irony was that Klein also beat up on the Stones.'

In years to come, some said Mick beat up on me. I don't see it that way. The Stones got big money from CBS, but we profited. Outlandish profits, though, wouldn't come from the aging rock stars. They would come from that strange and brilliant man-child who kept calling me the Good Father.

Fifty

OUT OF LOVE AND CONCERN, A SCHOLARLY FRIEND OF mine gave me a copy of Dante's *Divine Comedy* for my fiftieth birthday.

'Thanks,' I said, 'but it's a long poem.'

'Just read the first line.'

'"Midway in the journey of our life, I found myself in a dark wood, where the straight way was lost."'

'Get it?'

I got it but forgot it. I gave away the book and disregarded my friend's warning. I knew what he was saying – I'd have to be a moron not to – yet wasn't even close to accepting the truth. The truth was that in the first quarter of 1983 Columbia Records was enjoying its best quarter ever. Profits doubled. Michael Jackson's *Thriller* had taken off like a bat out of hell. Self-reflection about my moral decay was the last thing on my mind.

Friends like Tommy Mottola were continually propping me up with praise. 'No one could have nailed the Stones like you did,' said Tommy. 'No one but you could have brought back Marvin Gaye.'

One of my first encounters with Marvin was in L.A. Boom Boom and I had been indulging in a bungalow at the Beverly Hills Hotel for days. I'd wake up, get smashed, call my New York office, complain about being overworked and underpaid, bang Boom Boom and take a nap. On one smoggy afternoon, my head fogged up with weed, Marvin dropped by. He and Boom Boom were already well acquainted. They liked hanging out and posing for pictures; they got off on their ebony-and-ivory appearance. Maybe they were more than friends. I didn't ask.

Marvin was a tall, handsome man whose disposition would, at the drop of a hat, turn sour. He was well-spoken, highly intelligent, unusually charming. He and Boom Boom embraced before he began talking about his new songs. He wanted me to hear a couple. 'Certainly,' I said. When he handed me a joint, Boom Boom stopped him.

'My God, Marvin, please – put that away.'

'What's wrong?' he asked.

'Walter is vehemently anti-drug. He's spent his life warning his artists about the dangers. He's liable to make a citizen's arrest. He goes crazy when he sees an illegal substance.'

'I had no idea,' said Marvin, looking puzzled.

'Don't you realize,' I asked him, 'that pot can lead to coke?'

'I have some of that too.'

'Great,' I said, setting things straight. 'Bring it out.'

We spent the next few hours getting loaded as Marvin played his new songs with titles like 'Sanctified Pussy,' 'Savage in the Sack' and 'Masochistic Beauty.'

'Great stuff, Marvin, but radio will never play it.'

Next time I saw Marvin was in New York for his 'Sexual Healing' tour. After his eighth consecutive sold-out Radio City concert, I hosted a party for him at Studio 54. Marvin was on top, or should have been. After years of neglect, he had won his first Grammy; he had stunned a national TV audience at the NBA

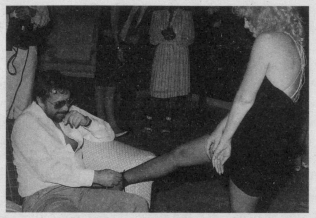

Boom Boom at Velvel's fiftieth

All-Star game with the funkiest version of the national anthem since José Feliciano; Marvin was back.

Everyone was in awe of him. Mick Jagger and Keith Richards looked at him like a god. As the reigning monarchs of pop paid their respects, Marvin handled his aristocratic status with notable ease. During the days and nights of his New York dates, though, he appeared frantic. He concluded each concert by doing a striptease version of 'Sexual Healing.' Throwing off his robe, he stood naked except for his briefs, an act sadly out of character for a character as cool as Marvin.

I had heard his entourage included dangerous men. When he invited me backstage at Radio City, I saw a veritable army of big bodyguards who looked armed to the teeth. The ambience was ominous. Marvin's dressing room, though, was empty.

'In here, Walter,' a voice called from the bathroom.

I opened the door. He was seated on the pot. I closed the door.

'Come in,' he urged.

'I don't have to see anyone take a shit,' I said, 'even if he is one of my artists.'

'I'm not taking a shit, I'm taking a hit.'

I opened the door again and saw that he was, in fact, fully clothed, a cocaine spoon up his nose.

'Have some.'

'No, thanks. By the way, I've always been curious. Did you ever want to fuck Diana Ross?'

'Yeah, when she was sixteen. And Walter, please don't give me that bullshit about how you don't want any blow.'

'I do, but not yours.'

'Why?'

'Because you're doing so much, you're going to run out. Then when you run out, you're going to get mad at me. With all these gentlemanly bodyguards you've employed, I don't want you mad at me.'

'I can't trust these guys, Walter. I can't trust anyone. They're trying to hurt me. They want to eliminate me.'

As he spoke, he kept zupping up the coke. His eyes were filled with fear.

'That's crazy,' I said. 'No one wants to hurt you. You're much loved.'

'I can't trust them, I can't trust anyone. They're lying to me, they're stealing me blind.'

'Who are "they"?'

He got up, came over and whispered in my ear. 'We can't talk here. The room is wired.'

I looked at him like he was kidding but saw he wasn't. His paranoia was raging. It was also contagious. I started feeling frightened myself.

'Will you meet me back in my hotel later tonight?' he asked.

'Sure,' I said.

I never showed up. Marvin Gaye was too out of control, even for me.

*

I liked controlling Allen Grubman, which is why I set him up with some of our biggest artists. In short order, the Grubber was representing Bruce Springsteen and Billy Joel. Dealing with a nonconfrontational lawyer made my life easier. I'd never have to worry about Grubman suing me. 'I don't know how,' he'd joke, though I believed the joke. Grubman also gave us first shot at new artists he was representing. It was a cozy arrangement, and also a little twisted. The guy would fall to his knees and beg me to do a deal. Nothing was beneath his dignity.

Nothing could keep me from wanting more money, power and prestige. All through the eighties, I had one foot out the door, hoping a competitor would lure me away with an offer I couldn't refuse. Enter David Geffen, yenta supreme. Geffen was another wheeler-dealer who played with power brokers in the hopes of becoming one. In the early eighties, he was certain I was the logical man to head up MCA. During one of his morning calls in which he manically redrew the map of the entertainment industry, he called to say that the big bosses, Lew Wasserman and Sid Sheinberg, were ready to meet me – and meet my exorbitant price.

I called Wasserman 'Papa Doc,' a tribute to his benign dictatorship over all Hollywood, and I referred to Sid as 'Shitty' Sheinberg. This didn't endear me to them, but what the hell. They needed *me* to run their music division; I didn't need them.

Geffen set up the meeting. I was prepared to answer questions about the future of the music business. I had been predicting, for example, that compact discs, a new innovation in which our Japanese partner Sony was heavily invested, would revolutionize the industry. At the same time, I'd been arguing with Sony that their double-well tape players made copying too easy. 'Your hardware is undercutting your software,' I kept telling them, and anyone else who would listen. Wasserman surely wanted to hear my views on the technological future. Not true. Wasserman just wanted to discuss Jewish delis.

'If you want to find a good deli,' he said, 'look inside to make sure it's crowded. A lot of business means fresh food. Nate and Al's has fresh food, much better than Canter's. Have you been to Nate and Al's, Walter?'

'Yes, Papa Doc, but what does this have to do with business?'

'A lot of business is done at Nate and Al's.'

'You wanna go to Nate and Al's, we'll go to Nate and Al's.'

At Nate and Al's we hammered out the basis of a deal. Once again, I was set to leave CBS. The money was practically double my present salary. The only problem was my current contract had a year to go. I needed a release.

'Release me,' I said to Tom Wyman. 'You've been a dime-a-dance executive for years. Now it's my turn to take a whirl. You understand.'

Wyman didn't argue. He said he'd authorize a release form. When it came, though, the form was the size of an epic novel. I speed-read it until arriving at one deal-breaking point: I could leave, it said, but I was not allowed to engage in any activities that even vaguely resembled the music business.

I went back to Papa Doc and explained the problem. If I left CBS for MCA, it might mean litigation.

'I'm not getting sued by CBS,' said Wasserman. 'CBS Television is a buyer of MCA products. If you can't work this out smoothly with Paley, the deal's off.'

So I went to Paley, hat in hand.

'You're strangling me,' I told the boss. 'This release form is so restrictive you could sue me for listening to music while I'm riding in an elevator.'

'What did you expect me to do, Walter, roll over and play dead? You have a binding employment contract. If you want to break it, you'll have to pay the price.'

'I'll willing to pay, but MCA isn't.'

'Then you have a problem. My problem, Walter, is that I don't understand you. I said I'll match their offer. What else does Wasserman have that I don't?'

'Movies.'

'You want to produce movies? Go produce movies. Your new contract will allow you to devote 20 percent of your time to independent movie production. Now is there anything else that requires my attention?'

'Adoption.'

PALEY ADOPTS YETNIKOFF!
Chairman of CBS Grants Music Mogul His 50th Birthday Wish

Boom Boom had mocked up the newspaper and presented it to me at my fiftieth birthday party, an event that reeked of industry decadence and Yetnikoff ego. It came off as a big surprise, thanks to Jagger.

Mick called to say he and Keith wanted to hang out. But when Jagger came by in his limo, Keith was nowhere to be found.

'Jump in, mate,' Mick urged. 'We're going to see Keith up at the penthouse on top of the Hilton.'

'What's he doing there?'

'That's the bloody life Keith likes to lead. The posher the better. Don't forget to ask him about his solo work, Walter. You know how sensitive he is. He thinks you love me more than him. You must be a good record exec and love all your children equally.'

'I love them in proportion to their love for me.'

'You'll love us even more when we're all high.'

He was right. I got high and loved everyone. I was relieved that the MCA business was behind me. Irving Azoff had taken the job. After all was said and done, I saw Paley as less interfering than

Papa Doc and Shitty Sheinberg. Riding up to the penthouse, I was feeling especially mellow. When the elevator doors opened, and the crowd screamed, 'Surprise!' my mellow turned to balls-out merriment. The joint was jumping. The great and near-great had come to kiss my ass. Naturally Grubman and Mottola were first in line. But there were also competitors like Ahmet Ertegun, who whisked me into a private room for a taste of birthday blow. Henny Youngman and Robert Klein were telling jokes. Moishe Levy and Fred DiSipio were trading stories. Even the Big Duck from CBS, Tom Wyman, honored me with his presence. Boom Boom, the party's prime mover, was in the center of the action. Male and female strippers strutted their stuff, satisfying the wide diversity of tastes. Boom Boom got a taste of one of the male strippers' crotch when she used her teeth to fish out a telegram from Billy Joel wedged inside his jockstrap. 'Happy 50th, Walter,' it read. 'You redefine insanity.'

I partied till the following day. I was wrecked. Among the remaining guests was my friend the Dante scholar. Like everyone else, he was sloshed.

'You read the rest of the poem?' he slurred.

'I've begun.'

'There are three parts – Hell, Purgatory and Paradise.'

'I'm stuck in Hell.'

'And you like it.'

'Hell, yes. I like it a lot.'

PART 3
The Pinnacle

Emmanuel Lewis, Michael and me

Michael and his Good Daddy

Iago Mottola, Jackson, Velvel and Dileo

Thriller

NO SINGLE RECORD CHANGED THE BUSINESS – AND MY life – as powerfully as Michael Jackson's *Thriller*. Springsteen's *Born in the USA*, Joel's *An Innocent Man*, Cyndi Lauper's *She's So Unusual*, Men at Work's *Business as Usual*, Boston's *Boston* – all huge career-defining records. But as a sales phenomenon, *Thriller* eclipsed them all. At one point the damn thing was selling a million copies a week. I'd never seen such figures. Michael had once again reinvented himself, only this time as the third prong of pop's Holy Trinity – now it was Elvis, the Beatles and Michael Jackson.

'I told you I'd do it,' he said. 'I told you I'd outdo *Off the Wall*.'

Thanks to Quincy Jones's stunning production and Michael's brilliant artistry, *Thriller* was wall-to-wall hits, silky-smooth rock-and-soul love-and-life songs with a pulsating magic that resonated with everyone.

'You delivered,' I said to Michael. 'You delivered like a motherfucker.'

'Please don't use that word, Walter.'

'You delivered like an angel. Archangel Michael.'

'That's better. Now will you promote it?'

'Like a motherfucker.'

Michael giggled the famous Michael giggle.

The stars were aligned, the planets in sync, the deities of high commerce directing Michael's destiny. When he performed the album's first single, 'Billie Jean,' on the Motown Twenty-fifth Anniversary television special, he moonwalked his way into a new stratosphere. Michaelmania spread around the world. Michael worked tirelessly, developing videos, short films, auxiliary products, anything to sell *Thriller*. He also became obsessed with how he looked. He literally resculpted his image, chose young children and chimps as companions, slept in oxygen chambers and consciously cultivated the crass mass media – including supermarket tabloids – to focus on his fame. I didn't object. Why should I? At twenty-four, Michael had become more than a master singer/dancer/songwriter. He was a supersalesman of his own mystique.

Michael's passion for world conquest was singular. I knew all about burning ambition – my own and those of other execs and artists. But Michael's drive bordered on the psychopathic. He lived, breathed, slept, dreamt and spoke of nothing but number-1 successes. He was possessed. He called me night and day for the latest figures. 'They're tremendous,' I'd say. 'They need to be more tremendous,' he'd reply. *Thriller* stayed number 1 for months. In the long period of its unprecedented success, however, when it occasionally fell to second place for a week or two, Michael panicked. Hysterical, he'd berate me for failing to pump up the promotion. 'I'm pumping, Michael,' I'd say. 'I promise you I'm pumping.'

And I was.

I screamed bloody murder when MTV refused to air his videos. They argued that their format, white rock, excluded Michael's music. I argued they were racist assholes – and I'd trumpet it to the world if they didn't relent. I've never been more forceful or obnoxious. I've also never been as effective, threatening to pull *all* our videos. With added pressure from Quincy Jones, they caved in, and in doing so the MTV color line came crashing down. The stunning creativity of Michael's videos – 'Billie Jean,' 'Beat It,' 'Thriller' – set a new standard and opened the door for black artists, including hip-hoppers and rappers, to the MTV crossover markets. Even more, Michael raised video to a new level. He redefined the relationship of dance to pop music. I'd always dreamed of a vehicle that would seamlessly wed audio/video with music and motion. Stigwood had beat me to the punch with *Saturday Night Fever*. But Michael came through with something even more exciting. His 'Thriller' video was as thrilling as *West Side Story*.

I had a Michael Jackson problem with Jann Wenner, publisher of *Rolling Stone*. I saw Wenner as a self-styled autocrat who took his role as tastemaker far too seriously. He probably saw me the same way. In the past, our conflicts had been so nasty I banned him from the building. He infuriated me when he ran a favorable review of a Dylan bootleg – hardly appropriate for a legitimate music magazine. In the early days of *Thriller*, though, I realized I needed Wenner. I needed Michael on the cover of *Rolling Stone*.

'I rarely put R&B artists on the cover,' Wenner said.

'He's not R&B, he's pop. And besides, you had him on the cover when he was a kid.'

'That was then. This is now.'

'This is going to be the biggest record in the history of records.'

'Black artists don't sell magazines.'

'I'm not sure he's black. He's not sure he's black. But that's beside the point. *You* think he's black, and your refusal to put a hugely popular black on the cover is nothing but blind prejudice. Keep him off the cover and I'll report your prejudice to every media outlet around the world.'

Wenner put Michael on the cover.

Thriller was loaded with radio-friendly singles. One after another, they all went top ten. Michael gave credit to our Epic promotion man, Frank Dileo, whom we called Uncle Tookie. Tookie took credit for everything, and was only too happy to accept Michael's gratitude. As long as Michael was happy, I was happy.

The truth is that Tookie, like all great promo men, could sell. He was a fast talker and slick operator who skillfully worked the indie promoters and radio programmers. Tall as a fire hydrant and twice as wide, Tookie was a physical phenomenon. His center of gravity was remarkably short and menacingly steady. With an enormous stogie permanently planted between his teeth, he seemed unmovable.

'I'm going to try to move you, Tookie,' I said.

'Try,' he urged.

'I'm charging at you full force.'

'Charge.'

I body-slammed him hard as I could. He didn't move an inch, but I did; I bounced off him and landed on the floor, breathless.

His salesmanship was equally as strong, the very quality that made him attractive to Michael.

'Will you be mad at me if I hire Uncle Tookie away from Epic and make him my manager?'

'Mad?' I asked. 'I'll be thrilled.' To have an insider – one of my own men – managing Michael could only make life easier.

'Tookie's a genius,' said Michael. 'With him, my albums will get bigger and bigger. Don't you agree?'

Thriller was already on its way to becoming the biggest seller in music history.

'At some point, Michael, the law of diminishing returns sets in for everyone. Bigness has its limitations.'

'Tookie says there are no limits. Tookie thinks the way I do.'

'Go with Tookie. Go with God. The way you're selling, maybe you'll rewrite the law of diminishing returns.'

'I will,' said the man-child. 'I have to.'

Momentum built. Michael's scary accident during the filming of a Pepsi commercial, when he was badly burned, only turned up the media heat. When I threw a black-tie party for him at the Museum of Natural History in New York, there were more security guards than guests. Donald Trump was Michael's new best friend. *The Guinness Book of Records* announced that *Thriller*, with 25 million copies sold, was the best-selling album ever. I introduced him as the 'greatest artist ever.' Only my Jewish roots kept me from comparing him to Jesus. The President and Mrs Reagan sent a telegram. When I saw Mr Paley, I said, 'Now you know who Michael Jackson is.' At the high point, at the very moment I was about to introduce Michael to the glittering crowd, he whispered in my ear, 'I have to tinkle. Can you take me to the potty?'

A few days after the party, I was on my way to California when Michael called.

'I'm not happy,' he said.

'How can you not be happy? You own the world.'

'My brothers want me to tour with them, and I don't want to.'

'Then don't.'

'But my mother says I should.'

'Do you always listen to your mother?'

'I try to.'

'Then tour.'

'She's working with Don King.'

'You're working with Uncle Tookie. It's an even match.'

'My brothers are broke. That's the only reason they want to tour with me.'

'That's a pretty good reason.'

'When I was a kid, they never stopped teasing me.'

'So you're angry.'

'Very.'

'I don't blame you.'

'But I don't want my mother angry at me.'

'You've got a problem, Michael. Ever think about therapy?'

'I could never tell these things to a stranger.'

'Then flip a coin. Heads you tour, tails you don't.'

'You flip.'

'Alright . . . I just did. It came out heads.'

In a few months, the Victory Tour, starring Michael and his brothers, hit the road.

Before that came the Grammys.

In February 1984, a week prior to the big event in L.A., I was in San Francisco, loaded and getting laid. I was with still another willing woman who swore undying admiration for my lovemaking.

'But beyond physical pleasure,' this one wanted to know, 'do you ever really love a woman?'

'Of course,' I said.

'How do you measure the love?'

'By how much she loves me.'

'That seems a little sad.'

'Do I seem sad?' I asked angrily. 'Do you have any complaints about the humping and bumping?'

'Underneath you do seem sad.'

'Just what I need. Postcoital psychoanalysis.'

'You're saved by the bell,' she said, referring to the ringing phone. Michael was on the line. God forbid he should ask whether he's interrupting.

'I think I'm going to win a lot of Grammys.'

'I think you're right.'

'But everyone says Quincy is going to win some, too. And I don't want him to. Quincy didn't really produce the record, I did.

Quincy has enough Grammys. He doesn't need any more. Tell them not to give him any Grammys for *Thriller*.'

'I can't tell them anything, Michael. The Grammys are run by NARAS. I have no influence over the National Academy of Recording Arts and Sciences.'

'You have influence over everyone.'

'Except God, NARAS and Michael Jackson.'

'You can call Quincy and tell him to withdraw.'

'No one withdraws.'

'If he doesn't, I won't let him produce my next record.'

'That'd be foolish.'

'People will think he's the one who did it, not me.'

'Quincy doesn't sing or dance. Quincy isn't in any of the videos. Quincy sits behind the board and produces.'

'*I* was the producer.'

'Michael, I was in the studio myself. I saw Quincy producing.'

'All he did was help out.'

'Fine. If you want to complain to NARAS, complain to NARAS.'

'That won't look good. You have to complain.'

'Get Tookie to complain.'

'He said to get you.'

'And I say this is a crock of shit. Go to the goddamn Grammys, Michael, and act like you're happy.'

He did.

Between Michael and Quincy, *Thriller* won a dozen Grammys. Michael acted like he loved Quincy more than life itself. Seated in the first row in spangled mock-military garb, his glittering single glove on full display, he had Brooke Shields on one side and child star Emmanuel Lewis on the other, a ménage à trois to make the Marquis de Sade blush. When his name was called as winner of one of the Grammys, he asked me to join him onstage. Few artists ask the head of the record company to share the spotlight.

Naturally I was flattered. The next day I called Tom Wyman to ask if he'd seen the show. He had.

'Don't you think that increases my visibility to potential new artists?' I wanted to know.

'Yes.'

'And don't you think Michael's gesture makes me more valuable as an executive?'

'Yes.'

'And don't you think that justifies a major raise?'

'No.'

Money was pouring in. Michael was making so much he went on a buying tear. He was especially intrigued by song copyrights. When he learned the Beatles catalogue was up for grabs, he wanted in on the action. McCartney and Yoko Ono had stopped bidding because the price was too steep. Michael asked my opinion.

'At forty-five million or so,' I said, 'I think it *is* too high. I'd be careful.'

Michael wasn't careful. He bought the catalogue. He was right to disregard my advice. The value of those songs has increased dramatically. Though he appeared impetuous – and at times was – Michael's business acumen was sharp. He suffered some fallout with McCartney, who protested that his friend Michael had somehow undone him. But the truth is that Paul had the resources to buy back his songs. He simply chose not to.

Michael made other decisions, though, that had me scratching my head.

The Victory Tour was billed as a grand reunion of the Jacksons, including Jermaine, who had left the group when the brothers moved to CBS in the seventies. But the reunion turned bad. Michael never overcame his bitterness toward his brothers. They bickered endlessly. Michael called me from practically every venue, complaining about his commitment, whining how his family was riding his coattails. Meanwhile, at his mother's urging, he had participated in a new Jacksons album, *Victory*, that included a duet with Jermaine. Michael had sung still another duet with Jermaine on Jermaine's Arista album. This evidence of brotherly love, though, was misleading. Underneath was raging sibling rivalry.

'I don't want to release any of those duets as a single,' Michael told me.

'Fine. Tell Jermaine.'

'I can't. I already told him that I would allow Arista to release a single. But I want him to think that Epic won't allow it.'

'By Epic, you mean me.'

'I'm telling everyone you think it'll hurt my career.'

'But I *don't* think that. I think you should do whatever you want.'

'I want to keep the family happy.'

'And lying to your brother will do that?'

'I'm not lying. I really do believe it'll hurt my career. And I believe you believe that too.'

'Doesn't matter what I believe. What matters is that you want me to be the bad guy.'

'That's a great idea for the title of my next solo album.'

'What is?'

'Bad.'

In every sense of the word, Michael *was* bad. As I watched him change over the next five or six years, I was alternately impressed and alarmed. His artistic brilliance stood in contrast to his personal behavior. He grew more isolated, evolving from strange to weird to outrageously (and perhaps calculatingly) bizarre. But if he did, as his 'Thriller' video projected, turn into something of a monster, so did I. His sense of self-entitlement corresponded with my own.

On some level, we enabled each other. I put the full force of a giant international record company behind his products. His unprecedented success strengthened my own notoriety. If he was intoxicated with the heady autonomy that accompanies celebrity, so was I. Being the corporate confidant of the biggest star in the world blew up my ego, not to mention my sense of self-deception, to outlandish proportions. When we spoke of violent fathers, we seemed to understand each other. I did his bidding, he praised my skills. His fame fed my power. We were convinced that we were, to borrow a title from a future Michael Jackson album, invincible. The truth was otherwise. The real question, which neither of us perceived, was who was crazier – Michael or me? I leave the question of Michael's craziness to Michael. But what about my own madness? What the hell was I looking for?

Torturing My Competitors

HERE'S WHAT'S HAPPENING IN MY OFFICE: MY ENGLISH barber, who's also my drug dealer, is dying my beard because I hate the gray. The dye is Lady Clairol medium brown #5. While the barber is sticking blow up my nose, he's asking whether I like this particular grade of cocaine. 'I like the grade,' I say. 'Don't breathe,' he says, 'or you'll breathe in the toxic dye.' 'How can I snort and stop breathing at the same time?' Before he can answer, I see the dye dripping into my glass of vodka which is turning purple. When I put a match to my Nat Sherman cigarillo, everyone screams, 'You're going to blow us up!' 'So we'll blow up,' I say. 'Barbra Streisand's on the phone,' my secretary says. Barbra is responding to my idea of boosting her overseas sales by recording with Julio Iglesias. She says, 'You mean you want me to record with him?' 'Yes, darling, he sells records.' 'Fine, Walter, I'll think it over.'

I'm thinking about my schedule – run over to Paris for a Cyndi Lauper concert, then back to New York, then off to Tokyo to see my friend Norio Ohga, who's telling me that, if he wanted to, Michael Jackson could be crowned Emperor of Japan. Ohga and

I are seriously thinking about starting an import company – Maine lobsters to Japan. Robert Stigwood is telling me that he's docking his yacht in Brooklyn and to come over for a drink. I tell him Brooklyn is too dangerous a spot to dock a yacht. 'Bring it over to the Seventy-ninth Street boat basin,' I say, 'and I'll be right there.' Boom Boom is gone but I've taken up again with Cynthia Slamar, my former girlfriend from California, who accompanies me to the boat. I'm ready for another night of serious debauchery.

I was touched by death, but not moved. I was hanging out with Alan Carr, the producer, and Julio Iglesias at Julio's house in Miami when the call came. Ma died. My feelings were frozen. My mother died and, out of respect, David Geffen came to the funeral. But a few weeks later that didn't stop me from teasing him about his sexual bent. I'd chase after him into gay clubs and demand his hand in marriage.

June was also at the funeral. Soon we'd formally divorce, but she still had enough feeling for me to express her fear of lung cancer. That's why she had stopped smoking. She had a met a man whom she'd soon marry. 'You don't look good, Walter,' she said, 'is there something I can do?' I said looks can deceive. I sat shiva for my mother, but kept my thoughts from the loss. Ma was dead. In spite of my dead feelings, fleeting thoughts ran through my head – *Did I please her by becoming a big shot? By moving her out of the Brooklyn ghetto, did I finally win her love? Did I satisfy her ambitions? Was I a good son?* – but several stiff drinks suppressed all questions.

My sons, from whom I felt disconnected, sat with me. They were smart and talented young men, but I hardly knew what to say to them. We didn't discuss their lives, we didn't discuss mine, we didn't talk about their grandmother, we didn't process our grief. It was small talk and more drinking and then time to go back to work.

*

My sons, Michael (on left) and Daniel

More death:

Marvin Gaye called from Los Angeles, saying the devil was pursuing him. He was incoherent and frightened. He babbled on for a half hour. He said he hadn't left his house for weeks.

'Get help, Marvin,' I urged. 'Get out of the house.'

'I can't leave. It's too dangerous. They're waiting for me out there.'

I made a few calls to see if there was anyone who could get through to him. No one could. The fact that the drugs were taking their toll was something I wanted to ignore. On April Fool's Day, his father shot him to death. That night, to ignore even more, I did what I did most nights, I got high.

For far too long, I had played with Ophelia in the fields of insanity. We'd stop, then we'd start, then we'd stop again. Though I was

Marvelous Marvin Gaye

drawn to her drama, she was the one woman whose excesses frightened me. I finally cut her off completely. Then years passed and word came to me: She had driven her car off the side of a mountain. I tried to think about her, tried to mourn, but I didn't know how.

I looked for distractions. I played games. I had to play games. One of my favorites was torturing my competitors.

The big labels loved to complain about the cost of indie promoters. In truth, the price of promoting *was* exorbitant. But as everyone knew, profits from a big hit justified those costs. Just look at Michael Jackson. And besides, attaining an industry-wide ban on indies had proven impossible. When it came to scoring hits, labels were simply too competitive with each other to restrain from using every available resource.

Shitty Sheinberg of MCA, though, was determined to change things. Along those lines, he went over my head and called my boss, Tom Wyman, to moan about independent promoters. When

I heard about the conversation from Wyman, I got pissed – and swung into action. I called Irving Azoff, who was running MCA's music labels.

'Did you know that your boss called my boss?' I asked him.

'No.'

'Did you also know that Sheinberg discussed the price of indie promoters with Wyman?'

'No. But so what?'

'*So what!*' I screamed. 'As a lawyer, Irving, I'm letting you know that's a serious legal violation. It's called price fixing. It could cost both you and Shitty your jobs.'

'Take it easy, Walter. It was a private conversation.'

'It was a *taped* conversation.'

'Who taped it?'

'Wyman.'

'And Sheinberg doesn't know?'

'Of course he doesn't know.'

'Holy shit.'

'I'm telling you, Irving. MCA screwed up. And CBS has proof.'

My price fixing theory had some merit, but the notion of Wyman taping the conversation was a piece of creative fiction that allowed me to sit back and watch the panic.

It didn't take ten minutes for Wyman to call me.

'What's going on here?' he asked. 'Sid Sheinberg is beside himself. He claims I taped a conversation that he and I had about independent promotion.'

'Did you?'

'Of course not. I don't tape private conversations. He's worried we've broken the law.'

'Did you discuss the promoters?'

'That's the reason he called.'

'Well, that could be seen as price fixing. Maybe *he* taped the conversation and is just trying to get you crazy.'

'You're the one getting me crazy, Walter. The point is – why should Sheinberg think I'm taping him?'

'I keep telling you, Tom. It's a competitive business. People get paranoid.'

'Now I'm feeling paranoid.'

'I know a good shrink. Call him before you get worse.'

As a competitor, Steve Ross haunted me. I saw how Steve, a silky-smooth operator, was much beloved by his artists and underlings. I envied the affection and admiration which the industry bestowed upon him. He also controlled a movie studio and a fleet of jets. When he wanted Barbra Streisand to visit him in the Hamptons, he sent his Gulfstream to Malibu. If I wanted to send for Barbra, I had to requisition the company plane, only to be told it was flying a group of sales reps to Cleveland. Ross made whatever movies he wanted. My new deal with CBS allowed me to exec-produce movies as well, but the only thing I did was *Ruthless People*, a comedy with Bette Midler and Danny DeVito, the beginning and end of my Hollywood career.

For all my jealousy of Ross, though, the man liked me. And even though the flirtation with Warner initiated by David Horowitz was not consummated, this time it was Steve himself who approached me, inviting me to dinner at an ultrachic East Side restaurant. Steve was in an expansive mood. I was in my usual drinking mood. Steve started talking about Ahmet Ertegun, the man who ran Warner's Atlantic label. The son of a Turkish ambassador, a songwriter, producer, industry pioneer and ultrasophisticate, Ahmet rivaled Goddard Lieberson as a certified legend. He hung out with Henry Kissinger. He hung out with Andy Warhol. When he wanted wild chicks and strong drugs, he hung out with me. He was a connoisseur of lofty literature and lowdown blues. But he was also high society. Steve saw him as a snob. Ross thought Ahmet looked down at him. 'I want you to replace him,' Steve told me.

I saw the idea of taking over Atlantic, a single label in the Warner world of many labels, as a comedown. After all, I was running both a domestic and international operation involving every label under the CBS music banner. 'I'll give you wider responsibilities,' said Steve. 'And besides, I'll make it worth your while.'

Over the next few weeks I discussed the move with my unofficial board of yes-men – Tommy Mottola and Allen Grubman. They were all for it. The Grubber, who at that point had become my part-time lawyer, was especially excited. Ross was talking about paying me $8 million in front and, even better, constructing the deal so that I'd wind up with $5 million in post-tax money. Such an arrangement would take me to another level. As Grubman and I looked in each other's eyes, we saw dancing dollars.

'I'm getting an erection,' said Grubman.

'Mazel tov,' I said. 'Try to put it to good use.'

A month later, negotiations with Ross were near conclusion. He and I had a handshake deal, with Grubman working out the details. We were set to meet Steve at his apartment for final deliberations. It had been a rough day. Always a borderline hypochondriac, I spent too much time compulsively examining my urine and feces for signs of blood. I was certain some fatal disease was galloping through my system. So I'd run to the doctor and the doctor would take tests and the tests would show nothing. God forbid I should have seen a doctor with the guts to call me a drunk or a drug addict. Anyway, during this particular visit my doctor wanted a urine test that would sample a day's supply. That meant carrying two big bottles with me wherever I went. By seven o'clock, when Grubman and I arrived at Ross's place, the second bottle was nearly filled.

Ironically, Ross pissed all over the deal.

'It's not me, Walter,' he said. 'It's my board. The board just won't approve it.'

The Grubber

'You don't control your board?' I asked.

'I wish I did.'

I looked over at Grubman, who simply shrugged his shoulders. For the second time in my dealings with Warner, I wound up holding my putz. I left without saying a word.

As fate would have it, not long afterward I ran into Ross's wife, the effervescent Courtney Sale Ross, at the driver's license bureau. We were standing on the VIP line to renew our licenses. I greeted her. She was cordial, and when I suggested we call Steve to say hello, she said fine.

'Steve,' she told her husband, 'someone wants to talk to you.'

'Mr Ross,' I said, disguising my voice to sound like an officious clerk, 'my name is Peter J. McDermott. I run the driver's license bureau, and I'm afraid we have your wife in custody. She's been using your influence to avoid bureaucratic procedures. When we told her she'd have to follow the regular rules, she responded by kneeing one of our agents in the genital area. She made an unfortunate choice because that particular agent suffers with severe heart disease. He immediately collapsed and was rushed to Lenox Hill Hospital, where he's in critical condition. The doctors say it's touch and go. If he dies, your wife will be charged with assault with intent to ill. We're holding her without bail. I can't talk any more because the television reporters are calling me to a press conference . . . wait . . . I'm getting late word . . . my God . . . the man *has* died. Yes, Courtney Sale Ross will be charged with murder. Would you like to speak with your wife?'

'Of course, of course . . .' said Steve in a panic.

I took a long time to hand the phone to Courtney. When she got on, she was hysterical. He presumed she was crying, but she was laughing so hard she couldn't say a word.

Both challenges were daunting:

The business challenge was to convince our Sony partners to pay us dividends owed for years. They claimed that the Japanese government restricted those payments; we claimed otherwise. The bill was mounting and the issues so important that Tom Wyman and Bill Paley were traveling to Tokyo with me. Which brought me to challenge number two:

How to avoid sitting next to Wyman and being bored for fourteen straight hours. Solution: Bring my girlfriend Cynthia and bring along a gift from Bill Graham, a giant chocolate cookie laced with hash. The plan worked – Wyman and Paley sat with *Fortune* magazines and I sat with Cynthia and the cookie.

'Easy on the cookie,' she said. 'It's strong.'

'Okay,' I said. 'You take half.'

I was sailing along, singing a song, enjoying the amenities of first-class travel – hot towels, fine wine, fresh sushi – when the cookie kicked in.

'Isn't the plane shaking a little bit more than normal?'

'No,' said Cynthia. 'That's the cookie talking.'

'Isn't the stewardess looking at me like I'm stoned?'

'Yes,' said Cynthia. 'That's because we both are.'

A well-dressed gentleman stood in front of me. He introduced himself as Bill Blass. 'It's a pleasure meeting you, Mr Yetnikoff,' he said. I began to get up but realized I couldn't. I was too plastered. I mumbled something, but was so out of sorts that the distinguished designer took his leave.

'We're going over the polar route,' I told Cynthia. 'That means we're in the same airspace where the Russians shot down a Korean jet.'

'Are we really in danger?'

'Big time. The Russians will shoot us down. I know they will. We're doomed. This is it.'

Cynthia huddled into her corner and started to cry. The more I talked, the weirder I became. I went over and woke up Wyman to alert him to the danger. He looked at me like I was nuts and fell back to sleep. I needed to talk to the pilot. The stewardess said, 'Go back to your seat.' I sat down and imagined what it'd be like to fall out of the sky. How long would consciousness last? How quick would it be? How agonizing the terror, how horrifying the final moments? I began to shake. I looked around my seat, I looked in my attaché case, I looked in the cuffs of my pants; all I saw were cookie crumbs. Those crumbs were loaded with hash. At customs, the dogs would surely sniff out the hash. The Japanese busted McCartney for pot. The Japanese would bust me. I started picking up crumbs, but where to put them? The guy sitting across from me looked like a drug agent. He knew what I was doing. He picked up the phone in front of his seat and made a call. He was tipping off the drug agents at the airport. My life was over. I'd spend years in Japanese jails.

When we landed, I was a mess. Before we reached customs, I went to the bathroom, took off my clothes and cleaned off every last crumb. The drug agents didn't get me, but Sony did. The

Sony brain trust – Norio Ohga and Akio Morita – were unyielding. They wouldn't alter the dividend payment plan. Even Wyman's quacking insistence made no difference.

'I'll find a way to make it up to you,' said Ohga when he and I were alone. 'In the future we'll do big business together.'

Sparring with Daddy

'WHAT DO YOU MEAN I'M SPARRING WITH DADDY?' I asked the therapist. 'That just sounds like glib shrink talk.'

On the recommendation of Cynthia, I was back on the couch.

'Listen to the stories you're telling,' he said. 'In every one you're sparring with an authority figure. You're beating up on Daddy the way he beat up on you. I see a great deal of unprovoked naked aggression,'

'That's *your* theory.'

'Forget my theory. Go back to telling your stories.'

'They'll just prove your theory.'

'Walter, what's bothering you?'

'It isn't what, it's who. The schmucks who run American business – that's who. The buzz brains who serve the CBS board. There's a guy named Harold Brown. Ever hear of him?'

'Whether I've heard of him is irrelevant.'

'Sure, you've heard of him. He was Secretary of Defense under Carter. Brown's on the board. And the other day, right there at the board meeting, Brown was challenging a report I was presenting about the worth of my record division. He said, "Why should we take your word on this? You have a vested interest in the outcome." So I challenged *him*: "Are you questioning my integrity?" He said, "Maybe I am." I flew out of my seat and went face-to-face with him. "Harold Brown," I said, "have you forgotten your handling of the Iran rescue mission? Have you forgotten the profligate defense establishment you ran? As Secretary of Defense for Jimmy Carter, you should have been indicted for treason. Don't move out of your chair, and keep your mouth shut."'

'And you consider that rational behavior?'

'Not at all. I think he acted like a pompous shit.'

'I don't mean his behavior, I mean *yours*.'

'My behavior was calm compared to what happened when they mentioned Dan Rather.'

'Tell me about it.'

'I call Rather Danny Doo Doo. Can't stand the guy. At some big corporate convocation, Danny Doo Doo and Charles Kuralt were talking politics in a public forum. To my way of thinking, they were bashing Israel. I took offense. I got up and told them so. Kuralt started arguing. I said, "Shut up, Kuralt. What kind of journalist are you with that Sunday morning show of yours? You find an old woman who embroiders daffodils on doilies and call that a story?"'

'Had you been drinking when you said this?'

'I'm always drinking.'

'Even at the board meetings?'

'If I don't get a little loaded before the board meetings, I can't get through them. One board meeting was devoted to whether we should build a company cafeteria. This is what a board should be worrying about? Then one board member started hocking me about Danny Doo Doo. If Danny Doo Doo is lured away from CBS News, he said, the consequences would be dire. We must be sensitive to Rather's celebrity. "Rather's celebrity!" I screamed.

"Danny Doo Doo is a manufactured product, a guy whose whole identity depends upon having a box around him. He's a talking head. Outside that box he's nobody." "He's a big star," said the board member. "You want to know from big stars?" I asked. "Take Danny Doo Doo out of the box and put him in front of the CBS building. Have him start talking into a megaphone. How many people are going to stop and listen? A hundred? Now put Bruce Springsteen in front of the building. Have him start singing. How many people are going to stop to listen? Twenty thousand? Fifty thousand? A hundred thousand? You'll have to call out the riot squad to control the crowds. Springsteen is a star, not goddamn Danny Doo Doo. Springsteen is entitled to a big ego. Doo Doo is not."'

'In telling this story,' said the shrink, 'are you identifying with your star?'

'What are you talking about? I can't sing a note.'

'In essence, aren't you saying to the board member – I'm a powerful man because I employ powerful stars. I have more power than you. I can beat you up. Verbally, Walter, you're going around assaulting people.'

'Only when they assault me. The CBS news anchors are pampered and overpaid. I also don't trust them. They're always looking for dirt on us.'

'That's beside the point.'

'That *is* the point.'

'You gave other examples that have nothing to do with news anchors. You mentioned someone named Diller.'

'Barry Diller. He runs Fox. We've been doing business together.'

'Another powerful man whom you verbally assaulted.'

'It wasn't an assault. It was merely an observation. We were meeting in L.A. with dozens of lawyers and accountants. I hadn't seen him in a long time and said, "Hello, Diller. You look like a prick." "I can't believe you're calling me a prick," he said. "I am not calling you a prick. I'm saying that with that bald noggin of ours, you *look* like a prick. Any moment now, I expect piss to come streaming out of the top of your head." Diller, a known screamer, started screaming. "You think you're a big shot," I said. "But if you don't stop screaming, I'm going to tell everyone how you hit on me in your hotel room."

'"I didn't hit on you in my hotel room."

'"I know, but if you don't stop screaming, I'm telling everyone you did."'

'And you don't consider that antagonistic?' asked the shrink.

'Of course it's antagonistic! The guy's my goddamn antagonist! But no matter how antagonistic I feel about Diller, I feel more antagonistic toward you. I'm paying good money to hear your canned bullshit.'

'What would you like me to tell you?'

'That you have a pill that eliminates all depression.'

'You suffer with depression?'

'After this session, deep depression.'

I fired the therapist but couldn't quite forget his sparring-with-Daddy theory when I found myself in the Dominican Republic. It was another CBS upper-management meeting put together by Tom Wyman, so enamored of the book *In Search of Excellence* that he decided to devote three days to its discussion. I devoted a minute to reading the first page before stopping. I told my assistant to summarize the book on an index card which I promptly lost. The *In Search of Excellence* conference turned into my Search for Excellent Dope.

During the seminars, Wyman went on forever, quacking like a duck. If I wasn't snoozing off, I was sketching pornographic drawings on the soles of my shoes. Then I'd stick my feet on top of the table, my artwork in full display. Though the conference was set up to exclude spouses and partners, I snuck Cynthia in. I stayed drunk, but wanted more. I'd been warned not to bring in drugs, but a bellhop told me they were readily available in a nearby village. I asked him to score for me, but he said he could lose his job. So he drew me a map indicating the dealer's house. 'If you want to,' he said, 'you can rent a moped.' I liked the idea.

An hour later I found myself racing through a maze of backstreets until I arrived at a hut, not a house, that corresponded with the map. There was no door – just a rug over an opening – and a half-dozen men inside smoking something that smelled good. Bags of weed were piled up on the dirt floor. I bought one of the smaller bags with American dollars. The dealer was pleased and invited me to smoke a giant joint with his crew. I didn't know Spanish, they didn't know English, but after a few tokes we were best friends. I got back on the moped and miraculously navigated my way back to the hotel where I was dreaming of a quickie with Cynthia. The pot had me hot. But Cynthia was gone for a walk. Her note read, 'They're looking for you. You're supposed to be at a private reception at Wyman's house.'

I decided to nap. I dreamt I was hanging out with Paul Gauguin in Tahiti. While he was painting the native women, bare-breasted and long-legged, I was telling them stories about Billy Joel and Neil Diamond. They were serving me ripe melons and tall exotic drinks, hanging on my every word. Gauguin grew jealous of all the attention I was getting. 'Keep painting, Paul,' I said, 'and I'll give you my leftovers.' Four of the local beauties slowly pulled off my shorts before carrying me to the ocean's edge, where they too dropped their clothing. The water was warm, their bodies even warmer. But just as the fun began, the spell was broken by the loud quacking of ducks. I woke up. The quacking continued. Where was I? For an instance, I was sure I'd fallen asleep at a meeting; I was sure the quacking was Tom Wyman discussing *In Search of Excellence*. But I saw I was in my hotel. I looked out the window and saw real-life ducks quacking like crazy.

Half-wrecked, I showered and dressed and decided to take the moped to Wyman's. Naturally I got lost on the way. That wasn't so bad – I finally figured out the right road – until I hit a rock and flew off into the bushes. Nothing serious, just bruises and bleeding scratches from the branches. Back on the moped, hurrying through town into the rich section where Wyman had his fancy hacienda. Knocked on the door. Mrs Wyman answered. When she saw me, her jaw dropped.

My pants were ripped, my face and arms caked in mud, streaked with blood. Inside Wyman was addressing a small circle of colleagues, still delineating the principles of *In Search of Excellence*. Everyone looked at me like I was a ghost. Mrs Wyman regained her composure and asked whether I'd like to clean up. I said yes, please. She took me to a bathroom with a bidet. She filled up the bidet with warm water and suggested I soak my arm.

'I'm not putting my arm in there.'

'Why not?'

'I'm afraid of getting arm clap.'

Mrs Wyman didn't find that funny. Neither did her husband, who was standing at the door.

'Walter,' he said, 'I'm not sure you're long for the corporate world.'

By year's end, though, it was Wyman who got the boot. His Reign of Excellence ended just as my Reign of Terror began.

On December 14, 1985, I converted to the Church of England. It happened at Synod Hall in the Cathedral of Saint John the Divine in New York City.

That was the night of the reception when James Taylor, divorced from Carly Simon, married Kathryn Walker. I was introduced to Bishop Moore, the renowned clergyman who ran the place.

'Bishop,' I said. 'Do you want a bump?'

'No, thank you,' he answered, giving me no indication of whether he understood my cocaine reference.

'You know, Bishop,' I went on, 'I work for a company overrun with WASP. They're everywhere. If you could convert me, my life would be easier. I'd then outrank the whole lot of them. Nothing's higher than the Church of England.'

'Fine. You're converted.'

'That's it?'

'Yup.'

'At least lay your hands on and bless my head.'

He blessed my head.

At the next Wyman management meeting, I led off with the shocking announcement. 'Gentlemen,' I said, 'you're looking at a member of the Church of England who outranks all you lowly Methodists and Presbyterians.'

'What about the Jewish holidays?' Wyman asked.

'I learned in the Army,' I shot back, 'always to keep two sets of dog tags.'

Whatever my religion, the pace of my life quickened: Mick Jagger was set to release *She's the Boss*, his solo album; Barbra Streisand had *The Broadway Album*; James Taylor was recording *That's Why I'm Here*; Springsteen was working on a live album. And Dylan was performing at Madison Square Garden.

As much as you could deal with Dylan, I dealt with him. I understood how hard he worked to protect his mystique. He was entitled. I saw him as a master poet, master folk rocker, voice of a generation, American icon and a guy who still sold a shitload of records. If he wanted to sulk in the corner, let him sulk in the corner.

After the concert, I hosted a private dinner for him at a swanky restaurant. We planned to eat at midnight. By 2 A.M. he still hadn't arrived. I was about to go home – the hell with him – when, just like that, he and his entourage walked through the door. His entourage surprised me. I was expecting Bohemian groupies and scruffy musicians. Instead he arrived with his family – his Jewish uncles, his Jewish cousins, his Jewish mother, Mrs Zimmerman, his Jewish girlfriend Carol Childs and his Jewish dog, an oversized mastiff.

Sitting next to Bob and his mother, I was astonished by their dialogue. The mysterious poet suddenly turned into little Bobby Zimmerman.

'You're not eating, Bobby,' said Mom as his girlfriend Carol was cutting up his food as though he were an infant.

'Please, Ma. You're embarrassing me.'

'I saw you ate nothing for lunch. You're skin and bones.'

'I'm eating, Ma, I'm eating.'

'And have you thanked Mr Yetnikoff for this lovely dinner?'

'Thank you, Walter.'

'You're mumbling, Bobby. I don't think Mr Yetnikoff heard you.'

'He heard me,' Dylan said sarcastically.

'Bobby, be nice.'

'Does your son always give you this much trouble?' I asked.

'Bobby? God forbid. Bobby gives me such naches. He's a good boy, a regular mensch. He calls, he writes, he listens to his mother. Every mother should have such a son.'

'Stop, Ma,' said Bob. 'You're embarrassing me.'

'You *should* be embarrassed,' I said to Dylan. 'You're a fraud.'

He looked at me quizzically. I explained, 'Aren't you the guy who wrote, "And don't criticize/what you can't understand/your sons and your daughters/are beyond your command . . ."? So why are you whining to your mother?'

'I wrote that a long time ago. Is it okay with you if I love my mother?'

'That's wonderful. I understand you've done the definitive version of "My Yiddishe Momma."'

He smiled.

Michael Jackson looked different. We were driving through L.A. in a limo, on our way to see Michael Eisner, the big mouse at Disney. It had been only a month since my last meeting with Michael, but his face had been altered, his skin lighter, his nose smaller. Compared to the handsome young man who had come to my office to argue for his autonomy back in the seventies, he was starting to look downright weird.

'What are you doing to yourself?' I asked him, sounding like Mrs Zimmerman.

'I never liked the way I looked,' he said. 'Now I do.'

'Fine, but enough's enough.'

'When I was a kid, my brothers teased me to death. They taunted me about my bad skin and my big nose.'

'So now you have good skin and a little nose. Leave yourself alone, Michael.'

'Surgeons these days can do wonderful things. They can perform miracles. They're like sculptors.'

'Except you're not made of clay. You're a nice-looking guy. You don't want to look like a piece of sculpture.'

'And I don't want to be seen holding hands with Pluto.'

Michael was referring to *Captain EO*, a seventeen-minute movie that cost $20 million. George Lucas was the producer and Francis Ford Coppola the director. The spectacular, in which Michael, modestly enough, single-handedly brings peace to the world, was to be shown at the California and Florida Disney theme parks, where special theaters were built to accommodate it. The thing had taken a year to make, and Eisner, worried about his investment, was frantic to have Michael promote it. Understandably, he wanted Michael to make appearances with

Disney characters inside the amusement parks. None of us thought this would be a problem since Michael was, in some ways, a Disney character himself.

'So what's wrong with Pluto?' I asked him.

'It's wrong for my image. You're the one who always says I'm supposed to have an adult image.'

'Then why'd you make the movie?'

'The movie isn't just for kids, the movie is for everyone.'

'And everyone goes to Disneyland. Eisner wants to get people into his amusement parks. You're the lure. There's nothing wrong with that, Michael. Disney is wholesome fun. The Disney market is the same as yours – the world, all ages, all races, everyone. Isn't that what *Captain EO* is aiming for?'

'I just don't want to look like a huckster. That'll cheapen my image.'

'You owe these guys,' I said.

'These guys owe *me*. Disneyland is the only place in the world my movie is going to play.'

'So what do you want me to tell Eisner?'

'I have too many other commitments to promote it.'

'Fine.'

A few minutes later, Michael and I were at Disney headquarters, where Eisner was waxing wildly enthusiastic about the prospects of *Captain EO*. He saw it as the greatest thing since God created earth. Michael agreed, I agreed, it was all lovey-dovey until I lowered the boom. 'Michael,' I said, 'can't go to the parks to promote it.' Eisner heard me, but he saw that I was merely Michael's mouthpiece. So he focused his attention on Michael, whom he flattered unashamedly. The only other time I'd seen such excessive and calculating flattery was when Tommy Mottola and Allen Grubman extolled my genius. When the praise was directed at me, I loved it. I couldn't hear enough of it. So who was I to begrudge Michael – whose talent, unlike my own, was real –

the joy of adulation? Eisner didn't prevail completely, but a compromise was reached. Michael would do some promotion.

I flew back to New York and thought about Michael, his changing face, his prodigious talent, his need for adoration, his self-absorption, his not-so-innocent innocence. All analysis aside, my job was to keep him happy while he put the final touches on his new album. If *Bad* did a third the business of *Thriller*, we'd still make a fortune.

I called Cynthia from the plane. She wanted to talk about getting married. I wanted to talk about getting high.

'Is there any milk in the house?' I asked, referring to coke.

'No. You know I don't even like milk.'

Great. I had to go looking for milk.

I flipped through a trade paper and saw a mention of strong earnings by Columbia Records. I was referred to as the architect of a well-oiled worldwide music machine that kept getting stronger. That called for a drink. The stewardess brought me a double. A little later I dozed off, comforted by an adamant sense of self-satisfaction.

What could go wrong?

'Everything's Gone Wrong'

TOM WYMAN WAS HYSTERICAL, CALLING ME AT HOME as though the world had just ended.

'What's wrong?' I wanted to know.

'Everything. Did you watch the evening news?'

'No, I'm having my evening drink.'

'So you don't know what happened.'

'Reagan and Gorbachev caught in bed.'

'It's no joke.'

'I know, they really love each other.'

'Walter, listen to me – *NBC Nightly News* broke a major story. They called it "The New Payola," and it focused on independent promoters and the mob. It showed two men in particular, Fred DiSipio and Joe Isgro. Do we do business with them?'

'Of course we do business with them. There's no major label that doesn't '

'They claim there are links to the mob.'

'They have proof?'

'They had the reporter, Brian Ross, standing in front of Black

Rock, that's what they had. He mentioned CBS. He mentioned you. He said how you tried to stop the Record Industry Association from investigating the indie promoters. Is that true?'

'Yes, it's true. And I'd do it again. The RIAA couldn't investigate their own grandmother. They're a trade group for record labels. They hand out gold records. What the hell do they know about criminal investigations?'

'Ross said you were the only company president to oppose the inquiry.'

'So what? I was the only president with the guts to speak my mind. The others approved an investigation because they were afraid not to. Personally, I welcome an investigation, but by professional investigators, not amateurs.'

'They had a music business lawyer on camera who spoke about heads of record companies who abuse cocaine. The direct implication, Walter, was that they were referring to you.'

'Screw them. Do they have pictures of me snorting? Do they have statements from a dealer? Anyone can say anything. But I want to see proof.'

'The appearance is terrible.'

'No more terrible than this scummy level of yellow journalism.'

'Just wait till you see the show.'

When I saw a tape of the show the next day, I dropped everything and stormed up to Wyman's office. I was enraged. 'It's bullshit,' I said. 'Not a shred of proof. No substantiation. They film these guys getting out of their cars like they're convicted killers. As president of CBS you gotta do something. You gotta put out a press release and call it what it is – a journalistic scandal worse than the scandal it purports to expose. You need to defend Columbia Records, and you need to defend me. You need to stand up.'

To Wyman's credit, he did. He issued a statement calling the story half-baked and unproven.

Meanwhile, the industry ran for the hills. DiSipio and Isgro were dropped by every label, including ours. I had no choice. Paley himself gave the order. Isgro retaliated by suing every major, *except* us, which made me look even worse. I suppose Joe thought he was doing me a favor, but the result was even more dirty looks from upper management. The truth, though, is that I didn't care and wasn't worried. I'm not saying I believe in the tooth fairy. The music business – and especially the cutthroat business of generating hits – has always had its shady side. What else is new? By the panic over the *NBC Nightly News*, you'd think we were all on our way to Sing Sing. I knew better. I knew that documents signed by our indie promoters protected the corporation. I also knew that this inscrutable promo-type sales system would remain the same – inscrutable. In the end, I was right. The cases against these guys collapsed. Despite heavyweight teams of killer reporters, despite overzealous prosecutors, despite an avalanche of investigations – even Al Gore got into the act – it all came to naught.

Even today some may suspect that I was enmeshed in the world of illicit paybacks. Bullshit. I was never involved in any wrongdoing. When it came to protecting the corporation against fraud and criminality, I was squeaky-clean. The music industry – no better or worse than its show business counterparts – got a raw rap. Even investigative geniuses like Mike Wallace and other CBS newsmen, dying to nail their sister CBS division (which made tons more money than News), came up empty-handed. Despite years of digging, a legion of writers wound up frustrated, their articles and half-baked books a study in erroneous facts and unproven accusations.

Now I'm not saying that I was naïve. I couldn't vouch for every negotiation on the part of every indie promoter. Promotion is the vulgar art of influence-peddling. The system wasn't based on the Sermon on the Mount. The system was the stark reality I faced – compete or collapse. In the rough-and-tumble business of selling entertainment products in cutthroat markets, promotion is the essential tool. Without it you're dead. The sensationalized news reports killed off that system, but only temporarily. Heavy-handed promotion would return. Today, twenty years later, radio station giants Emmis Communications, Radio One and Clear Channel Communications are being accused of forcing labels to pay promo firms to place songs on their stations' playlists, a variation of the same song and dance that, back in the eighties, prosecutors had vowed to discontinue. The more things change . . .

Did the *Nightly News* scandal change me? If anything, I became more defiant, more arrogant, more contemptuous of my adversaries. Michael Jackson's *Thriller* was still setting sales records; our roster of powerhouse artists was still highly profitable; Paley and Wyman still saw me as the key man in charge of the moneymaking machine. Who else had Michael's confidence? Who else could hang out all night with Mick? I charged full steam ahead. I might have been middle-aged, but I adopted the youthful battle cry of more sex, drugs and rock and roll. I wanted more of everything, and I wanted it with a vengeance.

My friend the Dante scholar was on the phone.

'You got to slow down, Walter, you're going to crash.'

'What are you talking about?'

'Peace of mind. Did you read the book of Robert Frost poetry I sent you?'

'Always with the poetry. Matter of fact, I did read it. Didn't Frost write, "I have miles to go before I sleep"? Well, that's me. I'm just getting revved up.'

'He was talking about walking in the woods. He was discovering his soul.'

'Well, I'm walking down Columbus Avenue and discovering my soul in a watering hole that's a magnet for beautiful blondes.'

'You and your blondes.'

'One wants to marry me.'

'They all want to marry you. You're rich.'

'Cynthia is serious about it.'

'Cynthia's a nice woman. But how well does she know you?'

'We've been off and on for years. She says she accepts me for who I am. She says it's time for me to settle down.'

'Not a terrible idea.'

'She's young, she's gorgeous, the sex is terrific. I don't want to lose her, but marriage scares me. So I called my main adviser in matters of the heart, Jon Peters.'

'You always called him a pussy hound . . .'

'Which is why he knows women. Peters said, "If you don't want to marry her, draw up a ridiculously one-sided pre-nup and then demand that she convert to Judaism."'

'And?'

'I said, "Brilliant idea, Jon." So I did it. I presented both demands to Cynthia, and guess what happened?'

'She agreed to both.'

'How'd you know?'

'Wild guess. So much for the wisdom of Jon Peters. What's the next move?'

'Have a drink and watch TV.'

I turned on the news and the anchorman started talking about the Mafia and the music business. He mentioned Morris Levy. Suddenly there was Moishe, being handcuffed. He was arrested and charged with extortion. Reporters were following him; flashbulbs were popping. This was serious. I knew nothing about the case. I hadn't heard from Moishe in a while. I never saw any more money on the racehorse we owned together, and ever since the ELO suit against Levy, our business dealings had ceased. It was troubling that the guy was in hot water, but I wasn't completely surprised. He never denied hanging out with his mob pals. He flaunted those friendships. Moishe had told me that his phone had been tapped for years. He loved antagonizing the FBI by telling his caller, 'There's a package coming in from Bogotá on the nine o'clock flight at Kennedy. Go meet it.' The cops would run out to Kennedy, frisk every arriving passenger and find nothing. Now, though, the cops apparently had found something.

I fixed another drink, took another hit and was lost in thought when the phone rang. I let my answering machine pick up.

'Walter, this is Moishe. Are you there?'

For a split second I hesitated. Did I want to talk to him? Did I want to get involved? Wouldn't it be easier to avoid him? Hell, he was a friend. I picked up.

'You alright?' I asked.

'I'd be a lot better if you could get Bruce Springsteen to autograph a hundred leather jackets for my stores. We're running a promotion.'

Among his many businesses, Levy owned Strawberries, a chain of retail record stores.

'That's why you're calling?'

'Why else should I be calling?'

'Well, I mean . . . I just saw you on TV.'

'Fuck TV. I'm asking you for Springsteen autographs. Can you get 'em or not?'

'I can try. I can ask him.'

'You can make him.'

'No, Moish, I can't make him. It doesn't work that way.'

'However it works, my managers are screaming for autographed jackets.'

'And everything else is okay?'

'Business is good, I can't complain.'

'Good luck, Moish.'

'I don't need luck, Velvel, I need Springsteen autographs.'

*

Certain things I can remember and certain things I can't:

I can't remember whether I asked Springsteen to autograph the jackets. I can't remember when I decided to marry Cynthia. I can't remember when my drinking went from excessive to extraexcessive to dangerously obnoxiously excessive. I can remember, though, when Bill Paley told me the most shocking news I'd heard since coming to work there twenty-five years before: that CBS was being threatened by corporate raiders. The fact that Paley might lose control would unleash a series of events that would drastically change my life.

It happened at one of our private lunches over boiled beef, cabbage, two kinds of potatoes and three kinds of desserts. I was hardly his confidant, but there were times, especially during heavy meals, when Paley felt comfortable enough with me to reveal his inner conflicts. After the death of his wife Babe, to whom he was deeply devoted, Paley was a different man. His steely determination was less steely; his self-assuredness, while always formidable, was noticeably diminished.

'Walter,' he told me, 'you've heard the rumors, and the rumors are true – Ted Turner is making a run for CBS. He wants to buy us.'

'Forget Ted Turner,' I said. 'You can buy him.'

'That's more trouble than it's worth.'

'Buying him or letting him buy you?'

'Both. In both cases, it's the brokers and bankers who walk away with millions.'

'Isn't it more than the numbers, though, Mr Paley? Isn't it a question of holding on to your lifetime's work? It's your creation. You're the reason they call it the Tiffany of corporations.'

Sure, I was ass-kissing the boss, but that's what employees do. Besides, I liked Paley.

'What do you think of Wyman?' he asked me.

'Not much.'

'He's not the man I thought he was. His response to our vulnerability to corporate raiders has been foolish. His maneuvering has only made us more vulnerable.'

'But what do *you* want to do, Mr Paley? Do you really want out?'

'No. This is my life's work. CBS is who I am.'

'And no one can take it away from you.'

'I'm afraid, Walter, that it's going to get worse before it gets better.'

'Why do you say that?'

'The vultures, Walter. They smell blood. They're circling the sky. The vultures are about to descend.'

Sparring with Daddy: Part II

IN THE MID-EIGHTIES THE VULNERABILITY TO WHICH Paley referred was infecting the corporate culture like a virus. The junk bond era meant little fish – like Ted Turner – could go after big fish – like CBS – thanks to a system that made raising huge sums of money easier than ever. Paley's crown jewel, the TV network, had slipped from first place, causing a precipitous fall in revenue. In the middle of this uncertainty, I found myself, as crazy as it seems, sitting pretty.

I say crazy because my lush life had gotten lusher. My privileged position came from the unrestrained profits generated by the record sales of superstars who, at least in the mind of the CBS board, were linked to my mysterious aura. Naturally I milked the situation for all it was worth. I had a hefty salary and a few bucks in the bank, but hadn't amassed anything comparable to men like Steve Ross or Lew Wasserman. Somewhere deep in my head I heard my mother's voice say, 'If you're so smart, why aren't you as rich as them?'

It was in 1986 that Tom Wyman finally fell off the high wire of corporate high finance. Or was shoved off by a guy named Larry Tisch, my new best friend, soon to be my worst nemesis. Tisch was a multibillionaire whose holdings reached from insurance to cigarettes to hotels (including the swank Regency in Manhattan) to movie theaters. When it came to financial manipulation, Tisch took the cake. He owned 25 percent of Loew's Corporation when he began buying up shares of CBS. Before long, he wound up with 25 percent of CBS, a block big enough to control the board. In other words, through supershrewd strategizing, he parlayed his 1/16 percent – his quarter of Loew's that owned a quarter of CBS – and wound up in charge. He promptly canned Wyman. At eighty-five, Paley had neither the strength nor the spirit to resist. Tisch took over.

At first I viewed the takeover as advantageous. Tisch came on strong as a landsman, a fellow Jew who was a well-known philanthropist and supporter of Israel. He started out leaning on me for inside information. He dropped by my office; he called me at home on weekends; he bounced new ideas off me; he treated me like an equal and understood my need to feel important. I liked being solicited by the new boss. I also liked his half-kidding half-serious attitude that it was us (as in 'us Jews') against the *goyim*. Tisch knew Yiddish. Like Morris Levy, he called me Velvel. He studied the Talmud. And, unlike Arthur Taylor and Tom Wyman, he was neither tall nor elegant. He was short and bald.

In seeking my counsel, he once invited me to his apartment. Cynthia was with me, but Tisch asked that we speak alone. So Cynthia waited downstairs in the lobby. Over vodka and lox, he let down his hair (even if he had no hair). He was all worked up about the television network and determined to make a clean sweep – fire this one, fire that one, rearrange management, streamline the bureaucracy. Heads were going to roll. I liked his plan because I didn't like the TV division. Their aggravation was my pleasure.

'But whatever you do,' said Tisch, 'don't say a word to anyone. These plans are top secret.'

'Mum's the word,' I assured him.

He put his arm around me and accompanied me downstairs. 'I feel like I can trust you, Velvel,' he said.

'Your trust is well placed, Larry.'

When the elevator doors opened, we saw Cynthia seated on a couch in the lobby.

'Honey!' I yelled 'Larry's firing half the TV network. Call the gossip columnists at the *Post* and the *News*. Spread the word!'

'Are you crazy!' Tisch shouted. 'No one can know.'

'Everyone *must* know,' I insisted. 'I can't stop myself! I can't control myself! I'm going to the media right now!'

His skin turned so pale Cynthia had to tell him I was kidding. 'Don't you know, Mr Tisch, you've been talking to Louella Hedda Liz Smith Yetnikoff?'

I spent considerable time discussing Tisch with Tommy Mottola and Allen Grubman. They were the kind of advisers I liked – the kind who agreed with everything I said. Grubman was looking for me to throw him more big-time clients while Mottola wanted me to make him head of the domestic Columbia Records division. I wasn't quite ready to give Tommy that prize, just as I wasn't quite ready to marry Cynthia. But I enjoyed being pursued and Mottola, as a connoisseur of guns, boats and wild women, was especially endearing. He and Allen were also confidants when it came to corporate intrigue.

'Tisch likes me,' I told them. 'He's going to make my life easier.'

'He's scared of you, Walter,' said the Grubber.

'He's intimidated by you,' said Mottola. 'You've got the guy wrapped around your pinkie.'

I smiled and downed another drink.

'I'm sitting pretty,' I said.

My henchmen agreed. Tisch was good for Yetnikoff and Yetnikoff, that brilliant and fun-loving fox, was only getting foxier. Tisch's rise meant more power for me.

'He trusts you, Walter,' said Grubman. 'And trust leads to power.'

So what went wrong? How did trust turn to vicious animosity? How did our relationship fall apart? Why, in just a few short months, did I start referring to Larry Tisch as the Evil Dwarf?

The answer may be in a bagel – one lousy bagel.

It began with a phone call from Tisch ordering me to California. His tone was different; he wasn't requesting, he was demanding. Until then we had enjoyed an easy buddy-to-buddy rapport. But now he was making it plain that I was his employee. In response, I made it plain that he could get lost.

'We have a meeting with Diller at Fox,' said Tisch. 'You've got to be there.'

'Send the CBS jet, the G2.'

'For one person? Do you know what that costs?'

'It's in my contract.'

'No G2.'

'No trip.'

'Walter, I need you at this meeting.'

'Say "please."'

'Please.'

'I'll slum. I'll take American Airlines.'

I took a commercial flight but booked the biggest bungalow the Beverly Hills Hotel was offering. Next morning Tisch called me to his room, which was the size of the closet in my bungalow. He suggested I have some of his orange juice.

'I'm hungry,' I said. 'I'm ordering up a bagel.'

'Do you know what they charge for a bagel in this hotel?'

'No, Larry, what do they charge for a bagel?'

I couldn't believe I was hearing this. A guy earning a million a day in interest was telling me I couldn't order a bagel. He had to be kidding. But he wasn't.

'Tell you what, Larry, I'll skip the bagel.'

'Good. Let's go.'

'I'll call Diller and have him send a car.'

'No, I want to drive myself.'

A bellman brought around Tisch's rented compact car. Tisch gave the bellman half a buck. I couldn't keep quiet.

'Larry,' I said, 'unemployed actors in rented Rolls-Royces tip these guys twenty bucks. These guys live on tips.'

'That's all I want to give him.'

On the way to Fox, we fought like a miserable old married couple. I said, 'Larry, let me drive. I know the way.' He said, 'I'm driving.' He kept bugging me about rising record production expenses. What are the detailed costs of manufacturing a CD? What's the average marketing cost per hundred thousand units? He hocked me so long we both got lost. 'Let me drive,' I reiterated. 'I'm driving.' 'Larry, go right.' 'No, I'm going left.' After prolonged wrangling, the two corporate titans wound up at the airport, miles away from our destination. By the time we found the Fox lot, we weren't talking to each other.

Barry Diller gave Tisch the royal treatment. He did everything but have Tisch carried into his office by Nubian slaves. It was another confrontational meeting about the fragile CBS/Fox alliance. At one point I remember Tisch telling Diller, 'I'll fight you for every last nickel.'

'Barry,' I said, 'the man's not kidding.'

Eventually the alliance fell apart. Eventually I fell apart. Eventually everything falls apart. Except the end of my relationship to Tisch wasn't eventual. It was immediate. After our California trip, all bets were off. We took off the gloves and started slugging it out:

Round One: A board meeting at Black Rock. All the uptight board members were there – prim, proper and dead serious. Tisch was sitting at the head of the table. Paley was present but only as a figurehead. The men looked like funeral directors in their black suits, white shirts and dark ties. Wearing jeans, a sport jacket and an open-neck sport shirt, I walked in late. As usual, I was drunk. Maybe everyone knew I was drunk, or maybe my brazenness hid my inebriation. I didn't care. Behind me a waiter was carrying a plate. On the plate was a plain bagel. I sat down. The waiter placed the bagel in front of me.

'This is my own personal bagel,' I announced. 'This bagel is not the property of CBS Inc. It was not purchased by CBS Inc. I was expressly told by Mr Larry Tisch that, given the exorbitant cost of bagels, I could not expect CBS Inc. to bear the expense of my bagel. Consequently, I have borne the expense myself. If any of you feel that your stewardship of CBS Inc. entitles you to free bagels, I suggest we discuss that issue now. I know that Mr Tisch is an expert in this area, so I suggest he give us his analysis of the alarming cost of bagels.'

Tisch ignored me. He started discussing cash reserves, proudly reporting that CBS was sitting on a couple of billion dollars in cash.

I interrupted his presentation with a question. 'Hey, Larry, when do you think you'll have enough money to buy me a bagel?'

My question was ignored as the board droned on with boring board business. After a half hour, I started suffering withdrawal. I snuck out, hurried to my office, downed a stiff drink, felt better and returned refreshed. Twenty minutes later, I snuck out a second time, had another drink and a healthy snort. Ah, that felt good. Back in the boardroom, the boredom was even more suffocating. So I was back out again for another drink and toot. This time paranoia crept in. I was convinced that my promiscuity had done me in. My dick itched. It must be a new venereal disease. I started searching for a bump in my crotch. If you study your crotch long enough, you're bound to find a bump. I found one. Certain I had only days to live, I returned to the meeting. Now my stomach was a mess. I had to take a dump. On close inspection, I saw that my feces were off-color. The pale green hue convinced me I had alcoholic hepatitis.

I wasn't close to calling myself an alcoholic then. Only later did I hear the phrase 'God protects little children and drunks.' Looking back, remembering the board members and their inane agenda, recalling that my division was making more than all of MCA combined, I can't help but wonder – was God running CBS Records?

Round Two: Cynthia, myself and Preston Tisch, Larry's brother, were on a company plane to New Orleans on our way to the Super Bowl. I didn't even know who was playing. I just wanted to party. The plane was small and looked outmoded. I was looped and looked outmoded.

'Why don't you buy a real plane?' I asked Preston. 'Why don't you buy a new jet?'

'Larry won't let me.'

'What do you mean, *Larry won't let you*? You control the company with him.'

'He controls the purse strings.'

'It's an outrage.'

'You tell him.'

I did. When we arrived in New Orleans I called him, complaining that his plane was a piece of shit. 'You're worth two billion dollars,' I said. 'You can afford something decent.'

'You want a new plane, Yetnikoff, buy it yourself.'

Suddenly I'm no longer 'Velvel'; I'm 'Yetnikoff.'

'You're the two-billion-dollar egg, Tisch,' I said, 'and you're about to crack.'

I stayed drunk all weekend. Don Johnson, the TV star, wanted me to go off to the Bahamas to chase broads. Cynthia didn't think that was a good idea. Instead she wanted me to take her to an elite Super Bowl party. I didn't have an invitation but saw some of the CBS sports executives on the inside. 'Get me in,' I shouted to them. 'No way,' they shouted back. 'Wait till you want tickets to Springsteen,' I screamed. I was pissed. With all my big-shot power, how can they keep me out of a lousy Super Bowl party? Then I spotted Lew Wasserman.

'Papa Doc! It's your baby brother Velvel! I've come to save you from boring yourself to death!'

Lew wasn't thrilled to see me, but, always a gentleman, he escorted me and Cynthia into the party. Cynthia, who had worked in L.A., acted like he was the Pope.

'Why don't you kiss his ring?' I asked Cynthia, jealous of her regard for Wasserman. 'Or his dick?'

'Please, Walter, do you have to be so obnoxious?' Wasserman chided.

'Obnoxious?' I asked, my voice booming with boozed-up courage. 'I'm actually being charming. If I wanted to be obnoxious, I'd talk about how for years you've been trying to hire me but didn't have the guts to take on CBS.'

'Walter, why do you always start up with me?'

'I start up with you in public forums because in public forums you're defenseless. I don't care about my image, but you do. I like the idea of a screaming match with you. But your image as a noble philanthropist won't allow you to scream back.'

'Please, Walter,' said Cynthia, pulling on my sleeve. 'Leave the gentleman alone.'

'Gentleman? You're calling this shark a gentleman? Why, Max is nothing more than . . .'

'*Max?*' asked Wasserman. 'Did you call me Max?'

His question silenced me. Max, I realized, was my father's name.

*

Round Three. The Evil Dwarf went on a cost-cutting tear. His people called me every day to hock me about expenditures. Tisch himself hammered me with memos about slashing overheads. I blew off his people and trashed his memos. Finally Tisch called me directly.

'I've been talking to Steve Ross,' he said.

'Congratulations. I can see the two of you going into the bagel business together.'

'He was extremely candid. He opened up his books and showed me the costs of running the Warner New York record operation. It's considerably lower than ours.'

'Of course it's lower than ours. Their big record operation is in California. The proper comparison is between our New York office and theirs in L.A. Or our L.A. office and theirs in New York. They're a West Coast record operation and we're basically East Coat. You're comparing apples and oranges.'

'I don't see it that way. Our costs are way out of line.'

'You don't see it that way because you don't know shit from Shinola about the record business. Sales are strong, profits are up, and Michael Jackson's about to release a new record. Meanwhile, you're significantly reducing overhead by removing free Kotex machines from the ladies' rooms.'

'That's not true.'

'I realize it's rough for you, Larry. Yesterday you were worth $2 billion. Today, with a dip in the market, you're down to $1.9 billion. That's scary stuff. You have my sympathy.'

'You know, Walter, you're a prick.'

'At least I'm not a cheap prick like you. I've warned you – if I walk away from this job, I take the superstars with me. They all have key-man clauses. And I'm the key man. You're about to blow your biggest asset.'

'I've looked at those contracts, Yetnikoff. My lawyers say no key-men clauses exist.'

'Do you think I'm stupid enough to put those papers in places where your lawyers would look? They're in my private files. I'm holding that file in my hand. Let me read you, for instance, just one letter. "To Michael Jackson. Dear Michael, I understand your concern about signing a new contract in the event that I am no longer at CBS to service your account. This is to assure you that if I indeed am no longer at CBS, you will have the option to terminate this contract, effective on thirty days' notice, and masters will revert to you. To clarify, this is an inducement for you to sign your contract. Very truly yours, Walter Yetnikoff." Eight titles follow my signature.'

'It's not binding.'

'Please, Larry, I went to law school. I know my business. It's binding precisely because it's an inducement to sign a contract. It's ironclad.'

Tisch stayed silent before finally saying, 'You had no authority to insert those clauses. I'll sue you for a billion dollars.'

'Go ahead.'

The conversation ended. I made my point. I also fabricated the entire thing. I made up the Michael Jackson letter on the spot. I had no such letters. On the other hand, I was having fun. I was driving the $2 Billion Egg crazy. Soon he'd see the only way to get rid of me was to sell CBS Records. Maybe I'd raise money to buy it myself. Or maybe I'd find a friendly buyer who, unlike Tisch, would leave me alone. Either way, I was in control.

Shadow and Light

AMONG THE WRECKAGE OF MY PAST ARE MEMORIES that haunt me like bad dreams. I wish, in fact, they simply *were* bad dreams. I'm talking more about my personal life than my professional conduct. That I was an arrogant would-be tough guy on an ego trip destined for disaster was evident to everyone except myself. That I was a prick in business was one thing. I can live with that. I can own up to my prick-dom. But what's far more difficult to face is my conduct toward June, the woman who saw me as a boy, then as a man, then as a man who deserted her and our sons.

June remarried a man far more caring than me. She found a degree of domestic happiness. Then sometime in this period when I found myself rising (or sinking) into a frenzied state of celebrity, she called me. Her worst fear, she said, had come true.

'Walter,' she said, 'I have lung cancer.'

This was the cancer she had always feared, the cancer that, years earlier, had motivated her to quit smoking, the cancer that was now invading her body. I don't remember what I said. I'd like to think I offered words of comfort. I'm sure I tried. But on the deepest level I couldn't reconnect to the one woman who was surely my soul mate. The truth is that I was – and would remain for a long time to come – toxic. The toxins of drugs, drink, reckless lust and unbridled self-aggrandizement were firmly in charge of my life. I could offer her, or, for that matter, anyone else, little of substance. I listened; part of me must have wept; but my response was tepid. My visits were few and far between. I blamed God, of whom I knew nothing, for his blatant injustice. If I felt pain, the booze would blot it out; if I felt remorse, the coke would relieve it. If I felt anything, my high-powered lifestyle annihilated all feelings except those that fed the endless loop mantra that played inside my head: '*More, more. Give me more. I want more.*'

If you'd asked me at the time, I'd say I was bathing in the light of good fortune. If you'd suggested – as my poetry-loving pal did from time to time – that I was operating in the shadows of unexpressed desperation, I'd only laugh. I'd question your own sanity. The facts were plain. My exalted position and extravagant privileges were evident for all to see. And if June happened to call on a summer's afternoon, if her news was alarming, if tragedy threatened her very existence, I could only listen for a short while before putting it out of my mind. The world was spinning too fast for me to slow down. The world was calling me . . .

Barbra Streisand was calling. Barbra liked to kvetch. Barbra *is* a kvetch. She was complaining I wasn't giving her the attention I gave my other artists. 'I'm always seeing pictures of you with Michael Jackson or George Michael or Mick Jagger or Bruce Springsteen,' she said. 'I've been with the label since the early sixties. When were they signed?' I assured her that she was right. I was guilty. How could I make amends? She was doing a concert in L.A. for the fortieth anniversary of the founding of Israel. Zubin Mehta was conducting. Would I be there? 'Of course,' I said, 'and I'll personally present you with an award.'

I went to the rehearsal, where Barbra was in top diva form. She didn't like the way Mehta was interpreting a song. Mehta heard it as 'doo-doo-*dee*'; Barbra heard it as 'doo-doo-*da*.' She stopped him five times until he finally turned 'dee' into 'da.' It was not a pleasant afternoon. Everyone was uncomfortable. During a break I went to her dressing room to let her know I was lavishing attention on her. She seemed pleased. We began chatting when I mentioned that I was thinking of getting married. Her response was to laugh hysterically.

'What do you find so funny?'

'You.'

'Why?'

'I don't know anyone less suited to marriage. The chances of you being faithful are absolutely zero.'

'Who said anything about being faithful?'

'Then why get married?'

'I like the idea.'

'You like the idea of a fancy wedding with pictures in *People* magazine?'

'If you're nice, I'll invite you. Would you attend?'

'I'd have to. Otherwise I'd never believe it really happened.'

Barbra attended. So did *People* magazine. So did Bruce Springsteen, Christie Brinkley, Mick Jagger, James Taylor, Norio Ohga, Ahmet Ertegun, Fred DiSipio and Moishe Levy (though Moishe was mad that his table was too far in the back).

Why did I do it?

Why not?

I could do whatever I wanted. Cynthia was sweet. Cynthia was smart. Cynthia was a knockout. Cynthia indulged my humor. When we fought, which was often, I said, 'Be careful because God is on my side.'

'How do you figure that?' she asked.

'Because God is an old Jewish man with a big white beard and you're just a pretty shiksa with big tits.'

'Which only proves your stupidity, Walter. Because if God is an old Jewish man with a big white beard and I'm a pretty shiksa with big tits, whose side do you think he's on?'

Thinking like that led me to appreciate Cynthia. I told her, 'Plan whatever wedding you want.'

It was a Jewish wedding. A rabbi officiated. We signed the Ketubah, the traditional Jewish marriage contract. I wore a yarmulke and danced the hora. I stayed stoned. Friends plied me with high-octane cocaine. Champagne flowed. The movers, the shakers, the stars all came out. The Plaza Hotel was filled with paparazzi. I realized they were interested in photographing Jagger, not me. But no one could deny the fact that Jagger and the rest of the crew showed up out of respect. Or maybe because they liked me. Either way, it was a day on which all feuds melted before the friendly warmth of good will.

'You really did it,' said Streisand. 'Now you better treat this woman right.'

'Mazel tov, Velvel,' said Larry Tisch. 'Let's put all the grief behind us.'

'Good idea,' I said, and then, as soon as my honeymoon ended, proceeded with my sabotage.

The sabotage was hardly subtle. When *Esquire* magazine profiled me, I came on like gangbusters, regaling the reporter with stories of my outrageous behavior – throwing plates at lawyers, throwing darts to determine deal points. If you read the article, you'd think a drunken lout was running CBS Records. Tisch read the article and tried to defend me. 'This isn't the Walter I know,' he told the press. In truth, the Walter he knew was far worse. All I knew was this: The more impossible I became, the better the chance of Tisch selling CBS Records.

'When you decide to spin it off,' I told Tisch, 'I want first shot. You owe me that.'

'I owe all my aggravation to you – nothing more. But if you can put a deal together, bring it to me.'

The first call came from Nelson Peltz, the billionaire owner of Triangle Industries and friend of high-flying junk-bond genius Michael Milken.

'Tisch said to call you,' said Peltz. 'Tisch is interested in selling.'

'I have no interest in talking to you,' I told Peltz.

I immediately got Tisch on the line. 'Tisch,' I said, 'you little putz. You're a liar. You said I'd have first option. So why are you sending me Peltz?'

'Just talk to the man. He's just exploring. You'll like him.'

I did like him. I'd never met anyone who got to the bottom line quicker. He looked over our books and said, 'I'm good with numbers, but these numbers make no sense. Who understands these numbers?'

'No one does, Nelson. The mystique of the music business is that, though profits are huge, accounting is incomprehensible.'

'Does that mean you're cheating?'

'I never cheat. I don't exaggerate sales, and I don't exaggerate profits. But calculating those profits requires decoding a system that defies normal scrutiny. All I can tell you is that we make the money we say we do.'

'And because your bosses don't have the vaguest notion of how you make that money, you become indispensable.'

'That's how it works.'

Peltz pursued me. I hung out on his yacht in Corsica. I met his wife, a religious woman with whom he had numerous kids, and urged her to divorce him and hire me as her lawyer. 'What do you need this old Jew for?' I asked her. 'I'll get you a billion-dollar settlement and a young stud. If the young stud can't last, I will.' Peltz thought I was funny. I was impressed by his money and macho ways. Sometimes we'd wrestle. I liked *mano a mano* combat, I liked the company of the super-rich.

So did David Geffen, who was excited by all the talk of selling CBS Records. The incorrigible gossip and kibitzer went wild when he heard that billions were in play. In fact, the day after I first spoke with Peltz, Geffen was on the phone, half-hysterical.

'I hear you're talking to Nelson Peltz.'

'What is it with you? You don't have enough phone calls of our own? So now you're bugging mine. Why don't you go bug your boyfriend instead?'

'Ivan Boesky says Peltz is no good. Boesky says Peltz is an ax murderer.'

'Who the hell is Ivan Boesky?' I asked. This was, of course, before the Boesky/Milken insider trader scandals.

'Boesky is about the most brilliant financier in the country. He's a super-rich stockbroker who knows everyone and everything. He says stay away from Peltz.'

'And why are you telling me this, David?'

'Because, whether you believe it or not, I care about you, Walter. I have better people who want to buy CBS Records. You don't need Peltz.'

'I don't need you.'

I hung up and called Peltz.

'Nelson,' I said, 'David Geffen says someone named Ivan Boesky thinks you're an ax murderer.'

Peltz was outraged and called Boesky. A few minutes later, Peltz called me back.

'Boesky denies saying any such thing to Geffen,' he said.

'Do you believe him?'

'No. He didn't sound right. So I ended the conversation. I've made up my mind to cut off all contact with Boesky.'

Boesky turned out to be taping phone conversations of colleagues and turning them over to the government in an attempt to save his ass. He went to jail anyway. And his battle cry – 'greed is healthy' – still stands for big business in the eighties. I never met

Boesky, I never even spoke to him, but I had no quarrel with his battle cry. I like to think that my conversation with Geffen may have saved Peltz.

My campaign to get someone to buy CBS Records – to install me as Super Czar and make me super-rich – heated up. Peltz was in the running, but Peltz was more Tisch's man than mine. I needed a player of my own. I found a billionaire investment banker who said he could come up with the billion-plus Tisch was demanding. If the deal went through, tens of millions were mine. The banker promised a done deal by week's end. I called him on Friday only to have his secretary say he was helicoptering his way to the Hamptons, where he was vacationing and accepting no calls from anyone except the Secretary of Commerce. In realizing he'd been toying with me, I also realized I'd overlooked a huge factor that, on the one hand, could destroy a deal and yet, on the other, could actually create one. That factor was Sony. Because of the joint venture I helped set up back in ancient times, Sony could block the sale of CBS's interest in CBS/Sony. That meant Tisch would never get his price. But what if Sony itself wanted to buy all of CBS Records?

'How about it?' I asked Mickey Schulhof, Sony's lackey in America, a guy I never liked.

'How much?'

'One point two five billion.'

'I'll ask Ohga and Morita.'

I realized chances were good because the yen was strong against a weak dollar. There was also a two-decade track record of heavy profits in the CBS/Sony alliance. Not to mention my friendship with Ohga, who never tired of praising my skills as an international operator. 'Walter is a master builder,' he once told his underlings in Tokyo. 'The others are carpenters.' Another key was Sony's debacle with their Betamax videotaping system. Beta was the best system, but because more software was available on VHS, VHS became the standard while Beta went bust. Sony wanted their own software. In that department, CBS Records was a gold mine.

Word was out. Everyone knew of the vitriol between me and Tisch; everyone knew Tisch wanted to dump the division; and everyone knew I was the man in the middle, the key player who could make or break a deal. The selling fever was contagious. I could hardly contain myself. I had three major-league deep-pocket players – Peltz, Sony and Disney. One early evening, just as a lark, just because I could, I rented three limousines and three drivers to accompany me to Columbus, the West Side bar where I held court. Each driver had a phone with a direct line – one to Nelson Peltz, one to Japan, one to Michel Eisner at Disney. In between drinks and come-ons to beautiful barflys, I'd run out to one limo or the other, where, while snorting lines of coke, I'd take calls from prospective buyers, hyping them up and pitting one against the other. It was a blast while it lasted. Sony never flinched. Sony wasn't about to lose the deal. The big boss himself, Akio Morita, called me to say, 'We want you to help us, Walter. This is honorable deal. We want to make honorable purchase.'

It's done, I thought. But it wasn't. Paley wasn't convinced. Tisch wanted more (although $1.25 billion was the price he set). The CBS board nixed the deal.

I was furious. Working for Sony would be a dream. Working for Tisch was a nightmare.

'Do not worry,' Morita said to me. 'We are determined. We are patient.'

Impatiently, I flew off to the U.S.S.R. in the summer of 1987, escaping all this sales madness – at least for a few weeks – to see my ancestral home and hear my friend Billy Joel give the Russians a taste of his rock and roll. What's more, I had a political agenda that turned into an adventure unlike any other.

Velvel and the Refuseniks

DELUSIONS OF GRANDEUR ARE ESPECIALLY INFECTIOUS for the semigrand. In the summer of 1987, I suppose you could call me semigrand. I held a prominent spot in a splashy industry. I saw my little world as a big world. I saw my little world as the only world. As I left that world and traveled to the U.S.S.R. I expected to be greeted like royalty. With my Russian name and high-profile position, I was expecting the Minister of Culture to greet me and Cynthia at the airport with a sign that said, 'Welcome home, boychick.' Instead I got a drunken taxi driver named Boris hustling rubles for dollars.

In the summer of 1987, Mikhail Gorbachev was running the show. The Soviet Union had begun to reform and restructure in the name of perestroika. The more radical phase of that evolution – glasnost – hadn't kicked in. Supposedly progress was being made. But refuseniks – Jews who were refused emigration from the Soviet Union under any condition – were still being persecuted. I had read their stories, which were heartbreaking and infuriating. After applying to leave the country, these people's lives were ruined. They were fired from their jobs, sent to Siberia, hounded by the KGB. Jewish scholars with graduate degrees were working as janitors. Families were destroyed – all because someone wanted to leave the country.

Before I left New York, I met with Larry Tisch, who also sympathized with the refuseniks. I told him that the American Committee on Soviet Jewry had approached me. During my upcoming trip, they wanted me to visit a refusenik. I admitted that the prospect of being followed by the KGB made me nervous. Could he offer any help?

'Don't be nervous,' he said. 'When I was in Russia, I went to see Andrei Sakharov in the company of the American ambassador. There were no incidents.'

'Of course there were no incidents,' I said. 'You probably had a division of Marines waiting outside. Very courageous, Larry.'

Tisch was no help. Neither were Armand Hammer's people. Given Hammer's close ties to the Soviet Union, I figured they'd have resources I lacked. I'm sure they did, but they sure didn't share them. 'If you get in trouble over there,' they said, 'call our New York office.' Thanks a lot.

Thanks to the United States/Soviet exchange agreement, Billy Joel was the first American pop star to take a full-tilt rock production to Moscow. This was big news. The minute I arrived in Moscow, I wanted to get to the hotel and see Billy. I was sure he'd help me get to the refuseniks. First, though, I had to get through customs.

Hardly surprising, but the Soviet Union excited my antiauthority streak. I resented the delays and the questions. I was furious that, rather than being seen as an important person, I was viewed as a suspicious one. I reacted by acting even more suspiciously. I thumbed my nose at the custom clerks and answered all questions with 'Nyet' and 'Double nyet!'

When we were finally cleared and heading for the hotel, I saw

Moscow as a deeply depressing city. In the hotel dining room, men in drab suits surrounded our table. I couldn't tell whether they were waiters or KGB.

'I want borscht,' I said.

'No borscht.'

'What do you mean no borscht? This is Russia. Give me borscht.'

'No borscht.'

'Then give me goulash.'

'No goulash.'

'If I can get goulash in the Russian Tea Room on Fifty-seventh Street, why can't I get goulash in Moscow?'

'No goulash. Chicken Kiev.'

'I don't want Chicken Kiev. I want borscht, I want goulash.'

They brought me Chicken Kiev that had me hungering for Colonel Sanders.

Up in Billy's suite, I saw he'd brought supplies of his own – tins of tuna fish, bottles of Evian water. Christie Brinkley and their daughter Alexis Ray had come along. Everyone was in good spirits. Because I had championed the return of his copyrights and took a personal interest in his business affairs, Billy saw me as a mentor. As a fellow Jew, he shared my concern about the refuseniks.

'I'd love to go with you,' he said, 'but I'd be recognized.'

'You're right. But help me get there. Find me a car and a driver.'

He did. Someone in his entourage, a Russian-speaking American who lived in Tashkent, made arrangements. It was up to me, though, to get the address. All the American Committee on Soviet Jewry gave me was a phone number. Furthermore, I was told not to call from the hotel. The phones were bugged and I'd be followed, with dire consequences for all concerned.

I walked from the hotel to a phone booth right in front of the Kremlin. It looked like everyone was looking at me. Although I wasn't crazy enough to take drugs to Moscow, my residual accumulation of stimulants kept me on edge. In a country likely to make anyone paranoid, I was a basket case. Part of me was scared; but another part kept shooting the shaft to guys who looked KGB. I was told that slipping in a dime and banging the phone box would get you an open line. I did. I reached a man I'll call Leon, whose father had suffered long years of repression. In plain English he gave me the address and said, 'Come over tomorrow.'

Next day Billy's guy, the American facilitator, had me and Cynthia meet him in an alley behind the hotel. An oversized sedan with flags flying from a radio antenna awaited. The driver was nervous. We all were nervous. We got in and roared off, merging into a VIP high-speed lane that seemed to accommodate any car that was big and bore a flag. I thought we'd be there in a few minutes. An hour later, we were still driving. The drab suburbs of Moscow were endless. When we got to a hill, the driver stopped the car and ordered us out. I was certain the driver was a KGB plant who, far from the city center, would now blow our brains out. When he put his hand in his pocket, I half-expected a weapon to emerge. Instead he pulled out a handkerchief. He was sweating profusely.

'What does he want?' I asked the facilitator.

'To help him push the car up the hill. Then he'll coast down. He wants to save on gas.'

'Tell him I'll buy him a gas station. Just get us there.'

We helped him push. When we finally arrived in the vicinity of the refusenik's apartment, the driver began to shout excitedly.

'He thinks we've been followed,' said the facilitator. 'He's afraid.'

'*He's* afraid!' I yelled. 'What about us?'

'He wants you to get out here. The apartment is just around the corner. He's worried the KGB will be waiting for him.'

'For him or for *us*?'

'You better get out.'

'Aren't you coming with us?'

'I'm going back with him. I'm a little concerned myself.'

'Oh great,' I said.

Cynthia and I got out. I looked around. Nasty gray apartment buildings in the middle of nowhere. We walked around the corner. A parked car with a man behind the wheel was sitting right in front of the refusenik's address. He had a moustache like Stalin. He had a scowl like the devil. He had to be KGB. As we walked toward the building, I eyed him eyeing us. What would I do if he stopped us? Offer him the bribe of choice, a pack of Marlboros? Kick him in the nuts? Scream bloody murder? When I reached his car, our eyes locked. I gave him the toughest tough-guy stare I could muster, imagining I was staring down Lew Wasserman or Steve Ross. He let us pass.

Up four flights and down a dark hallway we came to the apartment where Leon opened the door. He was glad to see us and ushered us inside. The furnishings were sparse, the rooms few, the lights dim. It seemed at least three generations were living in these cramped quarters – grandparents, children, grandchildren. Only Leon could speak English. I asked after his father, the refusenik whose name I had been given.

'He's out,' said Leon. 'I'm not sure when he'll be back. But he asked that I tell the story.' Leon's mother, a small woman who resembled all my aunts back in Brooklyn, sat beside him, nodding her head as Leon calmly conveyed the information. Years before, his father had asked permission for him and his family to leave the country. Both he and his wife were highly educated professionals, respected in their fields. Permission was not only denied, but the government, incensed by his public protestation, sentenced the father to prison and then exile.

'Exile must have been better than prison,' I said.

'Just the opposite,' the son corrected me. 'Exile meant living in a hut on the edge of the great Gobi Desert with little food and no medical attention. Exile was hell.'

The hellish stories went on – how his father could never work in his given profession again, how his mother was fired from her job and forced into menial labor, how the son was denied entrance into college, how every member was marked for exclusion, embarrassment and persecution. The stories were shocking. The biggest shock, though, came when Leon mentioned that I wasn't the first person from CBS whom he had met. He had also met Mike Wallace.

'The Mike Wallace from television?' I asked.

'Yes. He came for a story about the refuseniks. He listened to us carefully. But then he made us angry.'

'Why?'

'When my father said that he wanted to go to Israel, Mr Wallace said, "Why would you want to live *there*?" "Oh well," said my father, not wishing to argue, "I hope to see you sometime soon." "Not if the KGB sees you first," said Mr Wallace. Why would he say something like that?'

'Because he's a schmuck,' I said. 'Wallace will defend to the death the right to free speech – that's *your* death and *his* right.'

Before leaving, I embraced the family but couldn't put Wallace's comments out of my mind. Leon got me and Cynthia a cab back to the hotel. And though I was half-convinced the cabbie was KGB, my rage against Wallace outweighed my paranoia. The minute I got to my room, I called Tisch in New York.

'Fire Wallace,' I said.

'Why?'

I told him why.

'He'll deny it,' said Tisch. 'Then it's your word against his.'

'It's Leon's word. Why would Leon invent something about a man he hardly knows? Leon has no agenda.'

'Leon's not running a network. I fire Wallace and the ratings plunge.'

'Fuck the ratings.'

'Fuck *you*, Yetnikoff. I'm not firing Wallace.'

Frustrated but still fired up, I went to Billy's big concert at the Olympic Sports complex. Billy rocked. In fact, he rocked harder than the Soviets wanted him to rock. They told him no encores, but he did seven. He sang 'Back in the U.S.S.R.' and the crowd went wild. Fans rushed the stage. American rock and roll ripped up the iron curtain. Billy's nonstop performance so angered members of the Soviet Central Committee that Billy's tour manager, fearing arrest, hid in the men's room after the show. Moscow was never the same.

We flew off to Salzburg, where I was to meet Sony's Norio Ohga at a performance of Mozart's *Don Giovanni* conducted by Herbert von Karajan, one of Ohga's heroes. I knew von Karajan's musical credentials were incomparable but worried about his Nazi association during World War II. I had a hard time applauding him. I also had a hard time staying awake during the four-hour opera, although the subject matter – unencumbered promiscuity – was dear to my heart. The thing that woke me up, though, wasn't the sweet strains of Mozart's melodies; it was an awful grunt of pain that came from Ohga. In the middle of Act 2, my friend collapsed.

We carried him into the lobby, where I loosened his tie, opened his collar and called an ambulance. At the hospital I was told he'd suffered a heart attack, a semiregular occurrence for Norio. I sat by his bed while he experienced a speedy recovery.

'I'll be fine,' he said. 'But I'll be even better, Walter, if you get CBS to accept our offer.'

More motivated than ever, I flew back to New York. The plan was clear: Get Tisch out; get the Japs in; and, in the process, get rich.

Bad

'I HATE THE COVER,' SAID FRANK DILEO, MICHAEL Jackson's manager. 'It makes him look like a fag.'

'Did you tell him that?'

'How could I tell him that? You tell him.'

'If you couldn't tell him, how can I?'

'He respects you.'

'Look, Frank, I'm not telling him he looks like a fag. I'll just tell him he's wearing too much eye makeup.'

'He loves eye makeup. He thinks it's cool.'

'He also looks whiter than me.'

'He likes that too. He likes the new look.'

'Doesn't he know it's creepy?'

'Creepy is bad,' said Frank. 'And bad is good.'

Bad, of course, was the name of Michael's follow-up to *Thriller*. He and Quincy had been working on the thing for years. More than simply a new creative product, it was a corporate event. Stockholders were waiting. Tisch was waiting. Even Paley called to see when it was coming out. The press was crazy with anticipation. And Michael himself, always obsessed, was now obsessed by the fact that everyone else was obsessed with the release. The burning question, of course, was could *Bad* outsell *Thriller*?

'It's the wrong question,' I told Michael, who'd called from California. 'If it does half of *Thriller*' – which, in fact, is what it did – '*Bad* will be a huge success.'

'*Thriller* sold forty million,' said Michael. '*Bad* will sell a hundred million. I've written that on the mirror in my bathroom – a hundred million. Anything less than that is wrong, and anything over that is great.'

'From your mouth to God's ear.'

'Walter, you have to make it happen. It has to eclipse anything that's ever happened in the history of show business.'

'That's what we all want, Michael. And that's why I think you should reconsider the cover.'

'You don't like the leather jacket? The leather jacket is cool.'

'The jacket is fine. But all that makeup, Michael . . .'

'I'm hardly wearing any makeup.'

'It looks like a lot.'

'Everyone in Hollywood wears makeup, and everyone in Hollywood has plastic surgery. Compared to everyone else, I have very little. Why is everyone always picking on me?'

'Just a suggestion, Michael,' I said, knowing it was time to back off.

'I don't want to talk about makeup. Let's talk about promotion.'

'I want to bring out a group of CBS promotion people and key retailers to California. I want you to meet with them personally.'

'I don't like this idea.'

'The cover photo is one thing, Michael. That's your business. But now we're talking about selling your record. That's my business. If you want *Bad* to go through the roof, you'll listen to me. If you want it to stiff, you won't.'

He listened. My idea was to have a dinner party for fifty or sixty sales people who could make a difference. I wanted them wined and dined at the Jackson family home in Encino, the compound where he was still living with his mom and dad.

'I'm too shy,' Michael said. 'I couldn't give a speech or anything.'

'You just have to show up. I'll give the speech.'

The speech was a rousing success. It happened in July, just before the record's release. The guests were thrilled to be inside Michael's home. Michael was grateful I did all the talking – *this is the greatest artist, this is the greatest album, this is the greatest moment in world history*.

'How could you possibly think of all those things to say?' he asked.

'You're a genius, Michael. You sing, you dance, you write. That's called talent. What I do is called bullshit.'

'Your bullshit is your talent.'

'You better stop talking to me and start mixing with the salesmen,' I urged. But like a little child, he clung to me. The only other object of his attention was Bubbles the chimp, whose ass was covered with diapers. I finally dragged Michael from table to table to pose for pictures. It was hard for him to say a word to anyone; he wouldn't even look in anyone's eyes. Bubbles was holding Michael's left hand and I was holding his right.

The next time I saw Michael was in Tokyo. *Bad* was selling strong and Michael was off on his world tour. The Martin Scorsese 'Bad' video, shot in a Brooklyn subway station, was playing on every television set in Japan. I came over to see the show and prod Sony about buying CBS Records. Sony hardly needed prodding. When I walked into the office of Akio Morita it was nearly midnight, and he was just winding up a call to Paley. When he hung up, I saw him turn off a tape recorder attached to the phone.

'Mr Morita,' I said with all due deference, 'it's illegal to tape a call without the other party knowing.'

'In your country, yes. In my country, no. In my country taping is good. But don't tell anyone anyhow.'

'Did you get Paley to agree?'

'The price,' Morita replied, 'it keeps rising. I will not go higher than two billion.'

'Two billion! It's gone from one point twenty-five to two?'

'Our final offer.'

'Tisch is personally worth two billion. Now he's being offered another two and he's still hesitating?'

'Is it Mr Tisch,' asked Morita, 'or Mr Paley?'

'Mr Tisch,' I said, 'is the two-billion-dollar egg.'

That night Ohga and I went to see Michael's concert. Backstage, I saw that Michael's entourage included a cute young boy, not older than thirteen. I asked him what he was doing on the tour. 'I'm Michael's friend,' he said. Given Michael's discomfort with adults, I wasn't surprised. It was strange, but, then again, everything about Michael was strange. The Japanese loved his strangeness and called his visit 'Typhoon Michael.'

'Do you have the recent sales figures?' Michael asked me after his spectacular show.

'Don't worry. *Bad* is doing good. It's selling.'

'When will we reach a hundred million?'

'Keep touring and it'll keep selling.'

Back in New York, I figured I'd have to sell Tisch on accepting Sony's two-billion-dollar offer. I figured wrong. In October, the stock market crashed on Black Monday and Tisch, always prone to panic, thought the sky was falling in. Suddenly the two billion looked good. Within a month, he'd talked himself, the board and Paley into accepting the deal. CBS Records would soon be Sony's.

And I'd be President and CEO. I'd personally realize many millions. I'd soon be handing out million-dollar bonuses like a Good Humor man handing out Popsicles. I had known highs before – drug highs, sex highs – but nothing like this. I was over the top.

June was dying. I went to her home to visit her. I had to. A large part of me wanted to hide from the pain she was enduring, and from the pain her pain gave me. I was racked with guilt. I was also filled with the toxins that had fueled my life for so long. I was consumed with such self-concern and self-celebration that clarity – especially emotional clarity – was impossible. I came to visit June in a fog.

Somewhere in that fog, though, I still felt the pull of a love I had long lost. It was the love for a woman who had never harmed me but whom I had gravely harmed. While my head was buzzing with thoughts of ascension to new levels of power, my heart, if I still had a heart, silently cried for this good woman who knew me better than anyone.

The cancer had left her weak. Seeing me, though, seemed to bring a light to her eyes. Or maybe I was just flattering myself.

'Don't look so guilty,' she said. 'You didn't do this.'

'But I did other stuff.'

'I'm glad you came, Walter. I'm glad to see you. Don't worry about the other stuff. Not now.'

She took my hand. Hers felt lifeless. I grew afraid.

'You'll be okay, Walter. I know you've got a lot on your mind, but you'll be okay.'

I'll be okay. She was the one with cancer, and here she was comforting me.

'You make me nervous, Walter,' she said.

'I always made you nervous.'

'I love you,' she said, her eyes closing.

'I love you too, June.' But she was already asleep.

A few months later, she was gone.

I want to say that June's passing forced me into a period of calm reflection. It didn't. I was too far gone. The Sony sale had taken over every inch of my psyche. The thrill of victory, the certainty of serious wealth, the lure of absolute control – more than ever, I was crazed with ambition. The drinks and drugs only got stronger. And though I was married to a sweet young woman, I abandoned my vows on a whimsy. I took whatever I wanted.

To facilitate the Sony sale, I realized the artists had to be reassured. Part of the reason Ohga and Morita saw me as indispensable was my closeness to the big moneymaking stars. I had long-term relationships with Bruce, Barbra, Billy and especially Michael. Michael had to be personally reassured by me.

Cynthia and I flew to his newly acquired spread in California's Santa Ynez Valley, the place he named Neverland. Before serving us lunch, Michael gave us the tour. If you like llamas, this is your place. I don't like llamas. When he took us through a huge room filled with dozens of arcade-sized video games, I asked him why so many. 'My friends like them,' he said.

Business with Michael was always conducted at the lowest decibel levels. Michael is a whisperer. I'm a screamer. At times, I couldn't resist startling him.

'MICHAEL JACKSON!' I shouted at the top of my lungs. 'HAS ANYONE EVER YELLED AT YOU? HAS ANYONE EVER ORDERED YOU TO SPEAK UP?'

He winced. I thought the power of my voice had crushed him. He looked like he was going to collapse. On the verge of tears, he pleaded, 'No, no, no. Don't ever do that again.'

I never did. That day in Neverland, I saw Michael as a hothouse flower. Inside his controlled cocoon, he thrived. Outside, he wilted. I had wilted him enough. Time for the good news.

'Sony loves you,' I said. 'Sony buying CBS Records is good for you. Paley and Tisch are cheap. Ohga and Morita are spenders. They see you as their number-one asset. They're the best thing that could happen to your career. I call them the Happy Japs. And the reason they're happy, Michael, is because of you.'

'So I shouldn't be worrying?'

'You should be rejoicing. We all should be rejoicing.'

I said the same thing to all the artists. Sony was a world-class company as opposed to Tisch's tarnished Tiffany. Once the stars heard that Sony would boost their careers, nothing else mattered. The media, though, were skeptical. The media are always skeptical. They love scare stories. They painted a picture of the Japanese chewing off huge chunks of American business when, in truth, the phenomenon was overblown (and short-lived). CBS Records, however, was a particularly sexy purchase. It was seen as the all-American company of all-American music, from Bessie Smith to Bruce Springsteen. On its cover, *The New York Times Magazine* plastered a shot of Cyndi Lauper hugging Akio Morita. Morita complained that Americans, once inspired by John Wayne, were losing their edge. I waited until it was 3 A.M. Tokyo time before calling Morita on the private phone next to his bed.

'Mushi mushi,' he responded in a surprised and sleepy voice.

'This is John Wayne.'

'Who?'

'John Yetnikoff Wayne. You said Americans were losing their edge. But in the name of John Wayne, I'm calling to say there's one American who's alert, on guard and manning the battle station all night long. That American is me. And that American is proud to be fighting for you, Mr Morita.'

'Walter, are you a crazy man?'

'No crazier than John Wayne. Have no doubt, Mr Morita, the war will be won.'

Howling at the Moon

THERE ARE NERVOUS BREAKDOWNS AND THEN THERE are nervous breakdowns. I've had several. Problem is, I didn't know I was having them. Because I was a shaker and a mover, I was moving and shaking even when, to most objective observers, I was going nuts. Allen Grubman and Tommy Mottola were not objective observers.

In the twenty months or so between the sale to Sony and the physical collapse that forced me to rehab, Mottola and Grubman – Tweedledee and Tweedledum – gave me much love. And why not? After bugging me for years, Tommy finally convinced me to appoint him head of the domestic division of CBS Records. The press screamed that he wasn't qualified. I screamed back that he was a good record man and, besides, what the hell; he was my friend who never tired of extolling my abilities.

Grubman was equally adept at working me. With my help, he had built up a clientele that included Springsteen and Billy Joel.

When the actual Sony deal came down at the start of 1988, I was beyond ecstatic. I was so pumped up I almost blew it. I was blowing so many gaskets the people around me had to duck for cover.

The brouhaha centered on the bonuses due me and my management. The formula said those bonuses were based on earnings previously agreed to by the board of directors. After the deal had been approved – but before it was closed – I charged everything but the kitchen sink against earnings so that, according to another formula, Sony's purchase price would shrink as much as $100 million. Tisch was screaming bloody murder. He claimed I was screwing him. I claimed I was merely doing what anyone would do for a future employer. He wanted us to reduce our bonuses accordingly. But he couldn't because, as I said, they were based on earlier board-approved earnings. On the day of signing, he threatened to hold up the deal.

Naturally I was uptight. Waiting for my millions, who wouldn't be uptight? Tisch was adamant that I change the formula. I wouldn't. I explained that I couldn't – it was the board's decision, not mine. Tisch threatened to walk away. He was ranting and raving; I was ranting and raving. His people were demanding that I come to his office. I refused. I was yelling my head off. 'If the Evil Dwarf wants to talk to me, he can come to me.' I was yelling so loudly that I didn't see he was already in my office.

'You can call me what you want, Yetnikoff, but this thing isn't going through without my changes.'

'You know, Larry, I'm tired. I'm tired of your bullshit. I'm tired of your cheap-ass schemes. I'm tired of your whining. As far as I'm concerned, you can take these contracts and shove them up your ass. I'm going home.'

I meant it. I got up and left. Which is when Tisch stopped me. He saw I was serious and, just as I expected, he signed.

'Now are you buying everyone champagne?' I asked him.

He didn't bother to answer. He walked out without saying a word.

'The champagne's on me,' I said to everyone within shouting distance. 'Get a dozen magnums of the best.'

I got drunk, but not too drunk to forget to charge the champagne to Tisch.

Payday!

I called the bank manager to see if my money had been wire-transferred.

'Yes,' the manager said. 'The wire went through.'

The manager knew I was crazy. In the past, when I made outrageous demands, he'd send over a tall beautiful blonde named Nancy to calm me down. Nancy usually made me forget my outrageous demands. But not this time.

'I want my money in cash,' I said.

'That's impossible.'

'I want it in thousand-dollar bills.'

'Why?'

'Who are you to ask me why? It's my money.'

'We don't keep that kind of money on hand.'

'What kind *do* you keep on hand – Monopoly money? If it's been wired, it's mine. And if you don't have it, you're committing fraud. If it's not at your bank, where is it?'

'Why would you want it in cash?'

'Why would you ask such a question? Maybe I'm running to Argentina, maybe I'm buying Michael Jackson's Neverland, maybe I'm using it to wallpaper my bedroom.'

'So you're serious.'

'Of course I'm not serious. I'm never serious.'

Nothing seemed serious in that period between the Sony takeover and my breakdown. Even my last meeting with Paley, which I thought would be sad, turned out otherwise. On his desk was a bag of pickles and pastrami sandwiches from the Carnegie Deli. We spoke in between bites. The old man looked wrinkled and fragile, but was still elegantly attired. His eyes still sparkled as he recalled the days when Goddard Lieberson ran the most prestigious company in all the world. Then he started tripping down memory lane.

'Frank Stanton, Arthur Taylor, John Backe, Tom Wyman. You've survived them all, Walter. You've been down the long road. And I suppose this is where it ends.'

'Over pickles?'

'Over pickles. I just want to tell you that I admire how you pulled it off.'

'You give me too much credit.'

'I never gave you enough credit. I don't know too many people who could get rid of their boss, hire another boss and make a mint in the process. That's a hell of a thing.'

'I hate for it to end like this, Mr Paley.'

'No you don't. You love it. You've got Sony tied around your little finger. You're happy, and they're happy.'

'I call them the Happy Japs.'

'And they're probably calling you the Happy Jew. Anyway, I want to say good luck. You've made this company a lot of money. And in this office, that hasn't gone unnoticed.'

'Thank you, Mr Paley.'

'Now you can finally forget about Tisch.'

The odd thing, though, was that I couldn't.

I had to show up at the CBS annual stockholders meeting and heckle the man. It wasn't enough that I had my money and was rid of him. I had to make a public display of my animosity. I had to be the bad boy. As Tisch spoke from the podium, trying to reassure the stockholders that all was right in the CBS world, I walked over to the press. 'If you want the real scoop,' I told them, 'follow me.' Like the pied piper, I led them to a corridor where I conducted a spontaneous press conference, using the occasion to toot my horn and discredit Tisch's regime. I was drunk.

In the aftermath of the sale to Sony, in the aftermath of my ascension to the throne, I flew into Tokyo to see Ohga and Morita. This was my first meeting with them since I'd been anointed their Crown Prince. I'd been to Japan a hundred times before, but this trip was special. I was no longer representing their partner. I was their employee, though they did everything in their power to make me feel as though they worked for me. They made it clear that they needed me. I ate it up. I felt myself floating above the human race.

Ohga and Morita took me to one of those extravagant restaurants in the Ginza where dinner is a four-hour ten-course ordeal. The saki flowed. The geishas bowed. The world bent my way. And the goodwill, always strong between us, reached new levels of brotherhood. Just when I thought the positive vibes couldn't become more positive, my bosses started talking about their newest notion. They wanted to buy a Hollywood studio.

Usually it takes a beautiful woman to get my dick hard. But I suddenly found myself with an erection. Sony, with more resources than God, was asking me to get them in the movie business. This was better than sex. I immediately had visions of calling the heavyweights – Michael Ovitz, Michael Eisner, Lew Wasserman, Barry Diller – and letting them know that I had one of the world's richest entertainment concerns at my command. All roads to Ohga and Morita – all roads to Sony's inexhaustible riches – now went through Yetnikoff. Beyond that, Yetnikoff, who controlled records, would surely control the studio as well. Ohga and Morita, with whom I had worked for a quarter century, trusted me with their very lives. They'd buy the studio *I* suggested; they'd hire the executive *I* deemed appropriate; *I* – and no one else – would head this vast enterprise.

'I'll be happy to find the right studio and the right people to run it,' I told my employers. 'I'll set up meetings. I'll make sure you meet the cream of the crop. I'll run this operation for you.'

'Thank you, Walter,' they said in unison, bowing in my direction.

To celebrate this new pursuit, we drank. They drank discreetly; I drank excessively. They saw the twinkle of mischief in my eye. They'd known me long enough to understand that twinkle meant danger. They had two security men accompany me back to the hotel. Inside my suite, I cracked open a bottle of champagne.

'Tonight is the party of parties,' I told myself. With its glitzy prizes of power and prestige, the world had seduced me. I had seduced the world. Now I wanted to seduce a female. Looking out the window, excited by the buzz of Tokyo's neon sex, I hungered for action. There were gorgeous women on the streets, gorgeous women walking into swanky bars. I needed to mark this new phase of my career with something special. I needed to culminate my achievement. I needed a woman – maybe two, maybe three – to bring to orgasm. I needed to hear how wonderful I was in bed. I needed the excitement and reassurance that come with successful new sex. The eroticism of all Asia swept over me like a fever. I grabbed my jacket and headed out the door. I was going out to find it, do it, drain it dry. Except my door was locked. I kept turning the knob until, from the other side, I heard a voice.

'No can leave.'

It was one of the security guys.

'What do you mean, "no can leave"?' I asked.

'No can leave.'

'Open the goddamn door.'

The expression didn't change. I called the front desk to complain.

'We're sorry, Mr Yetnikoff,' said the clerk. 'But Mr Norio Ohga has stationed two gentlemen by your door for your own protection.'

'What does that mean?'

'You can't go out.'

I understood what they were doing. They were protecting their investment – me. Tokyo wasn't New York. Tokyo could do me in, Tokyo could lock me up; in one night on the town I could single-handedly destroy Sony's image. But that didn't matter. I still wanted out. I went to the window to see if there was a fire escape. There wasn't. I started screaming at the security guards, whose only English was 'No can leave.' I looked down at the patchwork of screaming neon. I looked up. A full moon – silver and fat and glowing with light – sat in the middle of the sky. I swear I saw the man in the moon. That son of a bitch was winking at me. 'I know what you want,' he was saying, 'but you ain't getting it. Not tonight.'

That's when I pushed open the window and started howling at the moon.

PART 4

Over the Edge

The Lion in winter

The biker

The monster tamed

'I Come Apart'

THE LIMO DRIVER WAS TAKING ME TO THE AIRPORT where a private jet, with a private nurse aboard, was waiting to fly me to rehab in Minnesota. It was the summer of 1989, two days after my fifty-sixth birthday. The radio was playing softly. The voice drew me in. It was Marvin Gaye singing 'Trouble Man.' He kept repeating the words that seemed to have been written for this very moment. 'I come apart, baby . . . I come apart.'

Coming apart took a while. Only now do I realize that the distance between me and a full-blown breakdown was negligible. I had blustered and bullied my way through years of self-abuse and abuse of others. I had so deeply deluded myself about drugging and drinking that only the cold voice of a doctor saying, 'Stop or you'll die!' grabbed my attention. Were it not for that voice, I would not have stopped. Why should I have? In the months since the sale of Sony, I was riding high. My second marriage might have collapsed, but my career was in overdrive. Jackie O was begging me to write a book. My superstars – Michael and Mick, Bruce and Billy, Barbra and Cyndi – were more indebted to me than ever. They were my friends, my allies, convinced that my brilliantly arranged Sony sale would benefit them immeasurably. In Tommy Mottola, I'd finally found a second-in-command whom I liked, a brother who'd take a bullet for me (or so I thought). Even if he couldn't handle the controversy between Public Enemy and the Jews, I could. I could handle it all – Geffen's rancor, Ovitz's duplicity, Sony's impatience to buy into Hollywood. I *was* handling it all. I had arranged meetings between Ohga and the major players in L.A. We'd focused on purchasing Columbia Studios and the deal, in fact, was coming together. Ohga, after suffering another heart attack and while still on the brink, had made a decision to buy. Everything was coming together. If that were the case, though, why was I coming apart?

Because the doctor said so. Because the doctor made me afraid. Because the doctor invoked the specter of death. Because the doctor destroyed my feelings of invincibility. Because the doctor triggered all my wildest fears and scariest insecurities. Because I was beset with nightmares, night terrors, gut-wrenching episodes in which I found myself shaking. Because I, once the balliest man in the music business, was so afraid of going to rehab I had to have a nurse accompany me.

I chose Hazelden, located in nowhere Minnesota, because the doctor praised its program. I didn't know what to expect. My goal was to get in and get out – rid myself of my bad habits as quickly as possible and hurry back to New York where I could continue taking over the world. I saw this stay as a small bleep on the radar screen, a minor inconvenience that, once endured, would have me back in circulation in no time. I was, in short, still self-delusional.

My rehab was hard. Maybe it would be hard for anyone arriving on a $30 million private jet.

'You'll be responsible for menial duties,' said the doctor in charge of orientation.

'I figured as much,' I said. 'I know what it means to be a good soldier. I've been through boot camp.'

'That's relatively easy, Mr Yetnikoff. What's far tougher is the physical detox. Our tests indicate you're still high.'

'But it's been days since my last drink.'

'And it'll be even many more days before you come down.'

I didn't know what he was talking about. I'd been self-medicating for so many years I'd forgotten what it was like *not* to be high. I pooh-poohed his prediction. And then came the agony.

After years of palatial hotel suites, I was now sharing a small room with four other guys. Hearing their snores and smelling their farts, though, wasn't the worst part. I simply imagined that I was back in the Army. What was unimaginable, though, was how long the detox took. I spent half my days and nights in the infirmary. I couldn't get straight. My stomach was a disaster zone; my hands shook; I drooled; I was dizzy, nauseous, feverish, diarrhetic. I was also foul-tempered. The doctors pumped me up with phenobarbital and Librium. Neither one worked. I couldn't sleep. One night during this horrendous period I got up from a dream. I was so disoriented that, looking for the hall bathroom, I pissed all over my pajamas. I wandered into the community room, where I collapsed on the couch. Just when I'd managed to fall asleep, I felt a sharp tap on my shoulder. Standing over me was a nurse with the face of a bulldog.

'You'll have to move,' she said.

'You'll have to make me.'

'You need to be in your room.'

'You need to leave me alone.'

'Move it.'

'You know something, lady, the way I feel right now I could kill someone with my bare hands.'

'Are you threatening me?'

'I'm not even talking to you. I'm just thinking about the joy I'd get from the sound of breaking bones and the sight of flowing blood.'

She ran out of the room. Minutes later, security came to force me back to my bed. The next day I carried on like a lunatic, telling the doctors that I was organizing a strike of all Hazelden patients. We'd take over the place; we'd hold the nurses hostage and make so much noise the Minnesota state police would come running. We'd make the national news and, once and for all, expose this tyrannical institution. They let me babble until the sound of my own bullshit put me to sleep.

When I awoke, I was told I was wanted on the phone. Incoming calls were reserved for life-threatening emergencies. Naturally my heart raced. I braced myself for the worst. Had something happened to my sons? Who the hell was calling?

'We've closed the Columbia deal,' said Mickey Schulhof, my least favorite executive in the Sony hierarchy. I contemptuously called him Little Meeekee.

'You're crazy, Meeekee. What are you doing buying the studio before you have management in place?'

'That's why I'm calling you. We like Jeffrey Katzenberg for the job. What do you think?'

'Jeff's not leaving Disney, at least not now.'

'How do you know?'

'When Disney made my movie *Ruthless People*, I got to know Jeff. You'll never get him.'

'We'll get someone.'

'Of course you'll get someone. Every half-ass producer and agent in L.A. would murder his mother to run a studio. But that's not the point. The point is that you've got your head up your ass.'

'Is this how rehabilitation is helping your emotional state?'

I hung up in his ear. Screw Meeekee. He knew as much about show business as I knew about the anatomy of eels. That's all I needed in the middle of my detox – a call from Morita's minion who, in my measured opinion, was a lamebrain. But who was I to talk? My own brain was in meltdown.

My own brain was being assaulted on every side: On the physical side, I felt like shit. On the emotional side, I felt like shit. 'I'm getting out of this shitty place,' I said after two weeks. But then something happened that surprised and encouraged me – my liver count returned to normal. My detox finally kicked in. I was no longer high, at least not in the conventional sense. I was calm enough to participate in the group therapy sessions that used the twelve steps as a paradigm of recovery. Just as I had detoxed in two weeks, in another two weeks I was certain I would master this business of recovery. Then back to work.

The plain fact is that, since my August 1989 stay in Hazelden, I have not had a drug or drink. That would seem to argue for the ease of my recovery. That argument, though, would be fallacious. Like my life before recovery, recovery itself was tumultuous, frightening and frustrating. It was marked by everything that came before it – my insatiable ego, my unfettered insecurities, my need to control everyone and everything around me – and then some. The only difference was that I was – and am – sober. That sobriety has saved, or at least extended, my life. On some levels, I became a better person; on many other levels, I became worse.

Back in Hazelden, when the first of the twelve steps was introduced I was puzzled. It asked me to admit my powerlessness over my addiction and admit that my life had become unmanageable. I could see the unmanageability. But powerlessness was anathema to me. I'd based my life on the accumulation of power. It was under my own power that I'd agreed to go to rehab. It was under my own power that I agreed to sit and listen to these notions of powerlessness. How could I ever rescind my sense of power? Because, said the leader, your addictions will not be assuaged by your own power. They will be assuaged by a Higher Power. Step 2 is believing in that power.

I was asked to accept the belief that only a power greater than myself could restore me to sanity. Higher Power, of course, meant God. So I was being asked to believe in God.

'I didn't know recovery had to do with religion,' I argued.

'It's not religion. It's spirituality,' the counselor argued back.

'I don't know anything about spirituality.'

'That's the problem. That's why you take these steps.'

Fine, I decided. *I'll take the steps, I'll go along with the program, I'll move to the third step that says I've decided to turn my life and will over to the care of God, as I understand God. Even though I don't understand God. Even though I don't even know if I believe in God. But I know I better believe in something because before, when I believed in nothing, I nearly crapped out.*

The fourth step had me taking a moral inventory, which, of course, became an inventory of my immorality. Helluva long list. Step 5 wanted me to admit to myself, to God and to another human being the exact nature of my wrongs. That was another ordeal. Those wrongs went on and on. The counselor suggested that 'the other human being' be a minister. I said I was Jewish; I wanted a rabbi. They said there wasn't a rabbi within fifty miles. I said import one from Minneapolis. They said it would cost. I said I'd pay. But the rabbi was booked up and finally I caved. I'd recite my wrongs to a goddamn minister if that's what they wanted. *Work the steps; work the program; stop being a prick.*

Night and day I attended meetings focusing on the steps. In fact, I bonded with a number of other drunks and druggies who seemed especially bright. I saw them as the elite addicts. I saw myself the same way. This was the first of my many mistakes in recovery. The notion of humility was still foreign to me. I couldn't be just another junkie. I had to be a *special* junkie with *special* junkie friends. I left Hazelden after a month, convinced that I had absorbed all the wisdom the place had to offer. But the truth is that, although sober, I was still pumped up with pride.

The story I'd love to tell would go like this:

Walter returns to New York a new man. He finds the patience, serenity and inner peace to alter his very character. As he continues working the steps and making amends for past behavior, he's free of guilt and full of compassion for his adversaries. His mood volatility dramatically diminishes; he turns mellow; he puts rancorous relationships behind him and, through the gift of sobriety, finds a harmony that transforms his soul.

The true story goes like this:

Walter returns to New York and all hell breaks loose. He's less patient, more arrogant and crazed with anger. Even with the gift of sobriety, he's more of a prick than ever.

Fools Rush In

'I'VE FOUND GOD,' I TOLD MY FRIEND THE DANTE scholar.

'Mazel tov.'

'I've got a spiritual path.'

'Double mazel tov.'

'I'm jumping back in my job with a clarity and determination I've never known before.'

'Your conversion was awfully quick.'

'Wasn't quick enough. It should have happened before. It set me free.'

'Be careful, Walter.'

'Of what?'

'Yourself.'

'What are you talking about?'

'You sound the way you've always sounded.'

'Fuck you.'

'See what I mean?'

Somewhere in the twelve-step literature I was warned. The text distinctly points out two pitfalls that trip up newly recovered addicts – the first is to rush back into business because you're convinced all your personal problems are solved; the second is to start talking about your spiritual renewal to anyone and everyone when, in fact, you don't know what you're talking about. Besides, people will think you're crazy.

I fell in both pitfalls, feet first.

When Ohga or Morita came to discuss vital business matters, I started off all meetings with the declaration that I had found God. I urged everyone to form a circle, hold hands and recite the Serenity Prayer. Having been saved, I felt compelled to spread the word. I was certain Righteousness was on my side. When, for example, I learned that Bruce Springsteen was giving a benefit concert for Amnesty International, an organization I saw as anti-Israel, I stopped taking calls from his manager and even from Bruce himself.

In virtually every area, I threw caution to the wind: I stridently criticized my own employer, Sony, for making consumer duplicating devices – such as dual cassette tape recorders – that cut into record sales. I was so vociferous that Akio Morita called to ask me whether, during an upcoming industry convocation in Vancouver, I would refrain from publicly feuding with him. I said I'd think about it. Morita had to plead before I capitulated.

Then came the infamous purchase of Columbia Studios.

Ovitz wanted to get Sony to make him Big Cheese at Columbia, but Ovitz would answer to no one, least of all me. Ovitz's overreaching soured him with Sony.

Norio Ohga wanted to interview Michael Eisner at Disney. We all met in L.A., but Ohga was so jet-lagged he kept nodding during Eisner's long-winded dissertation.

'Why is he sleeping?' Eisner kept asking.

'Don't worry, Michael,' I said. 'That's a sign of respect. He's really listening to every word you say.'

Sony lost interest in Eisner.

'Please,' Ohga urged, 'you must find someone.'

I called Peter Guber, who, together with Barbra Streisand's ex, crazy Jon Peters, had a successful production deal with Warner. With *Rain Man* and *Batman* under their belts, they were red-hot.

'Come to New York,' I urged Guber. 'I might have something interesting for you.'

Over dinner I spelled it out. Was he interested in running Columbia Studios for Sony, understanding that movies, like records, would report to me? He was interested. Was he interested in running it alone or with his partner Peters? Peters had to be part of the deal.

'However you want to handle it,' I told Guber. 'Just come back with a strong presentation.'

Ohga and Morita bought the presentation – lock, stock and barrel. The numbers were staggering – Guber/Peters would get $200 million for their production company; they'd each get $2.7 million in yearly salaries; deferred compensation approached another $50 million. And that's not counting the $3.4 billion Sony paid for Columbia itself. Guber/Peters, hot as they were, had never run a studio.

'What do you think of these numbers?' Ohga wanted to know.

'They're crazy, but no one consulted me about numbers. You just wanted names.'

'And you're sure Guber and Peters are the right guys.'

'Guber is the right guy. Peters gets a free ride.'

No one got a free ride. After being assured by Guber/Peters that Warner boss Steve Ross would willingly let them out of their contract, Ross threw a fit. Ross sued for $1 billion. Suddenly shit was flying everywhere.

Big-time lawyer Arthur Liman represented Ross. I couldn't stand the guy. In a meeting in New York, opposing sides were assembled in a conference room. Liman was making outrageous demands. During a break, with Liman out of the room, I went over to read his notes. As he walked back in, I was seated in his chair, carefully scrutinizing his papers.

'By God, Yetnikoff,' he screamed, 'those are my papers!'

'You're right.'

'You're reading my papers.'

'Right again.'

'I cannot believe you're reading my papers.'

'You're getting on my nerves, Arthur. If you don't want your goddamn papers read, take them with you.'

'Yetnikoff, you're a vulgar man.'

'Screw yourself, Liman,' I said, making his point.

If the point had been missed, I also spent some time insulting Steve Ross's wife Courtney, just for the fun of it. I spent half the meeting screaming at Sony's adversaries.

I was excluded from the rest of the negotiations. Mickey claimed that Ross wouldn't negotiate if I were present. I claimed that Meeekee, whose negotiating skills sucked, was threatened by me. Unlike Schulhof, I wasn't about to give away the store.

In the end, Meeekee settled by giving away, among other assets, half of the Columbia Record Club to Warner. This is the same asset I'd wanted to sell Warner for a half-billion. The final giveaway approached $800 million.

Ohga and Morita called.

'Do you think this is right?' they asked. 'Are Peters and Guber worth it?'

'Now you're asking me? I fought for Guber in the beginning because he's a smart guy. I was about to fight Warner when Meeekee took me out of the game. Now I don't give a shit. Do what you want.'

Some said it cost Sony $6 billion to buy Columbia and Guber/Peters. Some said it was all my fault. I said I didn't care. I was relying on my Higher Power. Besides, when all was said and done, Sony owned a major studio. That meant I was head of music *and* movies. Or was I?

'You're chairman of a steering committee that oversees the studio and you run the record company,' said Ohga.

'What does that mean?'

'The committee has eight members who vote on every major issue.'

'I don't like that.'

'Why not, Walter?'

'I don't mind eight advisory members, but I want the final vote. I want veto power over the committee.'

'I'm afraid it doesn't work that way.'

'Let me ask you this, Norio. How does the Sony board work? Aren't there thirty-four members?'

'Yes.'

'And how many of their votes count?'

'Well, only two votes really count.'

'Whose?'

'Mine and Morita's.'

'That's my point.'

'But Guber's point is that he is only comfortable with you as head of the steering committee.'

'A committee,' I pointed out, 'that's essentially ineffectual.'

'I hope you see his point, Walter.'

'I do. He's fucking me.'

Later Guber admitted to me that the committee concept meant he reported to no one. When Ohga fell for his scheme, my dream of being the boss of a studio boss was vanquished. Guber and Peters went on to lead Columbia down the road of ruin until Sony canned Peters and then canned Guber. In the mid-nineties, Sony dumped Schulhof, who by then had cost them $3.5 billion in lamebrained decisions. Of course the most lamebrained decision of all might have been Ohga's – to make poor Meeekee an entertainment czar.

Back at the start of the decade, Meeekcc was looking to undercut my power, not a difficult job given my what-the-fuck attitude.

My what-the-fuck attitude led me to shower favors on people I liked. On a trip to Tokyo in the old days, for instance, I was passing by a car dealer when an especially sporty Porsche caught my eye. I bought it for Ohga, a racing car fanatic. I charged it to the record division and called it a bonus for a man who had helped that division prosper. Norio was delighted. After Sony bought CBS Records, I called him and said, 'You should be rich. You should have million-dollar-plus bonuses.'

'I can't say that to Morita. But you can.'

'I will.'

I did. On a little scratch pad, I wrote out a list of superlucrative bonuses for Ohga, including the exclusive use of a New York luxury apartment paid out of record division funds.

When Morita came to New York, I showed him the list. He looked it over before quickly initialing it. Ohga became rich.

But in the last year of our relationship, Ohga also became a different man. While he expressed his gratitude for my largesse, he also – like Tisch before him – tried to make me feel like an employee.

'You work for me,' he said.

'No, I don't. I don't work for anyone.'

Mickey Schulhof didn't help matters. Meeckce was a man who, when Morita wasn't in New York, liked to sit in Morita's office and give guests the impression it was his.

Meeekee was always looking to undermine me. Example:

Because I was in charge of Sony's small fleet of private planes, I got a note saying that Schulhof wanted a jet to take him to Singapore. I refused the request. Rules said that only Morita could use the plane for a trip that long. Next thing I knew Ohga was on the phone, incensed.

'Who do you think you are, Walter? It's not your plane. It's Sony's.'

I was taken aback. He'd never talked to me this way before. 'I'm just playing by the rules, Norio.'

'Morita made the rules. If he wants to fly to Singapore, he flies to Singapore.'

'What does Morita have to do with it? It's Schulhof who wants the plane.'

'He's requesting it for Mr Morita.'

'He didn't tell *me* that. He made it sound like the plane's for him.'

'Well, it's not.'

'Well, maybe he wants people to think it is. He spends his life trying to impress people with his importance. That's his problem, not mine.'

'It's your problem that you turned down Morita's request.'

'No, it's your problem if you believe the false information that Schulhof's feeding you. It's your problem because that's going to ruin our relationship. And eventually Schulhof's going to ruin your company.'

With that, I hung up.

My relationship with Ohga, my friend for some twenty-five years, was never repaired. When it came time for me to sign a long-term contract for gobs of money, I refused. I said I wanted a short-term.

'Why?' asked Norio.

'I might not want to do this forever.'

'What else would you do? We need you.'

'You have Mottola. Tommy's doing a good job.'

'Tommy is nothing without you. Just like Sony is nothing without Morita. You know, Walter, I've given my life to Sony.'

'And I've given my life to God.'

'I don't understand your God.'

'I'm not sure I do either. But all I want is a short-term deal.'

Ohga saw Sony as God. I no longer did – and that made him nervous. I liked the fact that I was making him and Morita nervous. Let them just try and run this operation without me.

Ohga and I also fought over his idol, Herbert von Karajan. Ohga wanted to give him millions for the laser disc rights to the operas he conducted. I thought that was nuts.

'You're not a classical music expert,' Ohga told me.

'But I'm a money expert,' I told him. 'This will never earn back.'

'Pay it,' Ohga insisted.

'You pay it out of your budget, not mine.'

So much for my involvement with Hitler's favorite musician.

I took a winter vacation to the Loire Valley in France. I escaped with a girlfriend. In my still new state of sobriety there was neither booze nor drugs in sobriety – not a single drop, not a single joint – but lots of girlfriends. If sex is an addiction, I was still hooked. After a night of serious shtupping in an ancient castle turned luxury hotel, the phone rang at seven in the morning. Ohga was after me.

'You have no right to spend millions on copyrights from old Columbia movies,' he said.

'Who's spending millions?' I asked.

'Mickey says you are. You're about to make a major purchase without authorization.'

'Meeekee, Meeekee. Every time Meeekee hears a rumor he turns to you, the Great Ohga. "Oh, Great Ohga," he says, "Walter's being a bad boy again. Oh, Great Ohga, stop him before he ruins us all." Well, for your information, Norio, I haven't done a goddamn thing. I've been discussing buying some valuable copyrights – but that's all.'

'You are not to do anything of that size without me knowing about it.'

'I'm taking a big shit right now. Now you know.'

My unruliness was not restricted to business. I started going to twelve-step meetings on a regular basis. I still go. But in those first months after getting sober, I went with a vengeance. I went to hear myself talk rather than listen. I really didn't know what I was doing. I stuck with the one principle – don't use no matter what – but in every other regard was out of control.

I walked into a meeting on a stormy Manhattan night way downtown by the docks. The guys had been gathering in this location for fifty years. The leader was tough. He ran a no-nonsense agenda. 'We're here to talk about booze,' he said, 'and nothing else.' His audience was composed of a bunch of men who looked like lumberjacks. He spoke for a long time about his hard-earned recovery. I grew impatient and stepped to the front of the room, waving my arm in front of him. 'I have to share,' I said. 'I have to share.'

He finally gave up the podium. I got up and told my truth. 'I'm having a hard time,' I explained, 'because of this fantasy. This fantasy won't leave me alone: I'm called to California. They put me in a fancy hotel and invite me to the pool area where ten gorgeous women, completely naked, are waiting for me in a hot tub. I get in. I screw three out of the ten and give the other seven to my pals. My pals tell me I'm the greatest friend in the world – and that makes me feel great. The girls tell me I'm the greatest lay in the world – and that makes me feel even greater. But now a fresh crop of women show up, with bigger tits and wetter pussys than the first crop. The only way I can screw them is to get high on ludes. I need ludes. But if I take ludes, I blow my sobriety and lose my time. But fuck it – I take the ludes and screw the other broads.'

Before I could babble on any longer, the leader stopped me, saying, 'This has nothing to do with booze. Sit down.'

I went back to my seat, where an old-timer, a man in his seventies, turned to me. I also expected him to scold me. But all he said was 'Next time you go to California, take me with you.'

Humpty-Dumpty Had a Great Fall

'EVER READ *OTHELLO*?' ASKED MY POETRY PAL.

'Not recently.'

'You should.'

'First you hock me with Dante. Now Shakespeare. What do I want with *Othello*?'

'To learn about betrayal.'

'So now I'm being betrayed. Who's betraying me?'

'The way you describe your office politics, it sounds like half the company is plotting. They sense you're vulnerable.'

'They don't sense shit. When I stayed drunk, maybe I missed a beat or two. But sober, I'm sharp as a tack. My troops are loyal.'

'Allow me to quote the bard: "Nature would not invest herself in such shadowing passion without some instruction."'

'What does that mean?'

'Othello didn't see it coming either.'

'Am I Othello?'

'Maybe.'

'So who's Iago?'

'Look around you.'

'Mottola? Grubman?'

'You know those guys. I don't.'

'You don't know Sony. They'd give up sushi before they'd give up me.'

For all my cockiness, events were spinning out of control.

In early 1990, David Geffen sold his record company to Papa Doc Wasserman and Shitty Sheinberg at MCA for a half-billion. Now richer than God, Geffen went on a power tear. He was pissed at me for a couple of reasons: At Michael Jackson's whining insistence, I told Geffen that he couldn't use a Michael track for the *Days of Thunder* soundtrack; and I kept circulating the story that I wanted David to show my girlfriend how to give superior blow jobs. In short, I showed him contempt at every turn.

Meanwhile, Allen Grubman had become Geffen's attorney and partner in office politics. I didn't like that. I saw Grubman as my man. Out of whimsy, I had created him. I had handed him the industry's most prestigious client list – Bruce Springsteen, Billy Joel – on a silver platter. Why should he cavort with Geffen?

Besides, who was Grubman to test my power? I knew everything about the schmuck. I knew he was fucking a hooker, a close dog-walking confidante of one of my girlfriends. The hooker told me all the sordid details that he confided to her – his business finagling as well as his personal misbehaviors. The Grubber had reason to fear me.

Yet clearly the winds were shifting. But I was unclear. I miscalculated the shift. Or maybe just didn't care. Maybe my High Sobriety blinded me to the blatant facts. Maybe I was self-destroying and didn't know it. Either way, I was slipping.

'You know, Walter,' Grubman said, 'I'm tired of you throwing plates at my head when I don't give you the deal points you want.'

'You oughta be happy it's plates and not rocks,' I said. 'Geffen will wind up turning on you like he turns on everyone.'

'Geffen is a gentleman.'

'And Hitler's in heaven.'

'You don't need to aggravate the situation. You're making it hard on yourself. You're going against your own artists.'

'Who are you talking about?'

'Michael Jackson. He looks to Geffen like a father.'

'I'm getting sick.'

'You better get wise.'

I should have expected Grubman's Revenge. After all, I treated him like a schlemiel. If anyone had motive for revenge, it was the Grubber. And if anyone should have been able to read the tea leaves, it should have been me. The leaves spelled trouble:

Michael Jackson first fired Frank Dileo, my former employee and loyal supporter, and then fired his lawyer John Branca, another guy who liked me. Michael's new lawyer? Allen Grubman.

Grubman put together a new contract for Michael that I considered outrageous. It gave him his own label with the promise to earn his regular high-share royalties in addition to half the profits from his label.

'In my legal opinion,' I told Mottola, 'profits plus royalties could be violating every favored nation clause with our other artists.'

'No, it doesn't,' Tommy argued. 'His income from label profits are seen as separate.'

'Bullshit. Any accountant worth his salt will see it as disguised royalties. Springsteen's people will go crazy.'

'I'm giving Springsteen a full royalty rate on CD's.'

'What!' Because of what we claimed were high manufacturing costs, artists were usually paid half royalties on CD's.

'He deserves it,' Mottola said.

'What does "deserve" have to do with it? That's another favored nation dilemma. Do it with Springsteen and you'll have Billy Joel's people up your ass. You're losing it, Tommy.'

'I don't think I'm the one losing it, Walter.'

'I'll tell you who's going to lose it – Grubman,' I said.

'Grubman's irrelevant. Michael's the one who's not budging.'

'What if I call Michael and tell him that if his lawyer insists on this unreasonable deal, I'll put out a quickie CD of his greatest hits? There's nothing he wants less right now than a greatest hits collection – and we have all the necessary rights.'

'I wouldn't do that.'

'Then do this – call up Living Colour and tell them to fire Grubman.'

Living Colour was a hot rock band on Epic represented by Grubman.

'What's the point of that?' asked Mottola.

'I want to teach Grubman a lesson.'

'I can't tell a band to fire their lawyer.'

'Why not? Artists are more afraid of their label than their lawyer. Artists want to keep their label happy. The label makes them or breaks them. The lawyer isn't shit. The Grubber isn't shit.'

The Grubber was making me angrier by the day. He was power tripping, Hollywood social climbing, testing his mettle against mine.

Mottola was also tripping. After a secret love affair with a Japanese superstar singer on Sony – who was, in fact, Morita's goddaughter – he was also carrying on with his own superstar signing, Mariah Carey, while divorcing his wife, who had called me to complain how he was screwing her – financially. With my approval, Mottola had put in place a management team of his own. I'd thought he was the right guy to run Columbia Records. Now I was slowly getting the idea that he was getting ready to run me out.

Every time Tommy came near my dog, a benign and gentle spirit, the dog would growl like the devil himself was approaching.

I decided to read *Othello*.

''Tis here, but yet confused,' says Iago. 'Knavery's plain face is never seen till used.'

Even with the tide turning against me, I still couldn't get myself to believe that, after fifteen years of outlandishly profitable rule, the powers-that-be would show me the door. Even more convincingly, CBS Records was still making a mint. Net, not gross but *net*, profits for 1989 were a whopping $450 million. That fact alone told me there was nothing to worry about.

While Ohga had been more distant and adamant on letting me know that he, and not I, was the boss, he'd also reassured me about Mottola.

'Tommy loves you,' he told me when I questioned my lieutenant's loyalty.

Rather than reassure me, that statement worried me. Ohga never used the word 'love.' He doth protest too much. Maybe Shakespearean plots *were* being hatched.

Smelling blood in the water, the media sharks flashed their teeth.

Forbes wrote a piece about the Sony deal with Guber/Peters and called it 'Walter Yetnikoff's $300 Million Mistake.'

Billboard asked me if I was on my way out. Hell, no. I was there to stay. In the same issue, though, Jon Landau gave a statement that stunned me. He said that since the sale of Sony my relationship with him and Springsteen 'had ended.' Clearly, Landau had been talking to Geffen. Springsteen had been talking to Grubman. Grubman had been talking to Mottola.

But who the hell was talking to me?

The gossip items continued. Reporters read my short-term contract as proof that I was a lame duck. When I pointed out that the short-term was my choice, not Sony's, no one believed me.

The press made it sound like my two biggest artists, Michael and Bruce, were deserting me. Were they? All I had to do was call them and get them to issue a statement on my behalf. No big deal. So why didn't I do it?

Pride.

Why should I call Michael? He should call me. Same with Springsteen. Who was I to chase after these troubadours? I was the President and Chairman of the Universe. Let them come to me.

Fear.

I was afraid that they wouldn't take my calls. Afraid that they wouldn't call me back. Afraid that they had, in fact, transferred their loyalty to Geffen, Grubman and Mottola. I was afraid of the truth.

Moral superiority.

I was sober. I went to a meeting a day with other sober people. I was on a spiritual path, I was on higher ground, I was above and beyond. I was clean.

I tried acting like all was well. I faked it. I went to the Hamptons with a girlfriend – this was the summer of 1990 – with rumors whirling around my head. I was looking to relax, to spend a pleasant weekend on the beach, to forget what everyone was calling the impending crisis. Walking down the main street of East Hampton on Saturday afternoon, nonchalantly eating an ice cream cone, I ran into Peter Guber. We hadn't spoken in weeks.

'How's everything, Walter?'

'Fine. Why shouldn't everything be fine?'

'Just asking.'

'I didn't know you were on the East Coast. How come you didn't call me, Peter?'

'I was going to but . . .'

'What are you doing out here?'

'Mickey Schulhof has a place out here. He called me for some meetings.'

'What kind of meetings?'

'Company meetings, planning meetings.'

'Meetings that don't include me.'

'It's about movies, not music. Relax, Walter, you're too worked up.'

That night I couldn't sleep. I kept envisioning the gathering storm. Next morning I tried to call Mottola. It was time to have it out with Tommy, who'd been assiduously avoiding me. I'd put it to him point-blank – was he with me or against me? Was he with Geffen or with me? Was he with Grubman or with me? I'd made a place for him, just as I'd made a place for Grubman, in the highest ranks of the music business. He owed me. The very least he owed me was the truth about his backbiting. I had to talk to Mottola. But Mottola was nowhere to be found. Someone said he was on his boat sailing somewhere around the Hamptons. I had a friend with a boat who agreed to help me find Mottola. I spent all day Sunday sailing from dock to dock, searching for Mottola's boat.

What was in my head? If I found him, what would I do? Cajole him? Kill him? Force him to tell me the truth? Win back his loyalty? Call him a cad? Get him to confess his betrayal?

What was I doing on a sunny summer's day chasing after my underling's boat like a spurned lover? Wasn't that beneath my dignity? What did I hope to gain?

Was I spinning out of control?

I never found the boat.

Back in the city on Monday morning I found myself being called to Norio Ohga's office. I was told he'd be accompanied by a lawyer. Does that mean I should bring a lawyer as well? 'Use your own discretion,' I was told.

I brought a lawyer.

Norio Ohga, my forever friend, the man who had graciously hosted me in Tokyo a hundred times, the man who had slept in my home and trusted me with the most intimate details of his life, the man I made wealthy, gave me the news standing up.

'I'm sorry, Walter,' he said, 'but this hurts me more than it hurts you.'

That was the first lie.

'The board of directors has met and decided you should take a sabbatical.'

That was the second lie.

'How could the board meet without me?' I asked. 'I never received legal notice. And besides, how could you meet with anyone? You said you were on an Alaskan cruise.'

'We had a special meeting. We were told that the artists are not happy with you.'

'Which artists?'

'Many artists.'

'They told you this personally?'

'They made it known.'

'By letter? Do you have the letters? Can you show me the letters?'

'You're making this difficult.'

'Oh, I should be making it easy. You want me to make it easy for you?'

'I'd like you to understand that your own behavior . . .'

'Now you're a psychiatrist, Norio. Now you're a behavioral psychiatrist.'

'I'm your friend . . .'

'You call this a friendly discussion? Your lawyer standing next to you looks extremely friendly.'

'It's a necessary discussion. And a final one. I'm talking to you with tears in my eyes.'

With that, he left the room. He didn't shake my hand. He didn't use the word 'fired.' He simply vanished.

'Please exit through the side door,' said a security guard.

'Why?' I wondered.

No one said why. Later I learned it was because in the adjoining room Ohga was meeting with Mottola and already planning the new regime.

'Ding Dong the Witch is Dead!'

SUPPOSEDLY THAT'S WHAT GEFFEN SAID, QUOTING from *The Wizard of Oz*, when he heard about my demise. Of course it stung. The whole goddamn thing stung. The sting was so painful, in fact, that I refused to admit the raw truth to my friends, or even to myself. I went around telling people I had actually quit. My rationale went like this: Because I had told Ohga that God and not Sony was my Higher Power, I had, in essence, resigned. By refusing their long-term contract, I reinforced that position. Rather than being pushed out, I had left of my own volition.

For years I offered that reasoning to anyone who'd listen. And on some metaphysical level, it may have even been true. But the plain fact of the matter – a fact my ego couldn't accept – is that I was unceremoniously canned. If I had wanted to stay, I could not have. The sabbatical that Ohga mentioned was an obvious euphemism. My enemies – by then too numerous to count – were right to relish my public humiliation. To them, I was the Bad Witch, the Big Bully, the Nasty Prick of Pricks. They were all too happy to flood the press with quotes celebrating my dismissal.

Every day a new headline took aim at my head: 'The Fall of Yetnikoff,' wrote *Rolling Stone*. 'Once thought the most powerful man in the business, the former head of CBS Records went on a self-destructive tear and lost his job.'

'A Music King's Shattering Fall,' wrote *Time*. 'How the brilliant builder of CBS Records spun out of control.'

I made the same foolish mistake fallen moguls often make. I figured that by entrusting a reporter with *my* version of the story, I'd win vindication. When I did that with *New York* magazine, their profile made me look like a pathetic putz. 'Spinning Out,' their headline screamed. 'How record heavyweight Walter Yetnikoff took the big fall.'

In contrast, I went around bragging how settling my contract had cost Sony tens of millions of dollars. I'd emerged from the fray wealthier than ever. My parachute was 18K gold. I was free of corporate headaches, corporate intrigue and endless corporate bullshit. I was, after all, victorious. When *Forbes* magazine asked me what I was going to do now, I answered, 'Count my money. And, believe me, that's going to take some time.'

The old Yetnikoff was still giving 'em hell. The old Yetnikoff wasn't about to be beat down by a bunch of carping reporters. The old Yetnikoff was too resilient to crumble. Underneath, though, the old Yetnikoff was devastated. At the end of the day, after I'd made my hundredth phone call where I told still another acquaintance how I was sitting pretty, I fell apart. If I had still been drinking, I'd have drunk myself to death. But without drink or drugs to annihilate my true feelings, I had to cope with a condition that had existed for much of my adult life: acute depression. While I was running the free world, I could assuage those dark spells by ranting and raging, by antagonizing associates and turning daily tasks into high drama. By yelling, I could move mountains. Suddenly there was no one to yell at.

I was given an office in the Coca-Cola building owned by

Columbia Studios. They put me on the zombie floor. The place was deserted. Dark hallway, flickering fluorescents, just me and a secretary. Cut off from everyone and everything, I'd come in, call my broker to make sure my money was still there, lean back in my chair and stare into space. I had nothing to do. I could have called Barbra, Billy, Bruce, Mick or Michael, but hell, they could call me. No one called me. The years of relationships, the comradeship, the good vibes, the mutual admiration, favors done and favors received, zipping here, zooming there, the world at my feet, the stars at my disposal. Now nothing. Wouldn't one of them want to reach out to commiserate? Wouldn't one of them want to say, 'I won't forget how you helped me, and I just want you to know I care'?

Instead, my secretary just sat there, attending a silent phone.

I read the paper. Morris Levy, convicted to ten years in prison for the extortion of a small-time music wholesaler, died with the case on appeal. It was the only way for Moish to beat the rap. Moish died a broken man. I felt broken.

One day Bill Graham showed up with a big jar of pickled herring in cream sauce.

'I'm just back from the Catskills,' he said. 'And I figured you could use a little soul food.'

We sat and ate herring together. Bill was sensitive enough not to mention my past, present or future. He saw how I was hurting.

'You'll be back,' he said and then, after patting me on the back, left me to face the empty afternoon.

Jon Peters called.

'I realize what you did for us, Walter,' he said with apparent sincerity. 'We wouldn't be here if it wasn't for you. Move out of that dreary building before you go nuts. We'll give you a beautiful suite over here.'

The offer heartened me. I made plans to move. The next day, though, Peters called back.

'Sorry,' he said, 'Ohga nixed my offer. You better stay put.'

I sighed and said it didn't matter. I didn't need an office. I could afford the most splendiferous office in the city. I rented a huge space atop Trump Tower on Fifth Avenue with a commanding view of Central Park. All of Manhattan was at my feet. I bought a Rolls-Royce. I employed a full-time driver. But where did I have to go? I was chauffeured to twelve-step meetings where I heard speakers talk about humility. 'Humility,' one of them said, 'comes from *humus*, meaning soil, ground. Humility means being grounded. It means having an accurate perception of who we are.'

Who was I? The answer was clear – an untalented piece of shit who got lucky in business and wound up rich. A growing sense of self-contempt deepened my depression. How to escape the morass?

In typical addict fashion, I got compulsive. I went to weights. I hired a trainer, a huge Italo-American I'll call the Great Bambone who pumped me up to look like Popeye. I attacked the barbells and dumbbells as though they were my old enemies. I squatted and lifted, grunting and groaning and reciting a mantra inside my head – no pain, no gain – that led to massive muscles. I grew excited by the bulge of my triceps and biceps, by my ability to bench-press 300 pounds. I lost my gut and regained my old attitude that said, *Don't fuck with me*. I saw that as mental health. It was, in truth, mental decay. Narcissism taking a new turn. Flexing in front of the mirror, I beat back the bad feelings with the guise of a warrior.

An old associate at CBS called to invite me to lunch. We talked about the old days. 'The business is boring without you,' he said. 'The excitement is gone.' I ate up the flattery. The next day Mickey Schulhof from Sony called to say that my severance agreement forbade me from discussing the music business with former employees.

'What are you doing, Meeekee – snooping during lunch? Do you have spies following me around?'

'The agreement is enforceable.'

'I'm tired of your bullshit. If you don't like who I eat lunch with, sue me.'

Of course they never did. And I suspect, given their fear of what I know, they never will. But I didn't know that at the time. In fact, when I told my girlfriend the story, she got worried. 'So they *are* following you. Maybe they're afraid you'll divulge company secrets.'

'Which secrets?' I asked.

'Accounting practices, strange associations.'

That's all I needed to hear. My girlfriend's paranoia triggered my own. The Great Bambone, paranoid himself, got on the bandwagon and claimed he was followed every time he came to see me. When we went to jog out in the country, he had me convinced we were being tailed by a big black sedan.

'Let's take 'em on,' said Bambone. 'Let's force 'em out of the car and beat the shit out of 'em.'

'Let's not,' I said. 'They'll have guns.'

'I have heat of my own.'

'Great. I'll be gunned down in a shoot-out with Sony.'

Somehow we lost the black sedan. But it took a long time to lose the feeling that I was being pursued by the evil forces of a company I once led. I felt the same way about the moguls who, in my mind, had betrayed me – Geffen, Wasserman, Mike Ovitz. I'd read that Steven Seagal had been Ovitz's personal trainer in the martial art form of aikido before Ovitz made him a movie star. The Great Bambone scoffed when I told him that. 'Brute force will kill aikido,' he said. 'I can teach you enough so you can kill Ovitz.'

I liked the idea. I relished the details. 'Aikido is a soft form,' Bambone explained. 'Ovitz won't hit or kick. He'll just use his leverage against you. He needs you to make the first move. To make you move, he'll scream his head off. The key is, don't react. Just smash him in the mouth. You'll break his jaw and he'll never recover.'

It's hard to explain my motivation. It was hardly reasonable. But then again, when is madness ever reasonable? I was mad. I was also jealous of Mike Ovitz's rising status and power in a world that had rejected me. I so relished the notion of breaking Ovitz's jaw that I hired a graphic artist to design an ad I was prepared to place in *Variety*, a public challenge to Mike Ovitz.

*******FIGHT TO THE DEATH!*******
WALTER YETNIKOFF TAKES ON MIKE OVITZ
MADISON SQUARE GARDEN
APRIL 15, 1991
NO-HOLDS-BARRED
ALL PROCEEDS DONATED TO
THE UNITED JEWISH APPEAL
THE WINNER PAYS THE LOSER'S BURIAL COSTS
****

I was dead serious. If anything would restore my deteriorating public image, this was it. Ovitz dare not refuse. With one lethal chop to his throat, I'd kill the motherfucker Hollywood had crowned its most powerful player.

'I didn't think you could get any crazier,' said my poetry pal. 'But you have.'

'What are you talking about? My mind is crystal clear, my body is a killing machine. I've never been better.'

'Run that ad in *Variety* and the men with the straitjackets really *will* be coming after you. They'll stick you in a padded cell and swallow the key.'

'I'm dead certain this fight will come off.'

'Last time we talked you were certain that the banks holding your money were conspiring against you. Next you were sure that the police were about to bust you for some unregistered shotgun you stashed in your attic. Now this.'

'This is cathartic. Aren't there entire epics based on the power of catharsis?'

'Superman was not a sixty-year-old Jewish guy looking for redemption.'

'Fuck redemption, I want blood.'

I dropped the ad and went to California. I had another idea guaranteed to chase away my blues. I'd become a movie mogul. With my enormous resources and managerial skills, I'd become a producer's producer. I'd seek the advice of Marvin Worth, a famous producer himself who made *Lenny* and *The Autobiography of Malcolm X*. Marvin had been sober for twenty-five years, a good man with a hip style and Hollywood muscle.

'Marvin,' I said, 'I have an idea.'

'What is it?'

'A biopic on Miles Davis.'

'I knew Miles.'

'I did too,' I added. 'He was one of my artists. He'd come by my office from time to time to call me an asshole. I liked him.'

'The Prince of Darkness. Miles is a great idea, Walter. I'll help you. I'll put you in touch with Spike Lee. He'd be perfect.'

'I want Wesley Snipes for Miles. What do you think?'

'Another good call. But you gotta get the music.'

'I got it. I got a free option on wall-to-wall music rights with a buy-out of two hundred and fifty thousand dollars.'

'Cheap.'

'What about the script?'

'I'll hook you up with a Pulitzer prize winner.'

'It can't miss.'

'It's good to see you moving, Walter. Once you get sober, you gotta keep moving.'

'What happens when you stop?' I wanted to know.

'Then you gotta sit with yourself. In my case, I can't stand that. I can't be with myself for more than a minute.'

I related. I swung into action. Nailed down an option on Miles's autobiography. Talked to Spike. Broke bread with Snipes. Hired a writer, insisting that he write me into the script as the exec who encouraged Miles to record his breakthrough landmark album *Bitches Brew*. Everything was set, all systems go. It was just a matter of getting major funds to produce that film. That meant enlisting a studio.

The golden rule of Hollywood is, of course, don't spend your own money. I'd spent a modest amount on music and options, but nothing alarming. With Marvin Worth's help, with Spike Lee directing and Wesley Snipes starring, with the drawing power of Miles's charismatic character and incredible music, I knew I had a winner. I had hold of the jazz equivalent of *Amadeus*. Like *Amadeus*, it would sweep the Academy Awards. As producer, I'd win best picture. I'd get back my reputation as a winner. I'd be lauded and applauded by everyone who figured I was dead. I couldn't lose.

While I was out chasing money for the Miles movie in L.A., I went to a meeting. I was – and am – always going to twelve-step meetings. They ground me. This particular meeting in Pacific Palisades featured a famous speaker. When he was through, an attractive woman came around with a basket for contributions. As is customary, I dropped in a buck.

'A man like you should give us at least twenty dollars,' she said.

'What d'you mean, "a man like me"?'

'I know who you are.'

'We're supposed to be anonymous here.'

'I used to work for you. But I was too low down on the totem pole to be noticed. I'd hear about those wild parties of yours, but I never got invited. You're lucky to be here. Guys like you usually don't make it in this program.'

'Why?'

'Too goddamn arrogant. You have to eat humble pie in this program. This program is about service. In order to keep what you got, you have to give it away. You get a daily reprieve from your addiction based on spiritual maintenance. How's your spiritual maintenance?'

'I'm working on it.'

'Good. Give us at least ten bucks.'

I dropped in five.

I wound up fumbling the Miles movie. It never got made. My mess-up came from that very thing my twelve-step lover had pointed out – arrogance. I saw it as a slam dunk. With a prestigious director, star and script, no one could resist. After nearly a year of shopping the thing, everyone resisted. The story was tricky, the screenplay never exactly right. As a money raiser, I was lame. In the name of rigorous honesty, I kept telling potential investors that, as a recovering alcoholic and drug addict, I had great vision. No one wanted to hear about my recovery; no one cared. Investors and studios either saw profit potential or didn't. Exasperated, frustrated, filled with even more self-contempt, I discovered a fact that should have been obvious: I knew nothing about producing a movie. My period of energized hustle ended. My comeback came to a screeching halt. No flattering articles about me in the trades, no buzz celebrating my ingenuity. I was just another schmucky would-be producer who never cracked the Hollywood safe. I wound up selling the rights to Marvin Worth, who cut a deal with Sony. But when Marvin died, the deal died with him.

Back in New York, I sulked. An old drinking partner slipped me
a copy of some saloon singer doing Cole Porter's 'Down in the
Depths on the 90th Floor.' From my Trump Tower perch, I
offhandedly considered the long leap. Then I considered a drink.
Then I went to a meeting. The old-timers said, 'Keep coming
back. It gets better.' But it was getting worse. When I initiated my
Hollywood scheme, I was convinced that my fortitude would see
me through. I could reclaim my power. Now there was nothing to
do except go back to square one. I had to relearn the first step of
a program that continued to both sustain and baffle me:

I had to admit I was powerless.

Hot Mantra

'MEDITATE,' SAID MY POETRY PAL. 'IT'S GOOD FOR YOU.'

'Fine, I'll meditate.'

The cloud of depression fogging my brain wasn't lifting. A shrink had given me Prozac, but it wasn't working. Why not meditate?

I found a transcendental meditation teacher who was supposed to be the best. Three hundred bucks a session – plus another hundred for my own private mantra. It sounded like highway robbery, but what the hell. Everyone wants top dollar these days, so why not a guru? The guru was a lady. Her guru was pictured on her wall, a man with glowing eyes and a long flowing beard. He looked stoned. She assured me he wasn't. She started talking guru talk – 'the beauty of the balance of the cosmos and the symmetry of the soul.' She had me look into the heart of a red rose sitting in her vase. She gave me a mantra. I gave her a check.

I went home and tried to meditate, twenty minutes in the morning, twenty minutes at night. My mind roamed. My depression returned. I called up Madame Guru to complain.

'Come back for another session,' she said. 'You might find a group session more helpful.' I came back. This time it was me, the guru and another would-be meditator, a foxy young woman, dark hair, big boobs, short skirt. 'Close your eyes,' said the guru, 'and picture your mind on the surface of a rough sea. You're riding on the waves. You're moving up and down. Now picture the sea beneath the waves. Dive down into the sea. Picture clear blue water. Picture perfect calmness.' I couldn't picture shit. But when I opened my eyes, I saw a welcome sight: With her legs spread wide, my fellow meditator was on full display. I liked the picture. And I could tell she liked that I was looking. When I closed my eyes to return to the meditation, I was diving down into a different sea.

I found an apt metaphor for my condition. I was a bird flying around with nowhere to land. My life lacked structure and purpose. One shrink said I had posttraumatic syndrome. I was traumatized by failure – first Sony, then the Miles movie. I had a wonderful twelve-step sponsor who tried to help. He stressed gratitude. He was especially impressive because he had tremendous reasons for resentments. He was losing his sight; he was suffering with impotence; his business had gone broke; he and his wife, a nag, lived in a crummy little apartment. Darkness was literally closing in on him, and all he could do was talk about his good fortune.

'My sobriety is a blessing,' he said. 'My worst day in sobriety is better than my best day drunk. I've been out of the prison of addiction for forty years. What greater gift could I be given? I'm joyous, happy and free.'

And he was.

When he asked me to prepare a daily gratitude list, I easily filled up two pages. My sons were still part of my life, my finances secure, my program friends supportive, my health good. The list went on. When I was through listing, though, I felt worse.

'Why?' my sponsor asked.

'Because seeing all these reasons not to be depressed makes me more depressed.'

'I don't understand.'

'If the gratitude list doesn't make me grateful, that means I'm nothing but an ungrateful asshole.'

'You're judging yourself.'

'What else do I have to do?'

'Celebrate your sobriety.'

'You bring the champagne, I'll bring the coke.'

'You really don't even want that stuff anymore, do you?'

'I really don't. But I do think I want a job.'

'Then create one for yourself With your resources, that shouldn't be hard. Ask yourself what you want – and then go get it.'

When I asked myself, the question came amazingly quickly: I wanted back in the music business. It was the biggest thing I had done – run an international music operation – and done well. Besides, the period designated by the noncompetition clause of my Sony agreement had expired. By the mid-nineties, I had made up my mind. I was going for it – a big-time label of my own. It was risky and also high-profile. The media would eat up the story. Yetnikoff's return. Yetnikoff's revenge. Yetnikoff's big gamble.

If one thing defeated depression – at least temporarily – it was hyperactivity. I threw myself into the project with all I had. I reasoned that this was different than my film fiasco. I hadn't known Hollywood, but I did know the music business. I had over thirty years of experience. Once I broke through that pall of depression, I had energy to burn. In my early sixties, I was road-tested and ready to run.

With the help of a brilliant businesswoman who also became my lover – clear proof that clear boundaries between work and play still didn't exist for me – I went running around the world looking for funds to underwrite this enterprise called the Velvel Music Group. I wasn't going into the thing half-assed. I envisioned an internationally distributed record company with a number of associated labels. I envisioned an empire. If I had any model, it was Geffen Records when David had Guns N' Roses, Whitesnake and Aerosmith. My concentration was on alternative rock. Because I wasn't an A&R man, I assembled an A&R team I was convinced could find hitmakers. Following the time-honored edict – to make money you have to spend money – I coughed up a sizable chunk to concoct a master plan. I took that plan to London, Paris, Berlin, Brussels, Geneva and finally Tokyo, talking up my company to well-heeled financiers. No one bit.

'I'm going to take a bite,' said Jon Peters, who'd fallen from the heights of Hollywood power, a fall cushioned by a settlement for tens of millions.

'That's great, Jon. I'm looking for about twenty million.'

'I don't know of a sharper record exec than you, Walter. I'm going to kick in fourteen million.'

Jon liked to play the big man. He liked throwing around big numbers.

'I'd be thrilled with ten million,' I said, figuring if I asked for ten I might get five.

'You underestimate me. I'm flush right now. We'll swing, we'll spling, we'll bing. I'm ready to take a fling with this thing. I believe in Velvel.'

'I'm counting on you, Jon.'

'I'm here.'

Here today, gone tomorrow.

I never spoke to Jon Peters again. I called him a good dozen times to see about the check. No check, no nothing. Peters bowed out without as much as a 'sorry.' Of course Jon wasn't alone. A half-dozen of my high-powered contacts claimed that they'd be buying in; they just needed a little time.

After a year of solicitation, though, I felt myself running out of time. Out of a lethal mixture of frustration and determination, I started hiring. In spite of reluctant investors, I set up the company and forged ahead. I realized I was ignoring that hallowed edict – don't spend your own money – but what choice did I have? My need to reinvent myself as a major mogul defeated my reluctance to dip into my pocket. I dipped plenty. I hired a marketing team, accountants, publicists. I assembled a team of two dozen top pros. 'The Velvel Music Group,' said our press release, 'has the savvy of a major and the soul of an independent.' It went on to tout me as 'one of the architects of the modern music industry.'

We took office space and hit the ground running. I was cutting deals left and right. We were signing acts. We were buying catalogues. We were working overseas. I was back in my element. Our letterhead made Velvel look bigger than Sony, showing logos of all our affiliates – Bottom Line Records, EagleRock Records, Fire Records, Gypsy Records, Konk Records, the soundtrack imprint ReelSounds Records. We bought the rights to the Kinks catalogue; we cut a distribution deal with BMG: we signed an English group called the Candyskins, who'd had a hit on Geffen. We were strong in New York underground bands – Talking to Animals was one – and recorded a gal named Natalie Farr. We were firing on all cylinders.

Or misfiring.

The misfiring went on for some three years. There was always a reason to keep going – an investor was about to come through; a hit was about to drop. But nothing we recorded had any sales impact. The plain truth is that Velvel never had a hit. Not one. Meanwhile, the numbers grew more alarming with each day. At first I was pouring hundreds of thousands into Velvel. Then it became millions. To keep the ship afloat, I had spent my *own* millions. For a guy who's supposed to be smart, that's awfully dumb. I had to stop before I blew everything.

In selling Velvel for peanuts, I also had to admit something to myself that may have been obvious to others: I was adept at manipulating the giant resources of an international concern, but I was less than adept at manipulating the fragile resources of a small company. Neither my investors nor my A&R people came through with the goods. I could blame them or I could blame myself. I had to blame myself. After all, Velvel was my idea. I did the hiring. I set it up. I watched it fall.

This fall was far worse than Sony the debacle. When Sony fired me, I had the satisfaction of leaving with a wad. Velvel was also far worse than the Miles movie, a minor blip on the Hollywood radar screen. This humiliation was high-profile. I had gone after stories in the trade. I had sought to create a buzz around my artists and myself. When it came crashing down, there was nowhere to hide. 'Velvel Crashes, Velvel Collapses, Velvel Vanishes' read the headlines in the trades. Well, Velvel was me.

The twelve-step programs talk about hitting bottom. They say that in order to enjoy the gifts of recovery, some people need to find themselves in abject despair. I'd figured my bottom came in 1990 when Sony kicked me out. I was wrong. When my producer career died an early death, I thought that was it. Wrong again. When Velvel failed, I wasn't even thinking about a bottom. I wasn't even thinking about getting out of bed. I drew the curtains, closed the blinds and stayed in bed for months. I was immobile. I was useless. I was racked with every lousy self-loathing feeling known to man.

I was through.

Heshie

I STARTED CALLING GOD HESHIE. I'M NOT EXACTLY sure why. Maybe because Heshie is a familiar Jewish name that I could easily say. When a rabbi pointed out to me that perhaps I wanted to say, 'Ha 'Shem,' a Hebrew word for God, I wondered whether my unconscious was playing games with me. Either way, I was trying to connect.

'Heshie,' I said in my morning prayers, 'I'm not sure if you're there. I'm not sure who you are. But I'm talking to you anyway. I'm saying that I'm having a hard time getting out of bed. I can't lift more than twenty pounds of weights. I'm seeing doom and gloom everywhere I look. My ego is crushed. My sense of myself is devastated.'

'It's good that you're talking to your Heshie,' said my twelve-step sponsor. 'Talk to him every morning when you get up. Talk to him on your knees. Pray and meditate before you do anything else.'

'Even if I don't mean it?' he asked.

'*Especially* if you don't mean it. Your spiritual muscles are weak.

Like any other muscles, they have to be strengthened to be effective.'

'I still wind up depressed.'

'Accept your depression. Don't fight it. The less you fight it, the quicker it dissipates. Like your addictions, you're powerless over it. Relief comes from your Higher Power and nowhere else.'

'Heshie has put me through a lot.'

'*You* put yourself through a lot, Walter. Heshie just watched. When you got through, he was there waiting for you. When you view yourself as a victim, you become a victim. When you view your life as a gift, you start relishing that life.'

'You sound like you've been writing Hallmark greeting cards.'

'Make fun all you like, but wisdom isn't complicated. It's about service. You serve God by serving others. The only way of escaping the dead-end trap of self-absorption is service. Read Bill Wilson.'

I'd been reading Bill Wilson for years. As the father of all twelve-step programs and a writer with deep spiritual insights, Wilson commanded respect. Some consider him one of the primary social philosophers of our time. I can see why. This grassroots business of one drunk helping another was not only simple, but egalitarian. It was anti-elitist. All were welcome, all were equal. There were no leaders, only trusted servants. There was no profit motive, no room for megalomaniacs. If anything could destroy my program, it was ego. Ego and willfulness. The idea was to let go and let God.

Because my desire to be a big shot was ingrained, because I viewed control as much a necessity as food and water, it took heavy humiliation to pound the program through my thick skull. If Velvel had been a hit, I may well have wound up crashing completely. But because Velvel crashed, I had a chance of surviving. I had a chance because I had no choice. No pills in the medicine cabinet were lifting my spirit. My only choice was deeper commitment to the program.

'Okay, Heshie,' I said in my morning prayers, 'you got me. You brought me this far. I'm counting on you to bring me the rest of the way. I'm doing service. I'm turning into my grandmother.'

My grandmother was all about service. Her daily question was 'What have you done for someone else today?' Unlike my mother and father, who never posed that question, Bubbee was never depressed. Her focus was on others. Could it be that simple? If I were to find redemption for my rotting soul, if I were to escape the confines of my voracious ego, was it just a matter of serving someone or something besides my own needs?

'Faith is more than our greatest gift,' Bill Wilson wrote. 'Sharing it with others is our greatest responsibility.'

The twelve-step groups gave me the faith required to stay clean, one day at a time. That twelve-step faith, as the original program emerged in the thirties, came from Heshie. Now Heshie was saying, 'Share it!' I'd had sponsors; I'd been a sponsor; since getting clean I'd done occasional service. But I now realized it could no longer be occasional. It had to be continual.

In describing the edifice of recovery, Wilson wrote, 'Eager hearts and hands have lifted the spire of our cathedral into its place. That spire bears the name of Service. May it ever point straight upward toward God.' The symbolism of a church didn't thrill me. Couldn't Wilson have described a synagogue?

'Wilson,' said my sponsor, 'was the one who contributed to the third step that says, "Made a decision to turn our will and our lives over to the care of God *as we understood him*.' Wilson would have told you, "If you want to see it as a synagogue, see it as a synagogue. If you want to call him Heshie, call him Heshie."'

'I want to call a rabbi,' I said.

'Fine,' said my sponsor. 'Call a rabbi.'

Instead I called a priest.

I arrived at the Catholic church in Paterson, New Jersey, armpit of the nation, in an ordinary sedan.

'Last time you showed up here in a chauffeur-driven limo,' said the priest.

'How the mighty have fallen.'

'What happened, Walter?'

'I'm doing my own driving. I even got a MetroCard. I stood at the vending machine in the subway station for a half hour before figuring out how it worked. But I did it. You want to see my MetroCard?'

'No, I can read your aura. Humility has arrived. Your sanctification is certain. Heaven awaits.'

'I'm counting on your influence to get me in. Matter of fact, I'm *buying* your influence to get me in.'

The priest laughed. The priest was Reverend Monsignor Vincent E. Puma. I had met him years earlier at one of the T. J. Martell dinners that he regularly attended. Tony Martell, who began the yearly charity event, had worked for me at Epic. When his young son died of leukemia, he vowed to fight the disease by raising funds through a music-industry event. After some twenty-five years, Tony had raised nearly $12 million. The father was his spiritual adviser. The father reminded me of the priest played by Karl Malden in *On the Waterfront*. He was tough as nails and dead set on helping the poor.

'First time I met you,' he reminded me, 'was at a Martell dinner. I think you were the honoree. But I also think you were drunk as a skunk – and urging me to fix you up with the blonde sitting next to me.'

'Did you?'

'Of course not. She was one of my parishioners. I did my best to keep her out of your lair.'

'You did her a favor.'

'I did you a favor. She became a nun.'

'With that body?'

'I don't notice such things. But I do notice you appear less frenetic, Walter.'

'How frenetic can anyone be going from one twelve-step meeting to another? That's my life.'

'Sounds like a good life. Especially because it brought you to this meeting.'

The father went on to describe his vision for an expansion of his grassroots facilities in Paterson. He explained that, although he was a practicing Roman Catholic priest, this project would be independent of any church. He wanted to go from a simple soup kitchen to an entire recovery complex to benefit the poor, hungry and addicted. His aim was clear – to help the street people. 'First they need good food,' he said. 'Then good overnight shelter. Then good long-term shelter. And, underlining all this, solid rehabilitation. I'm talking about serving a thousand hot meals a day and housing hundreds of homeless.'

'And you want my money.'

'Sure, I want your money, but I want more than that. I want your heart. I want you to bring a twelve-step meeting here. And I want you to run it.'

'It's not enough to give you a check?'

'Not nearly enough. This is going to be a blood-and-guts operation. I need your blood and guts.'

Because I saw Father Puma as a gutsy guy, I was moved by his pitch. He was a rebel priest who had taken on the Vatican. He had eschewed a rich parish for an impoverished one. Like me, he had little patience with bureaucracy. I relished his story about how he took two thugs who threatened his female parishioners and slammed them against a wall, scaring them within an inch of their lives. The father was no bullshit.

'I'm not going to bullshit you,' I said. 'The idea of driving to Paterson every week doesn't thrill me.'

'It's not about thrills. It's about getting through to a hard-core group of addicts. These are rough characters right out of jail who weren't exactly educated in private schools on the Upper East Side.'

'I'd like to avoid the commitment, Father, but I don't see Heshie letting me out of this one.'

'Who's Heshie?'

'The guy who introduced us.'

A few years later, Eva's Village – Father Puma's dream – was built. He wanted my name on one of the buildings, but I flat-out refused. I figured if anyone saw me as a major contributor, every charitable facility on the East Coast would hit me up. Besides, humility humility humility. 'Don't give me that humility business,' the father said. 'You're talking at the grand opening ceremony.'

My talk was short. 'Honored guests,' I said, 'today I've become my Jewish grandmother. I want to thank her and Father Puma for teaching me about service. For me to serve someone besides myself is a major miracle.'

Paterson became part of my life. At the facility, they call it 'Walter's Meeting.' I've come to love the guys. I can feel their affection for me. I say just what's on my mind, and so do they. I show up telling my story. My recovery, though, is my ability to listen to their stories. That's the beauty of the program – simple listening. Listening with my heart and not my head. It took me a lifetime to learn to listen. I was always so busy mouthing off, so concerned with being heard, so desperate to dominate every conversation, I never heard anyone else. There's healing in speaking your truth, but even more healing in hearing others speak theirs.

I grew closer to Father Puma, as a mentor and a friend. It'd be easier for the Pope to convert to Islam than for me to turn Catholic, but that didn't stop me from hanging out with a priest who understood the need for redemption.

'There once was a scumbag music manager,' I told the father one night over dinner, 'who was a liar and a cheat. I ran into him after I got canned, and he asked me what I was up to. For some crazy reason, I told him the truth. "I'm trying to connect to God,"

I said. Then he said something that proves you have to listen to everyone, even scumbags. "Connecting with God isn't hard," he said, "because the target is so broad. You can have lousy aim and still hit the target because the target goes from A to Z. God said he's the Alpha and the Omega."'

'Christ said that, Walter.'

'You have to remind me?'

Today

'I WANT TO HAVE PHONE SEX,' SAYS THE WOMAN.

'You've got the wrong number,' I tell her.

'I thought this was the help line.'

'It is,' I say. 'Help for drunks and addicts.'

'I'm an addict.'

'Then we'll talk about what's bothering you and I'll tell you about some meetings nearby. Where are you?'

'In Queens. And I'm stark naked. What are you wearing?'

'A heavily insulated antibacteria protective suit and a gas mask. What do you care what I'm wearing?'

'Are you sexy?'

'I'm a drunk. Is that sexy?'

'Very.'

'Do you want help or do you wanna play?'

'Both.'

'Well, I'm not playing.'

'Then what are you doing?'

'Answering the emergency phone line for people who are desperate.'

'I'm desperate for sex.'

'Enough with the sex.'

'How long have you been sober?'

'Long enough to know that if I don't stop talking to you we're gonna wind up drinking in bed.'

'Now you're talking.'

I hang up. I look around the little room, where a few other volunteers are fielding calls from people trying to get or stay straight. I sigh. Sometimes I'm real good at this stuff, sometimes I'm not. By listening to the pain of someone else who's tempted to get high, I often feel more grounded. Once in a while, I can even say something to help the sufferer.

I take the subway downtown to the Bowery, where I run a men's group at a city-sponsored rehab house for guys just off the street. At ten in the morning, half the riders on the Lexington Avenue line look like street people. I study the faces. A guy wearing a moth-eaten fedora has hands caked with dirt. He's drinking wine out of a paper bag. Why him and not me? I'm thinking, *There but for the grace of God* ... A bag lady smells awful. A gorgeous redhead, dressed in a tailored suit, smells of fancy perfume. I smile at her. She doesn't smile back. But the bag lady smiles at me as she hits me up for money. I give her a buck. She says, 'Bless you.' I wonder how Heshie distributes the blessings. How some of us keep from falling off the deep end. How others don't. How fourteen years of sobriety has taught me that the tenuous cord separating sanity and madness is strengthened only by this singular notion of service.

Down in the Bowery, the men are waiting for me. They're pissed. Of the half-dozen participants, the guy I'll call Pete is angriest.

'Screw you, Yetnikoff, and screw the twelve steps you're always peddling,' he says.

'This isn't even a twelve-step meeting,' I say.

'Good. So don't mention them. You don't even know what the fuck they mean.'

'They're steps toward God.'

'So you know God?'

'I'm not saying I know him. I'm saying I'm stepping toward him.'

'Well, I'd like to step toward a fucking job. I been out of work for six months.'

'Last week, you were in the psycho ward, where you were out of your mind. Now at least it looks like you're back in your right mind.'

'Nothing's right without money.'

'Let's talk about gratitude.'

'You talk about gratitude. I wanna talk about money. I wanna talk about how once you get out of the joint, you can't find no work no way.'

'So you're here, living for free. That's something to be grateful for.'

'Here comes your fucking gratitude list.'

'Making a list ain't gonna kill you, Pete.'

'It ain't gonna get me a job.'

'You sure? The right attitude changes everything.'

'Money changes everything.'

'That's what I thought. I spent my life struggling to make millions. I was sure the millions would make me happy. But when I made the millions, I went nuts.'

For the remainder of the session, I listen to the other guys talk about their misery, fears and frustrations. A few have hope. A few are actually experiencing the healing of our fellowship. A few realize that talking about it helps. I realize that the group helps me. I'm still green at this counseling stuff. When I started, one of the staff professionals said I was talking too much. What else is new?

I carry inside my head a portion of a prayer that pleads to God, 'Relieve me of the bondage of self.' That goes back to listening to others. The elders say it's all about giving up my willfulness and heeding the will of God.

Understanding that will – at least for me – isn't easy. Heshie works in mysterious ways.

When I get back home, the phone's ringing. It's a big-shot Washington, D.C., lawyer considering suing the major labels for defrauding artists. He wants to sign me up as a *consigliere* for his case. This gets me excited.

'You know more about questionable accounting principles than anyone,' he says.

'I know that the artists are greedy and the labels are less than straightforward. If you ask me who's worse, I'll have to think about it.'

'What overall philosophy drives the companies?'

'Pay the artist as little as you can. Tie up the artist for as long as you can. Recoup as often as you can.'

'What are the most egregious ways that the companies cheat?'

'I'm not sure "cheat" is the right word. But I am sure, at least in my day, that royalties were never paid on 100 percent sales. You paid on 85 percent and called the other 15 percent breakage – even though the breakage applied to shellac records from the forties and fifties. What's more, you pay artists half royalties on their overseas sales. You say that's due to the cost of setting up your subsidiaries. Even when those costs have diminished, though, you keep paying the lower rate. On foreign sales, the company benefits from a tax credit on the artists' royalties. The royalties have nothing to do with the company, but the company pays less taxes. Meanwhile, the artist doesn't even know it's happening. You charge at least half of the video costs to the artists. You charge the artist the cost of packaging. That could be 10

percent – or one dollar on the wholesale ten-dollar price of a CD –
when actually packaging costs might be a quarter. It goes on and
on. Or at least it did in the music world of the seventies and
eighties.'

'And the artists' lawyers never objected?'

'In the age of excess, the artists' lawyers were as greedy as the
artists and the labels. The artists' lawyers were going for huge
advances for their clients and themselves. They didn't give a shit
about the small print. It was all about the big bucks.'

'So it was corrupt.'

'Morally maybe. But legally it was written out in documents no
one bothered to read.'

'But what about the big point – isn't it true that even when the
company goes in the black with a CD, even when massive sales
wipe out costs, even then the artist statement can still show red –
or a lot less black than it should?'

'There are ways to pump up those costs on paper so that
royalties are delayed or even permanently denied.'

'And you're willing to testify to those ways in a court of law?'

'I'm not willing to do anything but get off the phone with you
and try to regain my goddamn peace of my mind.'

'Can I call you again?'

'Let me call you.'

I put down the phone and start wondering. My mind wanders.
I'm thinking about royalties. The artists weren't the only ones who
got screwed. At the start of 1990, while I was still running the
world, Steve Popovich, one of my former in-house promo
geniuses, was screaming bloody murder. Back in the seventies,
Stevie owned Cleveland International, an indie label that brought
us Meat Loaf to distribute during the megahit days of *Bat Out of
Hell*. Steve was certain CBS Records had shorted his label on
royalties. The statute of limitations, however, prevented him from
auditing.

I liked Steve. He was instrumental in bringing me the Jacksons. He was a down-to-earth record man. So I agreed to waive the statute. Fast forward a couple of years:

Sony has taken over. Sony refuses to acknowledge my waiver. Steve asks me to intervene. I do. I write a letter confirming the waiver. Now Sony is pissed. I get a nasty letter from their lawyer saying I'm in violation of my settlement agreement, the United Nations charter and half of the Ten Commandments.

'If you don't like it,' I respond, 'sue me.'

The Sony lawyer calls. It's a she.

'Why are you so nice to Popovich and so uncooperative with us?' she asks.

'Because Popovich is a good guy and you're a bunch of assholes.'

'We have legal rights.'

'Fine,' I say. 'Serve me with a subpoena and get my testimony. But be careful – you have no idea what I might say.'

Sony never contacts me again.

Meanwhile, Popovich sues. An audit goes forward. Legal warfare breaks out. Giant Sony attempts to crush little Steve Popovich.

'Walter,' asks Steve, 'what should I do?'

'Hang in. Sony will settle on the courthouse steps.'

Which is just what they do – for several millions.

So in retrospect, I'm thinking maybe I should talk to this Washington lawyer digging into royalty practices. But I wonder about my moral culpability while I was the Great Honcho. Did I condone these practices?

Yes, like everyone else in the industry. Also, in the Age of Excess, what CEO was concentrating on royalty accounting? Ahmet? Clive? Mo? Hardly. Geffen? Less hardly.

I ask myself another question: If I had found a modicum of spirituality in the Age of Excess, would I have acted differently?

I hope so. The truth, of course, is that no one then – or now – has ever confused me with the Dalai Lama.

Yet my ego still tells me I can change the world. I can go where no alcoholic has ever gone before. I can right all wrongs.

Let me calm down. Let me stop envisioning myself as the brave iconoclast, back in the public spotlight, front-page headlines in *The New York Times*, blowing the lid off the music biz. Let me sit and talk to Heshie for a minute or two. Let me practice a little yoga, stretch my spine, open my heart chakra, remember to breathe.

Sun salutation.

Downward dog.

Hello, Heshie.

Goodbye, stress.

Well, at least less stress. At seventy, my life is busy as hell. I make a date with a woman. I'm always making dates with women. I call my sponsor. My sponsees call me. They help me. They bug me. I help them. I bug them. I go to Paterson. I go to the Bowery. I get involved with Road Recovery, an outreach program that helps young people see how the sober life is a good life. Seasoned veterans – from a lead guitarist to a carpenter who builds the stage – teach master classes on every aspect of the music field. Road Recovery arranges seminars at schools for disadvantaged kids where stars like Dr John and Doug E. Fresh come and speak.

Then there's commerce. Jews love commerce. I'm involved in everything from soundtracks to hip-hop to performance poetry to artist development. I've even toyed with major label acquisition. What would that do to my serenity?

Here comes another fax.

It's a reminder to attend the meeting of the Caron Foundation board. Caron is an addiction treatment and rehab center where I recently went for a week of self-examination. I didn't go because I had a slip, but because I saw how much I wanted to control everyone else's addictive behavior. Control is another addiction of mine. I got so involved with Caron that I wanted to help perpetuate their good work. Now that I'm on the board, I'm working hard not to try and control the other board members.

The phone keeps ringing. This time it's an extra-aggressive reporter from a major newspaper.

Iago himself – Tommy Mottola – has been fired by Sony. A scandal is brewing. Rumors are flying. Do I know anything about it?

'I know everything,' I tell the reporter.

'Shoot.'

'When I got fired, the company was making four hundred and fifty million a year in pre-tax bottom-line net profits. When Mottola got canned, it looks like they were losing two hundred and fifty million a year. Something may be rotten in the state of Denmark. For example, it was reported that they were putting DVD manufacturing revenues into the music operation. But DVDs include a helluva lot more than music.'

'Mottola had to deal with Internet piracy, though. You didn't face that.'

'No, I faced some real-life pirates. You want details?'

'Yes.'

I stop myself. Am I about to revert to rage and vengefulness? What am I doing? Where's my serenity? Is this Heshie's will? Should I really be ranting and raving about my old enemies? Aren't I beyond that?

'I'll call you back,' I tell the reporter.

'When?'

'When I have something to say.'

Meanwhile, I have something to read. Can't remember whether it was my poetry pal or someone in the program, but some high-minded friend gave me this book about the spirituality of being imperfect. I relate to the thesis:

I'm not okay, you're not okay, and that's okay.

There's a crack in everything. Even my recovery – especially my recovery – is full of cracks.

A rabbi says, 'In the world to come they won't ask you why you weren't Moses, but why you weren't the best Walter you could be. That means accepting your flaws.'

An eighteenth-century Jesuit says, 'Rejoice every time you discover a new imperfection.'

So I'm rejoicing, even as I'm still amending. I'm amending my behavior and actually writing out amends. The process has been going on for years. In the case of Junc, my ongoing amends take the form of acknowledging her soul when I do something especially righteous. In the case of Steve Ross, I was lucky enough to reach him before he died. 'I was a schmuck,' I said to Steve. 'I was jealous of you. I treated you and your wife like shit. I want to say I'm sorry.' I could have said the same thing to a thousand other people. Steve was gracious enough, even on his deathbed, to reply. 'You're a temperamental guy. I always knew that. I didn't take it seriously. But if you need for me and Courtney to forgive you, we do. I wish you nothing but the best.' Ross had class.

On my worst days, I regret lacking that class. I revert back to crass. I still want to blow the whistle on my adversaries, scream bloody murder, extract my pound of flesh, hoist the flag of my unconquerable ego. On my worst days, I'm still howling at the moon.

On my best days, I put on my helmet, rev up my Harley and hit the country roads outside the city. I go for hours. I've been asked to join a couple of biker clubs, but that's not me. I ride alone. The wind in my face, the power of the thing beneath me, the thrill of speed kills all thoughts. I just am.

On my best days, I try and treat myself the same as I treat the guys down on the Bowery. If I lose it, if I hear an angry voice inside my head, I just listen to it. I let it say what it has to say. I try not to judge it. I try to accept it, understand it and gently move on. If I feel that Heshie is listening, I speak to him. Even if I'm not feeling it, I get on my hands and knees and pray for calm. Sometimes calmness comes; sometimes it doesn't.

I get confused until my poetry pal reminds me that Saint Augustine said the most important things happen when we're in a state of confusion. If that's the case, everything in my life is important because I'm so often confused. But when the fog of confusion lifts, when the chattering voices inside my head – voices that argue, voices that demean, voices that drive me to distraction – when those harsh voices die down, I have a recurring vision that never ceases to amaze me:

I'm not living my life, I'm watching it unfold like a movie. I'm not the producer, not the director, not the screenwriter. I'm just a guy in the audience entranced by a story that keeps changing. As the story changes, so does the guy. In some ways, he's still a prick looking for that big emotional score that will set him free. But that's happening less and less. The prick is starting to see that the score is an illusion. The beauty of the story is in letting it emerge. The pressure of shaping it – controlling it, manipulating it – is no longer on me. Heshie is the writer, not me. And if Heshie is in charge, that means that I can finally relax.

INDEX